THE FUTURE OF SUSTAINABLE CITIES

Critical reflections

Edited by John Flint and Mike Raco

First published in Great Britain in 2012 by

The Policy Press
University of Bristol
Fourth Floor
Beacon House
Queen's Road
Bristol BS8 1QU
UK

Tel +44 (0)117 331 4054
Fax +44 (0)117 331 4093
e-mail tpp-info@bristol.ac.uk
www.policypress.org.uk

North American office:

The Policy Press
c/o The University of Chicago Press
1427 East 60th Street
Chicago, IL 60637, USA
t: +1 773 702 7700
f: +1 773-702-9756
e:sales@press.uchicago.edu
www.press.uchicago.edu

© The Policy Press 2012

British Library Cataloguing in Publication Data
A catalogue record for this book is available from the British Library.

Library of Congress Cataloging-in-Publication Data
A catalog record for this book has been requested.

ISBN 978 1 84742 666 6 paperback
ISBN 978 1 84742 667 3 hardcover

Cover design by Qube Design Associates
Front cover: image kindly supplied by www.alamy.com/www.istock.com
Printed and bound in Great Britain by Hobbs, Southampton
The Policy Press uses environmentally responsible print partners

Contents

List of tables and figures

Tables

Figures

Acknowledgements

John Flint and Mike Raco wish to thank Emily Watt of The Policy Press for all her support and advice. They are also grateful to Charlotte Skelton and Jo Morton for their assistance in preparing the typescript and to the anonymous reviewers for their insightful and constructive comments on earlier versions of the book.

Chapter Eight is a considerably revised and updated version of the previous article by Chris Pickvance (2009) 'The construction of UK sustainable housing policy', *Local Environment*, vol 14, no 2, pp 329-45, printed with the permission of the publisher, Taylor & Francis Ltd (www.informaworld.com).

Notes on contributors

Harriet Bulkeley is Professor of Geography, Energy and Environment at the Department of Geography and Durham Energy Institute, Durham University, UK (www.dur.ac.uk/geography/staff/geogstaffhidden/?id=929).

Allan Cochrane is Professor of Urban Studies in the Faculty of Social Sciences at the Open University, UK. He is a member of the Open Space Research Centre (www.open.ac.uk/socialsciences/staff/people-profile.php?name=Allan_Cochrane).

Tim Dixon is Professor of Real Estate and Director of the Oxford Institute of Sustainable Development (OISD) at Oxford Brookes University, UK (www.brookes.ac.uk/schools/be/staff/timdixon.html).

Iain Docherty is Professor of Public Policy and Governance at the Business School, University of Glasgow, Scotland, UK (www.gla.ac.uk/schools/business/staff/iaindocherty/).

Sarah Dooling is Assistant Professor in the School of Architecture, Environmental Science Institute at the University of Texas-Austin, Texas, USA. (www.soa.utexas.edu/people/profile/dooling/sarah).

Will Eadson is Associate Researcher in the Centre for Regional Economic and Social Research at Sheffield Hallam University, UK. He has recently completed a PhD in the spatial practices of governing carbon management in England (www.shu.ac.uk/research/cresr/postgraduate.html#will).

John Flint is Professor of Town and Regional Planning in the Department of Town and Regional Planning at the University of Sheffield, UK.

Mike Hodson is a Research Fellow in the Centre for Sustainable Urban and Regional Futures at the University of Salford, UK (www.surf.salford.ac.uk/page/Mike_Hodson).

Simon Marvin is Professor of Sustainable Urban and Regional Development and Co-Director of the Centre for Sustainable Urban and Regional Futures at the University of Salford, UK (www.surf.salford.ac.uk/page/Simon_Marvin).

Peter Newman is Professor of Comparative Urban Planning in the School of Architecture and the Built Environment at the University of Westminster, London, UK (www.westminster.ac.uk/schools/architecture/staff/staff-in-regeneration-and-planning/newman,-professor-peter).

Chris Pickvance is Professor of Urban Studies in the School of Social Policy, Sociology and Social Research at the University of Kent, Canterbury, UK (www.kent.ac.uk/sspssr/staff/academic/pickvance.html).

Mike Raco is Professor of Urban Governance and Development at the Bartlett School of Planning, University College London.

Jon Shaw is Professor of Transport Geography in the School of Geography, Earth and Environmental Sciences at the University of Plymouth, UK (www.plymouth.ac.uk/staff/jshaw1).

Mark Whitehead is Reader in Political Geography in the Institute of Geography and Earth Sciences, Aberystwyth University, Wales, UK (http://users.aber.ac.uk/msw/).

Section 1

The 'new' politics of sustainable urbanism

one

Introduction: Characterising the 'new' politics of sustainability: from managing growth to coping with crisis

Mike Raco and John Flint

Introduction

The financial crisis of 2008 and its subsequent fallout will have a profound affect on the content and character of urban sustainability planning. For much of the 1990s and 2000s policy thinking and practice was primarily concerned with managing the social and environmental effects of unequal growth and development. The emphasis in the UK and elsewhere was on tackling housing shortages, renewing urban centres, planning for growth areas and re-using brownfield land. Welfare reforms across the European Union (EU) focused on the promotion of social and spatial cohesion and longer-term environmental protection, in a political context of unquestioned neoliberal globalisation and economic growth. Sustainability planning became elided with 'sustaining success' or developing a series of policy interventions to support and enhance economic growth in a new era of global prosperity (see Manzi et al, 2010). It offered the promise of a win-win agenda in which governments could promise to meet the triple objectives of economic growth, enhanced social justice and environmental protection.

However, the sudden onset of the credit crunch in 2008, and the subsequent recession in many national economies, has opened up significant new challenges for policy makers and communities in cities across the world (see *The Economist*, 2009; O'Grady, 2009). The assumptions that underpinned planning systems and city strategies during the 1990s and 2000s have been rapidly undermined as welfare states are downsized and the availability of private sector investment becomes more circumscribed. As Zizek (2010, p 27) laments, 'after decades of hope held out by the welfare state, when financial cuts were sold as temporary, and sustained by a promise that things would soon return to normal, we are entering a new epoch in which ... crisis is becoming a way of life'. The boundaries between states and markets since 2008 have shifted in dramatic ways as the limitations and contradictions inherent in the neoliberal policy orthodoxies of the late 20th century have been exposed by the chill winds of economic crisis.

As the chapters in this book will show, the effects of these changes on cities, communities and policy makers will be significant. As governments roll out emergency 'austerity' agendas, the principles and programmes that formed the heart of the postwar Keynesian welfare settlement have come under renewed attack, with significant implications for social justice and urban change; the emphasis that governments place on private sector-led economic recovery and the respective roles for the state and voluntary sectors in addressing the social consequences of austerity will vary between nations, however.

At the same time, the crisis will also open up new opportunities for creative forms of sustainability planning to emerge in a context where market-led, property-driven agendas may not dominate development policy in cities to the same extent as they have since the 1980s. As Bourdieu (2005) argued, neoliberalism is founded on a series of politically constructed myths, imagined certainties and power-infused assumptions. The events of 2008 and its aftermath have generated new questions and new uncertainties, the outcomes of which remain to be determined and argued over.

In the following chapters leading writers in the field address these issues and explore the future prospects for sustainability policy in western cities. Their contributions address the following core questions:

1. What impacts will the financial crisis and its economic affects have on conceptions of urban sustainability?
2. How will these changes shape evolving urban forms and processes of sustainable city building?
3. What are the implications of change for the politics, governance and management of cities?
4. How might we characterise the evolving relationships between states and markets and their impacts on cities?
5. What might definitions and conceptions of urban sustainability look like in the future?

In this introductory chapter we outline some of the key themes that inform these questions, and also introduce the contributions that make up the remainder of the book. We begin by discussing the changing political and economic contexts brought about by the financial crisis and some of the core implications for sustainability planning more broadly. We also examine the effects on processes of governance. We argue that the crisis represents a significant blow to the rolling out of Third Way, 'post-ideological' political projects that during the 1990s and 2000s promoted consensus-based constructs, such as sustainable development, as a panacea for the challenges faced by modern societies. The post-2008 crisis not only raises broader questions over who governs and with what ends but also calls for a fundamental re-think of the forms of governance that are still possible.

From globalisation to recession: the changing contexts of sustainability planning

The contexts within which sustainability agendas are being rolled out have changed markedly since the late 2000s. The financial crisis has had a profound impact on the economies and political priorities of western countries. In the UK, for example, the economy shrank by an unprecedented 6 per cent of GDP in 2008–09, after 16 years of growth (National Statistics, 2010). During the same period the US saw a drop of 1.7 per cent, while the Eurozone saw falls of 4.1 per cent (see Eurostat, 2010; US Bureau of Economic Analysis, 2010). And while the global economy showed signs of picking up again in 2010–11, it was also prone to new inconsistencies and uncertainties, with the Organisation for Economic Co-operation and Development (OECD) (2010, p 5) still fearing that the 'risks to the global recovery could be higher now, given the speed and magnitude of capital inflows in emerging-market economies and instability in sovereign debt-markets'.

This reversal of economic growth has particular resonance for sustainability policy in cities as in most OECD countries the period of the 1990s and 2000s saw a close correlation between enhanced private sector profitability and increases in state spending on a broad range of social, economic and environmental programmes. Thus, in the UK, at the same time as sustainability planning agendas were being rolled out, the Labour government was increasing overall government expenditure at a significant rate, from £362 billion in 2001 to commitments of £661 billion in 2010 (see Figure 1.1). This was matched by institutional changes that saw a mushrooming of organisations with a stake in promoting sustainability strategies, including voluntary and community sector bodies, state quangos and local authority departments. Indeed, by the mid-2000s urban sustainability planning had become a wide-ranging policy field that was developed and implemented through complex institutional networks of actors, often working to different time frames, objectives and priorities (see Bevir and Trentmann, 2007).

With the onset of recession, however, this period of expansion has rapidly come to an end. Governments across the EU are now looking to slash spending in the wake of recession and imagined threats to the credit-worthiness of government finances. In the UK the Coalition *Spending Review* of October 2010 set out plans to reduce state spending significantly over a four-year period and instigated a set of changes that will have a colossal impact not only the capacities of state organisations but also on the number of voluntary and community sector intermediaries that emerged in the 1990s and 2000s (see HM Treasury, 2010). Social housing budgets, for example, have been cut from £8.4 billion in 2007–10 to just £4.4 billion in 2011–14. Local authorities across England will see falls of 28 per cent in their total funding in the same period, while spending on the environment will fall by 29 per cent, from £2.9 billion in 2010 to £2.2 billion in 2014. While it would be premature to talk of the 1990s and 2000s as a golden age in countries such as the UK, in which government spending and policy commitments to sustainability reached exceptional highs, there is a strong likelihood that these levels of expenditure will not be seen again in the short to medium term, and that this will lead to acute and unprecedented resource challenges for those working on the ground. As *The Economist* (2010a, p 11) notes, there is a trend of 'politicians cutting back on the basis that growth is assured … [and] planning tax rises and spending cuts worth 1.25% of the collective GDP in 2011, the biggest synchronised fiscal tightening on record'. New spatial patterns of economic decline will emerge at the same time as historical regional inequalities are likely to be exacerbated by welfare cuts that will disproportionately affect more deprived cities and regions.

Other longer-term trends are also beginning to erode some of the social and economic certainties of the neoliberal era. One of the affects of globalisation has been that commodity prices have undergone a significant boom during the 2000s, to the extent that the price of staple goods, such as wheat and oil, have begun to impact on the prospects for future economic growth (see OECD, 2010). Oil prices, in particular, have become increasingly volatile. This has direct impacts on the sustainability of global economic growth models that have been underpinned by relatively low, and decreasing, costs of trade, transport and distribution. With the strong possibility that the

Figure 1.1: UK public expenditure (£ billions) 2001–10

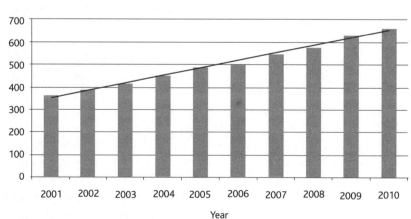

Source: www.ukpublicspending.co.uk/index.php

moment of global Peak Oil – where known supplies are unable to meet global demand and go into terminal decline – may be fast approaching, it seems highly unlikely that the conditions for future growth will return to those of the 1990s and 2000s (see Leggett, 2006; *The Independent*, 2007; *The Guardian*, 2010a). These shortages have been exacerbated by geopolitical changes in which countries such as China, India and Brazil have experienced rapid economic growth and expanded their consumption of commodities and raw materials. In the longer term the growing impacts of climate change, an increasingly erratic politics of energy production and consumption and projections of a rapidly expanding global population mean that the survivability of the capitalist mode of production in its existing form looks increasingly uncertain.

Other political trends are also changing the contexts within which sustainable development will take place in the coming years. New forms of protectionism are gradually emerging across the world, as governments come under greater domestic pressure to protect their own economies from global competition. There are new tensions, for example, over currency exchange rates and a greater emphasis on tariffs and trade restrictions (*The Economist*, 2010). Perhaps more significantly, in the wake of recession, demographic politics has re-emerged as a contentious political issue in many western countries. Across the EU there has been a resurgence of reactionary politics and a broader critique of policies that promote immigration and increased flows of people across international borders. In countries as diverse as the Netherlands, France, Italy and Germany there has been greater support for those who call for new restrictions on immigration (see Zizek, 2010).

This is not limited to those on the far right, with mainstream governments now openly challenging the cosmopolitan view that migration is of significant benefit to cities and countries. The EU's recent Pact on Asylum and Immigration in October 2008, for example, explicitly argues that,

> The EU does not have the resources to decently receive all the migrants who hope to find a better life here. Poorly managed immigration may disrupt the social cohesion of host countries. The organisation of immigration must consequently take account of Europe's reception capacity in terms of its labour market, housing, and health, education, and social services. (p 1)

Similar sentiments have recently been aired by powerful politicians such as Angela Merkel, who pronounced in October 2010 that multiculturalism in Germany was 'dead' and that the country needed to re-think its policies on guest workers and integration (*The Guardian*, 2010b). The longer-term implications of this reactive politics for social cohesion and sustainability could be profound.

At the same time, western governments are also grappling with another related demographic problem, that of rapidly ageing populations. As an *Economist Report* (2010, p 3) notes, in the absence of significant new immigration over the coming decades Western Europe's 'working age population, which until now has been rising slowly will shrink by 0.3 per cent a year'. In economic terms the *Report* draws together evidence that indicates that 'unless more immigrants are allowed in, or a larger proportion of the working-age population joins the labour force, or people retire later, or their productivity accelerates, the ageing population will translate into permanently slower potential growth'. There are likely therefore to be growing economic pressures on governments to increase immigration, at the same time as anti-immigrant sentiments and policies are growing in many countries in the wake of recession. Whatever the policy responses of governments turn out to be, it seems certain that demographic changes will have significant social, political and cultural consequences and may generate real tensions over the direction of migration policy and debates over sustainable communities in the coming years.

To summarise, this section has argued that:

- The combined impacts of these broader geopolitical, environmental and socioeconomic trends have potentially enormous implications for the sustainability of cities and western societies.
- In the short term governments and civil society may have to change their ways of thinking and move away from the dominant belief that policy is primarily concerned with managing the effects of growth.
- In some cases states and societies will be forced to consider the challenges involved in meeting short-term post-recession priorities at the same time as longer-term trends erode some of the socioeconomic 'certainties' of the era of globalisation.

In the next section we develop the discussion by focusing on the emergence of sustainability agendas in urban planning during the 1990s and 2000s and highlight some of the core assumptions that fuelled its seemingly relentless expansion. We explore the connections between the so-called Third Way politics of this period and the growth in sustainability as a post-political discourse, and assess its significance for policy making and implementation.

Post-politics of sustainability planning

The growth of sustainability discourses since the mid-1970s has been well documented in, and thoroughly interrogated by, the academic literature (for excellent assessments see Brand and Thomas, 2005; Gibbs and Krueger, 2007; Whitehead, 2007). Such work demonstrates how the term came to represent one of the key, binding policy discourses underpinning Third Way governance agendas across the EU, North America and elsewhere during the 1990s, in a period when globalisation was emerging and expanding. Sustainability provided a bridge between the competing objectives of economic competitiveness on the one hand, and social justice and environmental protection on the other. It enabled Third Way governments to propagate a politics of conflict denial, or a new post-political condition (cf Rancière, 2006), in which sustainability came to be defined as a modernised, consensus-based mode of thinking and acting.

The intellectual justification for the rolling out of these post-political agendas was to be found in broader debates within political science over the changing form and character of democratic politics under globalisation. Authors such as Beck (2000, 2006) proclaimed that societies had moved into a new era of modernity, characterised by post-industrialism and the emergence of a new 'sub-politics', in which individuals and communities now develop shared identities formed around specific interests and issues in place of economic class associations. For advocates such as Giddens (1994), this 'new' politics has replaced the traditional postwar antagonisms of left and right, with post-ideological discourses, such as those surrounding sustainability, providing an obvious grounding for consensus-based ways of working that look beyond divisions and focus instead on issues that unite disparate groups.

For instance, the Labour government in the UK rolled out a raft of policy measures that were intended to bring sustainability and sustainable development into the mainstream of spatial planning and urban development (see Table 1.1 for a list of core policy initiatives and rationalities). The new emphasis was to be on the consensus-based, post-political objectives of place building and the construction of vibrant sustainable communities. Planning policies became more 'holistic' in tone and imagined new possibilities for the creation of sustainable urban futures in which the objectives of environmental, economic growth and social harmony could finally be achieved. As Swyngedouw (2007) wryly notes, such visions constituted an 'impossible' construction, in which conflicts were imagined away as relics of a by-gone era of postwar, pre-Thatcherite class-based political systems. For post-politicists, the world had moved on, and sustainability issues provided a new focus for deliberation and action (see Mouffe, 2005).

However, these visions were based on a series of assumptions, many of which look increasingly redundant in the wake of the changes outlined in the section above. Perhaps most significantly, such discourses are premised on the acceptance that globalisation as a trend is here to stay and that the processes that brought it into fruition during the 1990s and 2000s represent 'realities' that are set in stone for the foreseeable future. Giddens (2003), for example, argues that we now live in a 'runaway world', in which the powers of national

Table 1.1: Key policy initiatives relating to sustainability planning in the UK, 2003–10

Key policy initiative	Year	Core rationalities/objectives
Sustainable Communities Plan	2003	• To define what is meant by a sustainable community and to enshrine it in policy plans and frameworks • To use spatial planning to sustain the economic competitiveness of the globally competitive London and South East of the England region • The designation of four Growth Areas around London in which new developments should take place • Designation of 12 Market Renewal Areas in English cities where markets have 'failed'
Egan Review: *Skills for sustainable communities* (2004)	2004	• Clarify what the term 'sustainable community' means • Identify who is responsible for leading the delivery of sustainable communities • Recognise the skills necessary to achieve sustainable communities
Barker Review of Housing Supply	2004	• Suggested housing targets of 70,000 new houses per year to avoid shortages • Building market affordability

Planning Policy Statement 1: Delivering sustainable development and planning policy; Planning Policy Statement 3: Housing	2005, 2006	• Set out core principles for the English planning system:
		  – make suitable land available for development in line with economic, social and environmental objectives to improve people's quality of life
		  – contribute to sustainable economic development
		  – protect and enhance the natural and historic environment, the quality and character of the countryside and existing communities
		  – ensure high quality development through good and inclusive design, and the efficient use of resources
		  – ensure that development supports existing communities and contributes to the creation of safe, sustainable, liveable and mixed communities with good access to jobs and key services for all members of the community

Establishment of Academy for Sustainable Communities	2005	• To promote enhanced awareness of sustainable communities • To establish core skills among practitioners and voluntary sector
National Brownfield Strategy	2006	• Enshrined principle of 'redevelop or re-use first' • Focus on provision of infrastructure for re-use in towns and cities • Full regard always taken of environmental impact of remedial work
Sustainable Communities Act	2007	• Promote the sustainability of local communities • Encourage the improvement of the economic, social or environmental well-being of local authority areas • Enhance 'social well-being' and participation in civic and political activity • Becomes the duty of the Secretary of State to assist local authorities in promoting the sustainability of local communities in the ways specified in this Act

Key policy initiative	Year	Core rationalities/objectives
World class places	2009	• Focus on quality of place and civic leadership • Ensure relevant government policy, guidance and standards consistently promote quality of place and are user-friendly. Actions include introducing new planning policy on the historic environment and green infrastructure • Put the public and community at the centre of place shaping • Ensure all development for which central government is directly responsible is built to high design and sustainability standards and promotes quality of place • Encourage higher standards of market-led development • Strengthen quality of place skills, knowledge and capacity

Enshrining of EU legislation/directives into UK law		• Water Framework Directive (adopted 2000):
		  – new requirements on planning to set environmental objectives for all water bodies
		  – comprehensive sustainable water and waterside development management
		• Landfill Directive (2002)
		  – '... to prevent or reduce as far as possible negative effects on the environment, in particular the pollution of surface water, groundwater, soil and air, and on the global environment, including the greenhouse effect, as well as any resulting risk to human health, from the landfilling of waste, during the whole life-cycle of the landfill'
		• The Conservation of Habitats and Species Regulations (2010):
		  – requires planners and developers to protect biodiversity through the conservation of natural habitats and species of wild fauna and flora
		  – new rules for the protection, management and exploitation of such habitats and species

governments have been hollowed out, leaving the nation-state as an empty shell, or what Beck (2000, p 80) describes as a 'zombie' structure, 'dead long ago but still haunting people's minds'. The implications of this assumption for policies and priorities have been profound as it has encouraged many governments to pursue neoliberal strategies, based on what Jones (1997) terms new forms of 'spatial selectivity'. This involves identifying the core needs of 'globally competitive' sectors, located principally in well-connected metropolitan areas, and developing policy interventions to address them (although this has, of course, recently necessitated enormous direct public subsidy of these sectors, most notably the bailout of the banking industry).

The focus instead has been on supporting growth centres and ensuring that spatial planning delivers the necessary infrastructure for their continued expansion, with the benefits eventually trickling down to all areas (see Chapter Three, this volume). In what Hutton (2010) characterises as a Faustian pact, the Labour government in Britain openly endorsed a growth-first policy, in which the needs of the South East of England and its clusters of financial services and cultural-knowledge industries became the centre-piece of development planning. Sustainability discourses and policy programmes became bound up with this wider set of neoliberal objectives and spatial policy interventions. Such an approach represents an inversion of traditional postwar policy that sought to even out economic growth and, to a lesser extent, populations across national spaces (see Parsons, 1986).

Another assumption that underpinned policy reform was the mantra of community empowerment. The devolution of political power has always been a key part of sustainability discourses. The pioneering work of Schumpeter (1973) and others in the 1970s saw the local level as the primary site for sustainability practices and policy experimentation. Likewise, the Brundtland Commission saw democratic reform and the devolution of powers and responsibilities to local communities as a fundamental building block for the reformulation of development thinking. Local activity was linked to what Massey (1993) would later call 'a progressive sense of place' in which ideas and imaginations forged at the local level would spread outwards to shape policy agendas across the world. At the international level the Agenda 21 programme established at the Rio Summit of 1992 institutionalised this localist emphasis. Planning, it was argued, should aim to create 'sustainable communities', or self-contained places in which people live and work, and where empowered individuals take on greater responsibility for their own welfare and quality of life. Policy's role was to encourage the ordered presence and absence of particular groups across space to create 'balanced', harmonious places, in which community-based identities and ways of working took centre stage.

With the onset of the recession, housing market decline, crises in pension provision and welfare expenditure and enormous uncertainties in the form and character of future globalisation, many of these assumptions look increasingly anachronistic. The irony of recent modernisation plans and reforms, in many cities and countries, has been that they were rhetorically designed to 'reflect 21st-century challenges'. However, there is the growing prospect that the pre-eminence of sustainability planning was, in fact, a creature of its time, or a manifestation of a broader conjunction of circumstances that will dissipate and fracture in the coming decades. Many of the ideas promoted with such fanfare in the 2000s suddenly seem dated and relevant to a different era, at least on the surface. The numerous strategies and plans that were written to manage 'growing cities' in a sustainable way imagined only one type of possible future. Despite their claims to represent practical frameworks, such plans look increasingly utopian in form, sprinkled with statistics, 'facts' and 'trends' that have quickly had to be re-drawn and re-interpreted.

In the next section we develop these points by exploring some of the core tensions over the future governance of sustainable cities. We suggest that while many of the assumptions that underpinned sustainability planning in the 1990s and 2000s have been overtaken by events, new political battles have broken out over dominant characterisations of emerging problems and the best ways to promote future forms of sustainability. The credit crunch has brought into sharp relief some of the underlying political tensions over sustainability agendas and opened up new opportunities for alternative ways of thinking and governing.

Governing the post-recession sustainable city: from managing growth to (re)creating growth

The reasons for the credit crunch have been discussed in detail elsewhere and we have no intention of rehearsing such debates at length here (see, for example, Krugman, 2008; Peston, 2008; Hutton, 2010; Reinhart and Rogoff, 2010). What is significant to our discussion, however, is the ways in which dominant discourses and understandings of the policy 'problems' and 'solutions' caused by the subsequent recession have shaped ways of thinking about sustainability, continuity and change. As Bourdieu (2005) argued, one of the key sources of political power in modern societies rests in the (in) ability to shape dominant definitions of reality and create collective truths and understandings. In establishing such truths, the narratives of the powerful come to have a far bigger impact on framing mindsets and approaches to policy problems than those of the less powerful. Dominant understandings of sustainability, crisis and change never start from a blank slate but are, to some degree, path-dependent, and reflect broader structures and dynamics of power. This explains why in the aftermath of the credit crunch, authors from different perspectives have sought to propagate their own narratives with the aim of extolling specific and power-infused explanations, diagnoses and policy cures for the economic system within which cities operate.

Thus for critics on the left, the events of 2008 represent the latest phase in capitalism's intrinsic crisis-ridden structure which has historically been characterised by periods of boom and bust. The work of the economist Hyman Minsky (2008 [originally published in 1984]), for example, has been 're-discovered' by some critics to explain how and why recent changes have taken place. Minsky (2008, p 11) argued that financial instability and economic fluctuations are not a consequence of 'unfavourable events ... the work of outside forces', but 'a result of the characteristics of the economic mechanisms of capitalism itself'. The ways in which capitalism generates rewards and returns therefore makes it inherently unstable and in the longer term undermines its sustainability. Similar arguments have been made by David Harvey (2009) for whom capitalism's tendency to crisis has simply been delayed by the ability of firms, supported by powerful nation-states, to maintain profitability and control over workers by re-scaling their activities on the global level. It is a process, however, that also exposes the system to enhanced risk of crisis as new forms of interdependency are created so that events in one part of the system, such as the sub-prime mortgages crisis in the US in 2008, have structural implications for economies across the globe. Over the longer term, as Reinhart and Rogoff (2010) argue, individuals and governments also tend to over-extend themselves when times are good and are then exposed when financial bubbles eventually burst.

For such writers the explicit failure of market systems to prevent crisis necessitates a radical overhaul of capitalist modes of (re)production. Such interpretations seek to open up new political spaces in which *alternative* forms of economic and social development could and should be promoted in the name of sustainability. For example, in some EU countries, including the UK, governments have started to establish industrial policies that seek to build on the strengths of existing manufacturing industries (see *The Economist*, 2010). The crisis could also act as a springboard for the promotion of new types of economic activity such as those connected to green technology (for example, the Scottish Government's National Renewables Infrastructure Fund to grow the offshore green economy) and/or new job creation programmes that seek to re-skill population groups that fared poorly in the 1990s and 2000s (Friends of the Earth, 2008; Cabinet Office, 2010; Scottish Government, 2010). New calls for tighter regulation on global industries have emerged since 2008, so that even in the US, President Obama has launched policy initiatives designed, ostensibly, to change the governance and regulation of the global financial services. Similar debates have arisen in the UK where the previously unquestioned dominance of the financial sector and the City of London has been increasingly challenged in mainstream political discourses (see Osbourne, 2010).

And yet, as Zizek (2010) argues, the financial crisis has also stimulated new rounds of conservative thinking, with capitalist interests, mainly in the US and the UK, seeking to characterise it as a contingent 'blip', resulting from the reckless and anomalous actions of a small group of rogue and irresponsible financiers alongside profligate public sector growth. There is less of an emphasis on recessions as a structural feature of capitalism or a consequence of the neoliberal programmes of reform that have systematically enriched the minority at the expense of the majority (see Davis and Monk, 2007 for an excellent discussion). Instead, the argument is that markets have not been free *enough*, and that if there are to be new modes of state intervention and regulation then these should primarily be concerned with re-establishing earlier modes of accumulation and a 'natural' capitalist order. As Krugman and Wells (2010, p 2) put it, 'it's now an article of faith on the right, impervious to contrary evidence, that the crisis was caused not by private sector excesses but by liberal politicians who forced banks to make loans to the undeserving poor'. While the first crash of the 1930s 'was followed by major reforms, it's not clear that anything comparable will happen after the second ... the consequence will be more and quite possibly worse crises in the years to come' (Krugman and Wells, 2010, p 2).

Indeed, under the guise of a post-crisis recovery agenda, conservative administrations have already introduced controversial reform measures across Europe such as increasing the retirement age of citizens, creating leaner and less generous welfare state systems, challenging the power of organised labour and erecting new institutional barriers to the flow of international migrants (European Commission, 2008; *The Economist*, 2009). Globally, these measures are also being implemented autonomously at city levels as mayors and municipalities, for example in Italy and the US, seek to erect 'internal borders' and limit migrants' access to local services (see Gilbert, 2009). Far from representing a moment of neoliberal dissolution, in some places the financial crisis has provided new opportunities for the rolling out of even more draconian, neoliberal programmes of action (see Peck et al, 2010). And as Whitehead's chapter in this volume will argue (see Chapter Two), the crisis thus far has demonstrated that the primary objective of many western states is now an explicit commitment to support and sustain the neoliberal economic system, whatever the costs of such action, in financial, environmental and social terms, turn out to be.

A further key factor that will influence the direction of post-recession sustainability politics will be the role of the private sector on the development and implementation of welfare and development policies. During the Third Way era of post-political governance, public–private partnerships were seen as a role model for how corporate interests, government agencies and civil society could work collectively towards sustainable and mutually beneficial ends. Across the EU, North America and elsewhere partnership working was promoted by national and city governments as an effective, efficient and democratically accountable mode of governance, built on direct forms of participation. It was contrasted with the representative political structures of electoral local politics that were a product of the postwar Keynesian welfare era.

However, in a post-recession context, it may be that public–private partnerships in cities become even more development-focused as policy priorities shift and policy makers become more concerned with promoting growth and development interests. New types of urban regime may emerge through which city-wide sustainability planning agendas will be forged. During the 1990s and 2000s residential and commercial property investments were fundamental components of the asset boom that fuelled economic growth. But as Tim Dixon shows in Chapter Five, with the onset of the credit crunch property investments were among the first areas of economic activity to suffer. The market for much of the speculative housing constructed on brownfield sites in British cities and elsewhere, under the banner of sustainable and compact urban development, rapidly fell away, leaving city centres with unfilled apartments and abandoned sites. Projects earmarked for suburban neighbourhoods and growth areas stalled. High profile development projects have also been affected, with developments being frozen mid-project, leaving empty, half-completed and/or derelict buildings in their wake. In the longer run there is also the possibility that urban environments will become less well maintained by public sector bodies as austerity measures begin to limit the resources of local authorities and others. Funding for environmental improvements, expensive remediation projects and infrastructure upgrades look likely to be cut, at the same time as sustainability programmes call for new forms of investment and environmental improvements.

On a broader scale, the role of the private sector may also become much more significant in the wake of post-recession austerity cuts. There will be a temptation for governments to privatise large parts of the welfare state in order to the shift the burden of costs from central and local governments to welfare users and claimants. In the relatively mild recession of the early 1990s the UK government, for example, introduced a Private Finance Iinitiative (PFI) in which welfare capital spending projects, such as the building of new hospitals, roads and schools, would be built by the private sector and then leased back to the public sector over a period of 25–30 years. In the short term the attraction for state authorities and politicians was that the infrastructure would be built quickly and would not be counted as state expenditure. In the longer term, however, this mortgaging of state investment has created new inflexibilities in the ways in which welfare is provided. Writers such as Allyson Pollock (2005) have demonstrated that PFI projects give private sector investors enormous influence over welfare spending priorities. They are also often relatively expensive for the public sector and carry prohibitively large long-term payback liabilities. One estimate is that public bodies in the UK will have to make £285 billion in PFI payments to private investors between now and 2025, thereby limiting the ability of local communities and future policy makers to take greater control of local services as envisaged by post-political thinkers (see Monbiot, 2007; Norman, 2011). Despite this, the short-term temptation provided by privatisation across the world, in a context of austerity cutbacks, may prove to be too tempting for policy makers to ignore. There is the likelihood that whatever the longer-term costs and democratic implications, the role of private companies in post-recession welfare provision looks set to expand.

It also seems likely that some of the key tenets of sustainability thinking will come under growing strain as societies experience the fallout of economic recession. For example, one area of contestation is likely to be over the moral and practical emphasis of sustainability discourses on the needs of 'future generations' as opposed to the short-term requirements of existing populations (see Bullen and Whitehead, 2005). Sustainability has often been characterised in 'light green' terms, as a win–win policy agenda in which economic growth and rising standards of living are presented as being compatible with environmental conservation. However, the perceived short-term threat of economic crisis and the negative consequences of the austerity measures now being rolled out across developed countries means that abstract concerns about the future are arguably becoming less relevant and more difficult to sustain. There is, of course, nothing new in this. Sustainability has long been presented by critics as a 'luxury agenda' that is, in itself, a symptom of western affluence and the movement away from the 'real' concerns affecting societies in poorer parts of the world (see Martinez-Alier, 1995; Goldie et al, 2005). There is some evidence that green agendas have, indeed, been pushed down the political agendas of governments in the wake of recession and that the behaviour of consumers has started to become less focused on ethical trading and more concerned with cost (see *The Guardian*, 2009). Chapters throughout the book engage with this broader set of issues.

The growing attention given to the short term may also help to explain the growing interest in resilience planning that, as Bristow (2010, p 153) argues, 'is rapidly emerging as an idea whose time has come in policy discourses around localities and regions'. Much of the literature on resilience has traditionally focused on the ways in which economies, environments and communities are able to 'bounce back' from major external shocks such as natural disasters (see Folke et al, 2002; Folke, 2006). In the wake of recession, there has, however, been a renewed focus on what makes places economically resilient and able to withstand the impacts of recessions. Resilience has long been a parallel discourse to that of sustainability in the varied writings on vulnerability and risk (see, for example, Pelling, 2003), and its recent rise has been directly connected to a changing understanding of sustainability, with a greater emphasis on how existing modes of activity can be 'sustained' and how societies should adapt to the needs of new forms of capitalism. There are also, however, some interesting discussions afoot in cities like London on the theme of more radical modes of resilience planning and using the crisis to launch very different modes of activity.

And yet if, as some of the early evidence indicates, the emphasis of sustainability policy is shifting towards more *competitiveness-focused* agendas, then where will this leave broader concerns with social cohesion, (in)equality, environmental protection and recent shifts towards place building and the use of planning to promote a better quality of life? It may be that urban politics becomes less holistic and strategic in form and more focused on project-by-project developments within cities. There may also be additional pressures on planners and policy makers to prioritise private sector profitability and growth creation, over and above other forms of (welfare) state intervention. In many cities social and urban policy has, at heart, become focused on the training and mobilisation of poorer, welfare-dependent individuals to improve their skills and access available employment opportunities, with a decline in the use of area-based initiatives that attempted to achieve regeneration and renewal in a spatial (neighbourhood) form, including addressing the social and environmental dynamics of exclusion. This form of welfare has been very much part of the 'managing growth' agenda of the 1990s and 2000s (see Imrie et al, 2009). But in the absence of employment opportunities, urban policy may have to shift its emphasis on to job creation programmes in order to support social and environmental sustainability. Governments do not seem willing to pursue this course of action at present, but it may become a priority in the continued absence of economic growth.

A final area of policy contestation relates to that of urban security in post-recession cities. Urban policy, since its earliest days, has been concerned with the maintenance of urban order and control. Earlier rounds of de-industrialisation and economic restructuring brought about social fracturing and disorder in many cities (see Cochrane, 2007). One of the rationales for sustainable urban and social interventions within different cities has been to mitigate some of the worst affects of capitalist development, growing inequalities and tensions between different social groups (see Atkinson and Helms, 2007). But with the onset of recession and its aftermath the potential for urban disorder and community conflict is likely to rise, threatening urban order. There have already been signs of growing community tensions within cities and conflicts over public sector cuts and unemployment. With the rolling out of an 'austerity' agenda, and growing political tensions between diverse communities, as outlined earlier in this chapter, the causes of urban conflict are likely to be exacerbated in the coming decade, with urban and social cohesion and sustainability increasingly threatened. And as Zizek (2010) argues, the rolling-out of consensus-based post-political agendas across cities and societies means that the formal political avenues for conflict that characterised the postwar period are rapidly disappearing (see also Mouffe, 2005).

In summary, then, the discussion has highlighted the following:

- The financial crisis has precipitated a series of structural changes that threaten the growth models that have dominated development thinking since the early 1980s.
- Third Way agendas promoted sustainable development as an inclusive, 'post-political' construct.
- The recession has exposed the limitations in such thinking and highlighted the systematic inequalities and differences that exist within modern societies.
- In a range of policy fields including urban and social policy, welfare provision, demographic policy, (im)migration and environmental protection, policy makers are having to rapidly re-think their priorities, objectives and capabilities of action.

Contributions and the structure of the book

The contributions in the rest of this book examine different aspects of these tensions, and the discussion is divided into three sections. The first examines the politics of sustainable urbanism, including the rationales and conceptualisations of sustainability and the role of cities and urbanism with structures and techniques of governance. Following this introductory chapter, Mark Whitehead presents a 'pre-emptive' obituary for the sustainable city. He highlights how rhetorical political commitments to urban sustainability are not manifested in the actual social, economic and environmental practices within cities. In charting a series of processes that threaten and challenge the status of the sustainable city, including hyper-localism, neo-localism and municipal pragmatism, Whitehead considers conceptually the impacts of reconfiguring a sustainable urban development paradigm.

Locating the emergence of sustainable urbanism in the ecological and urban crises of the late 1960s and early 1970s, Whitehead shows how the identification of the spatial form and functioning of cities as key centres for environmental and ecological regulation and social welfare provision created paradigms and spatial frameworks within which it was assumed that economic development, environmental protection and social justice could be achieved and indeed were mutually reinforcing. Through studies of Mesa, Arizona, Totnes, England and the Meriden Gap, England, Whitehead problematises these assumptions, and shows that, while contemporary forms of governance are unique and offer opportunities to re-think the logic of urban development, they also risk restricting the conditions for alternative mechanisms and possibilities for achieving more sustainable cities.

Allan Cochrane continues the discussion by reflecting on sustainability as 'a language of governance' framed by 'spatial imaginaries' which influenced the Labour government's spatial policy programmes, including the rise of sustainable communities planning in England in the 2000s. He, like Mark Whitehead, critiques the policy assumptions that tensions between economic growth, environmental renewal and social justice (including addressing regional inequalities) could be resolved. Cochrane argues that while some of the language and rhetoric that characterised this period has dissipated in the wake of recession and regime change, the theme of 'sustainability' as a model for future growth firmly remains. The chapter reflects on the limits of English spatial planning as 'even in a context where the promise of growth might have been more realistic, the assumptions of unproblematic development were questionable'.

The legacies for the post-credit crunch era, which undermines policies premised on the 'assumption of market-driven economic growth', are profound, and 'the utopianism of basing policy around the potential of market development is all too apparent'. However, Cochrane also highlights new directions for the sustainable communities agenda. Drawing on recent contributions by Ed Soja, he argues that there is much potential in taking the most progressive features of the move to sustainability and incorporating them 'in a wider strategy that repositions sustainability as part of a drive towards forms of … spatial justice beyond the neighbourhood and the (South East) region'.

Will Eadson investigates the emergent and potential politics underpinning the construction of the carbon city. He draws on the sociology of accounting to examine experiments in urban carbon calculation in English cities. These calculations produce a range of actors and activities deemed to be either within or beyond the city. Eadson questions the extent to which calculative practices, including carbon management and local area agreements (LAAs) and the currencies and objects of carbon control, will be sufficient to achieve long-term behavioural and technological changes. Conceptualising cities and nations as spaces of governance, Eadson's chapter suggests that the urban and rural hinterlands of cities will be disconnected from new modes of carbon accumulation with consequences for spatial carbon inequalities. He urges a need to move beyond conceptualising cities as focal points towards understanding the behavioural and material networks within the politics of urban sustainability.

The second section explores the building of the sustainable city through specific policy fields, including the property industry, low carbon cities, transport and housing policy and the current themes, conflicts and issues arising. Tim Dixon discusses the property development industry and its role in the creation of new, and the regeneration of existing, urban environments. The chapter examines whether or not the recession represents a crisis or an opportunity for the property industry, both in terms of residential and commercial development. Dixon examines the changing nature of the property market in UK cities over the last 50 years, before turning to the existing legislative landscape and the opportunities and barriers that now exist for developers and investors.

The chapter highlights the primary role of land ownership and asset management in (sustainable) development processes and the corrosive affects of recession on property and land markets. This, in turn, has undermined the reliance of planning policy on private investment in cities. Planning gain measures, for example, are now in crisis, as are broader objectives for the provision of affordable housing and brownfield remediation/redevelopment. Over the next decade or so, Dixon argues that we may see a new plurality of land ownership and development models such as community land trusts and new forms of public–private partnership in addition to the reconfiguring of concepts such as 'responsible property investment'. The chapter highlights how environmental risks will create a changing geographic distribution of property investment and development in the UK and realigned responsibilities between developers, landlords and tenants. Whatever forms the development industry takes, the growth assumptions that characterised investment in the 1990s and 2000s have been undermined by the recession with uncertain outcomes.

In the following chapter, Harriet Bulkeley, Mike Hodson and Simon Marvin critically explore the interconnection between the climate change agenda and cities. They seek to examine whether cities are conceived as sites where partnerships and innovation can 'accelerate' national low carbon policy priorities or conversely whether cities are conceptualised as urban arenas that will prevent or slow the implementation of environmental policy goals and targets. The chapter draws on analysis of the 2009 UK Low Carbon Transition Plan to develop a four-part typology of urban strategies: eco-targets for sub-national governance, strategic eco-localism, implementing changes in socio-technical systems and carbon budgets and locales competing for eco-status in national competitions.

The typology developed by Bulkeley, Hodson and Marvin provides an important analytical and conceptual tool for examining how cities' roles in urban sustainability are conceived, enacted and contested, and the complex relationships between top-down and bottom-up responses and universal standards and selective and specific urban contexts. The chapter argues that new spaces of governance have emerged that increase the scope for innovation and experimentation at the city level as the UK government has 'sought to enrol the urban as a key site in the pursuit of a low carbon economy'. However, the selective prioritising within national policy frameworks and the envisioning of multiple and diverse roles for urban contexts remain highly contested and are manifested in conflicts between groups and interests within cities. The specific roles for selected urban areas will create a varied landscape of climate change response within and between cities, although continuing neoliberal rationales may be complemented by a more explicitly interventionist role for the state.

Transport in a sustainable urban future is the focus of the chapter by Iain Docherty and Jon Shaw, who identify how transport and transport systems were symbolic of a 'new modernity' linking sustainable urban development to city competitiveness. The chapter charts the evolution of transport policy perspectives in the last 30 years and then turns to exploring what the uncertain conditions of the post-financial crisis period will mean for urban transport and its contribution to the sustainable city. Like Bulkeley, Hodson and Marvin and Whitehead, Docherty and Shaw argue that the urban, and transport in particular, were and are sites and fields of experiments ('trailblazers') in neoliberalism, but the assumptions on which these policies and techniques were based have been undermined by the recession.

The chapter discusses the rationales and effects of 'new realism' and the competitiveness agenda, including more complex patterns of governance and relations (and regulation) between the state and private sectors. Although Docherty and Shaw acknowledge examples where transport investment has 're-engineered the city to make it more vibrant, diverse and socially inclusive', they suggest that continuing public investment is uncertain (despite having a historical precedent in previous periods of economic decline). They argue that, regardless of whether any economic recovery would facilitate a 'return to business as usual', there is a need to pose more fundamental questions about societal organisation and the role of transport in urban sustainability, including 'rediscovering and renewing the concept of accessibility and considering the social value of urban journeys and mechanisms such as road charging'. Docherty and Shaw suggest that it is the territory of public value and instruments of welfare, rather than neoliberalism, on which transport's contribution to urban sustainability should be conceptualised.

Chris Pickvance concludes this section with a description and explanation of the development of sustainable housing policy in the UK. He examines the complexities of the definition of 'sustainable housing' and classifies four main types of housing policies: domestic energy-saving measures, sustainability rating schemes, building regulations and planning policy. Pickvance identifies how each are informed and enacted through state interventions of exhortation, regulation and economic measures, arguing that the former two are more prevalent than spending commitments or taxation techniques.

The chapter then turns to explaining these forms of sustainable housing policies and their influences, including international commitments, and the roles and power of key actors such as the house building, building supplies and energy industries, housing associations, local government and pressure groups. Pickvance suggests that the key drivers of sustainable housing policies have been central government commitments to international targets and effective lobbying by the building supply and energy industries (and a key pressure group). The chapter concludes by highlighting how the recent abolition of regional housing targets and new localism are likely to reduce the prospects for achieving sustainable housing, within a policy rationality that ignores the lifestyle and social justice elements of definitions of urban sustainability.

The third section examines how practices of, and conflicts over, sustainability play out and are influenced by specific urban localities at the city and neighbourhood scales. Sarah Dooling uses a study of Austin, Texas to explore the intersection between parks and green belts and homeless populations. She argues that homelessness presents a particular challenge for concepts and policies of urban sustainability and indeed, the vulnerability of groups such as the homeless may be conceived as the antithesis of sustainability. Dooling shows how the interactions between social groups and the negotiations between them make visible the limitations of the rhetoric of sustainability in an urban settlement such as Austin which, through the Save our Springs ordinance and 'green city councils', has cultivated an image as an environmental city.

In critiquing current rationales that situate homelessness outside the scope of 'legitimate' spheres of planning for sustainability, the chapter argues for a more robust conceptualisation of urban sustainability which enables a focus on poverty and exclusion to challenge and re-imagine existing notions of the characteristics of sustainable cities. In particular, Dooling unpicks the inconsistencies between holistic notions of sustainability based on accessible and liveable urban cores that, in reality, ignore issues of social equity and result in the further spatial exclusion of vulnerable populations. She concludes that a new calculus of planning and 'urban accounting' is required that addresses the difficult dialectics between equity, economics and ecology.

John Flint's chapter seeks to complement the other studies in this volume by exploring how residents themselves understand and conceptualise neighbourhood change and the elements required for sustainable urban neighbourhoods. Based on a study of six low-income neighbourhoods in Britain, Flint frames his analysis within the social sustainability identified as a central component of urban renewal, sustainability and resilience in UK planning and social policy. Residents used a series of drivers, symbols and indicators of sustainability, including the (national and local) economy, population shifts and housing and physical infrastructure to generate complex narratives of positive and negative dimensions of change, including the impact of regeneration initiatives.

Residents viewed future economic development as underpinning any prospect for positive trajectories for their neighbourhoods. A powerful finding was the extent to which neighbourhood sustainability was crucial for residents as they viewed their futures within their current places of residence, although they felt powerless to influence the drivers of change occurring within them. Flint concludes by arguing for a basic level of infrastructure and service provision to be provided to all urban neighbourhoods, and suggests that the current Coalition government's emphasis on residential mobility and private sector investment are directly contradictory to other governmental approaches to securing social and economic sustainability in urban areas, such as the promotion of localism and the Big Society of civic engagement and voluntary endeavour.

The concluding chapter in this section, by Peter Newman, describes how London has been conceptualised as a global city and how this understanding has been a powerful driver of national and regional policies within the UK. The chapter argues that the fortunes of cities including London would be dependent on how national and local governments and the urban infrastructure would respond to market failure. Newman assesses London planning strategies and suggests that although there was an emphasis on economic development and a competitive global city agenda, this did not extend spatially or politically to the idea of a global city region.

The chapter explores the new rationalities of planning and sustainability in London following Boris Johnson succeeding Ken Livingstone as Mayor, but suggests that, although there has been some re-imagining of the spatiality of the city and sub-region, there has been less significant fundamental change, with the continuing city-centric focus of previous sustainability strategies. Newman concludes that new financial limitations on (public and private) investment in infrastructure will provide the context within which new and complex planning relationships and partnerships between the national and local state, private and voluntary providers and community interests will evolve.

In the final chapter of the book John Flint and Mike Raco identify key conclusions and set out a prospective future research agenda.

References

Atkinson, R. and Helms, G. (2007) *Securing an urban renaissance? Crime, community and British urban policy*, Bristol: The Policy Press.

Beck, U. (2000) *The cosmopolitan perspective: Sociology in the second age of modernity*, Oxford: Blackwell .

Beck, U. (2006) *The cosmopolitan vision*, Cambridge: Polity Press,.

Bevir, M. and Trentmann, F. (2007) 'Introduction: Consumption and citizenship in the new governance', in M. Bevir and F. Trentmann (eds) *Governance, consumers and citizens: Agency and resistance in contemporary politics*, Basingstoke: Palgrave Macmillan, pp 1-36.

Bourdieu, P. (2005) 'The mystery of ministry: From particular wills to the General Will', in L. Wacquant (ed) *Pierre Bourdieu and democratic politics*, Cambridge: Polity Press, pp 55-63.

Brand, P. and Thomas, M. (2005) *Urban environmentalism: Global change and the mediation of local conflict*, London: Routledge. Bristow (2010)

Bristow, G. (2010) 'Resilient regions: re-"place"ing regional competitiveness', *Cambridge Journal of Regions, Economy and Society*, vol 3, no 1, pp 153-67.

Bullen, A. and Whitehead, M. (2005) 'Negotiating the networks of space, time and substance: a geographical perspective on the sustainable citizen', *Citizenship Studies*, vol 9, no 5, pp 499-516.

Cabinet Office (2010) *The Coalition Agreement*, London: The Stationery Office.

Cochrane, A. (2007) *Understanding urban policy: A critical introduction*, Blackwell, Oxford.

Davis, M. and Monk, D. (eds) (2007) *Evil paradises – Dreamworlds of neo-liberalism*, New York: The New Press.

Economist, The (2009) 'Turning their backs on the world: the integration of the world economy is in retreat on almost every front', 19 February, accessed at: www.economist.com/node/13145370, 8 December 2010.

Economist, The (2010) 'The quest for growth', 9 October, p 11.

Economist Report (2010) 'A special report on the world economy', 9 October.

European Commission (2008) *The European Pact on Asylum and Immigration*, accessed at: www.euractiv.com/en/socialeurope/european-pact-immigration-asylum/article-175489, 5 June 2011.

Eurostat (2010) *Eurostat News Release – Euro indicators* (http://epp.eurostat.ec.europa.eu/cache/ITY_PUBLIC/2-13082010-BP/EN/2-13082010-BP-EN.PDF).

Folke, C. (2006) 'Resilience: the emergence of a perspective for social-ecological analysis', *Global Environmental Change*, vol 16, pp 253-67.

Folke, C. et al (2002) *Resilience and sustainable development: Building adaptive capacity*, Background paper commissioned by the Environmental Advisory Council of the Swedish Government.

Friends of the Earth (2008) 'Unemployment figures should need for green stimulus for green jobs', accessed at: www.foe.org/unemployment-figures-show-need-green-stimulus-green-jobs, 3 August 2009.

Giddens, A. (1994) *Beyond left and right: The future of radical politics*, Cambridge: Polity Press.

Giddens, A. (2002) *Runaway world*, Cambridge: Polity Press.

Gilbert, L. (2009) 'Immigration as local politics: re-bordering immigration and multiculturalism through deterrence and incapacitation', *International Journal of Urban and Regional Research*, vol 33, no 1, pp 26-42.

Goldie, J., Douglas, B. and Furnass, B. (2005) *In search of sustainability,* Collingwood, Victoria, Australia: CSIRO Publishing.

Guardian, The (2009) 'Recession takes a bite out of ethical and green retailing' (www.guardian.co.uk/sustainability/blog/ethical-shopping-green-consumerism-sustainable-purchasing-csr-sustainability).

Guardian, The (2010a) 'US military warns oil output may dip causing massive shortages by 2015', 11 April (www.guardian.co.uk/business/2010/apr/11/peak-oil-production-supply).

Guardian, The (2010b) 'Multiculturalism has failed, says Merkel', 18 October (www.guardian.co.uk/world/video/2010/oct/18/angela-merkel-multiculturalism-germany-video).

Harvey, D. (2009) *Cosmopolitanism and the geographies of freedom*, New York: Columbia University Press.

HM Treasury (2010) *Spending Review 2010,* London: The Stationery Office.

Hutton, W. (2010) *Them and us: Politics, greed and inequality – Why we need a fair society*, London: Little & Brown.

Imrie, R., Lees, L. and Raco, M. (eds) (2009) *Regenerating London: Governance, sustainability, and community in a global city*, London: Routledge.

Independent, The (2007) 'World oil supplies are set to run out faster than expected, warn scientists', 14 June (www.independent.co.uk/news/science/world-oil-supplies-are-set-to-run-out-faster-than-expected-warn-scientists-453068.html).

Jones, M. (1997) 'Spatial selectivity of the state? The regulationist enigma and local struggles over economic governance', *Environment and Planning A*, vol 29, no 5, pp 831-64.

Krugman, P. (2008) *The return of depression economics and the crisis of 2008,* London: Penguin.

Krugman, P. and Wells R. (2010) 'Our giant banking crisis – what to expect', *New York Review of Books*, May, pp 1-2.

Leggett, J. (2006) *Half gone – Oil, gas, hot air and the global energy crisis*, London: Portobello Books.

Manzi, T., Lucas, K., Lloyd Jones, T. and Allen, J. (eds) (2010) *Social sustainability in urban areas: Communities' connectivity and the urban fabric*, London: Earthscan.

Martinez-Alier, J. (1995) 'The environment as a luxury good or "too poor to be green"?', *Ecological Economics*, vol 13, pp 1-10.

Massey, D. (1993) 'Power-geometry and a progressive sense of place', in J. Bird, B. Curtis, T. Putnam, G. Robertson and L. Tickner (eds) *Mapping the futures: local cultures, global change*, London: Routledge, pp. 59–69.

Minsky, H, (2008) *Stabilising an unstable economy*, New York: McGraw-Hill.

Monbiot, G. (2007) 'This great free-market experiment is more like a corporate welfare scheme', 4 September, *The Guardian* (www.guardian.co.uk/commentisfree/2007/sep/04/comment.politics).

Mouffe, C. (2005) *On the political*, London: Routledge.

National Statistics (2010) Annual Abstract of Statistics – National Income, Expenditure and Output, accessed at: www.statistics.gov.uk/hub/economy/index.html, 5 June 2011

Norman, J. (2011) *The Big Society: The anatomy of the new politics*, Buckingham: University of Buckingham Press.

OECD (Organisation for Economic Co-operation and Development) (2010) *OECD Economic Outlook 2010*, Paris: OECD.

O'Grady, S. (2009) 'Next stop in the crisis could be the collapse of the euro', *The Independent*, 1 April 2009.

Osbourne, G. (2010) 'We will lead the economy out of crisis', Speech to Conservative Party Conference, Birmingham, 6 October.

Parsons, D. (1986) *The political economy of british regional policy*, Oxford: Blackwell.

Peck, J., Brenner, N. and Theodore, N. (2009) 'Post-neoliberalism and its malcontents', Antipode, vol 41, no 6, pp 1236-58.

Pelling, M. (2003) *The vulnerability of cities: Natural disasters and social resilience*, London: Earthscan.

Peston, R. (2008) *Who runs Britain? How Britain's new elite are changing our lives*, London: Hodder and Stoughton.

Pollock, A. (2005) *NHS plc: The privatisation of our health care*, London: Verso. .

Rancière, J. (2006) *Hatred of democracy*, London: Verso.

Reinhart, C. and Rogoff, K. (2010) *This time it's different: Eight centuries of financial folly*, Princeton, NJ: Princeton University Press.

Schumpeter, E. (1973) *Small is beautiful: A study of economics as if people mattered*, London: Blond and Briggs.

Scottish Government (2010) 'Building an offshore green economy', News release, 2 November, Edinburgh: Scottish Government (www.scotland.gov.uk/News/Releases/2010/11/02131033).

Swyngedouw, E. (2007) 'Impossible "sustainability" and the post-political condition', in R. Krueger and D. Gibbs (eds) *The sustainable development paradox*, New York: Guilford Press, pp 13-41.

US Bureau of Economic Analysis (2010) *Real GDP change* (www.bea.gov/).

Whitehead, M. (2007) *Spaces of sustainability: Geographical perspectives on the sustainable society*, London: Routledge.

Zizek, S. (2010) 'Liberal multiculturalism masks an old barbarism with a human face', *The Guardian*, 4 October, p 27.

two

The sustainable city: an obituary? On the future form and prospects of sustainable urbanism

Mark Whitehead

Introduction: Urban economic recovery and/or sustainable development

I recently encountered an interesting example of the irony that so often surrounds sustainable urban development. While visiting the city of Birmingham, an early morning local news segment caught my attention. Set against the backdrop of a traffic-laden M6 motorway, the newsreader earnestly reported that new statistics indicated that the Birmingham metropolitan area was finally heading out of economic recession. I immediately stopped what I was doing in order to hear what I assumed would be a rare piece of good news: unemployment down, I thought; perhaps welcome new investment in the city's ailing manufacturing sector? Without a flicker of apprehension, the newsreader reported that heavy goods traffic on the West Midlands section of the M6 motorway (already one of the busiest sections of road in Western Europe) was up, and associated congestion levels on the predominately elevated section of the urban freeway had increased by 33 per cent. Needless to say, I returned to morning ablutions in a less than positive mood.

This story is ironic because Birmingham is now, purportedly, a city that is dedicated to the long-term ambition of creating the *first sustainable global city in Britain* (Birmingham City Council, 2008; Whitehead, forthcoming). Perhaps I should not be too surprised by the paradox that is thrown up by Birmingham's ambiguous relationship with urban sustainability. With one or two notable exceptions, the rhetorical commitments that many cities have now officially made to sustainable development routinely contradict the actually existing social, economic and environmental practices of these places. It is precisely in this context that Krueger and Agyeman (2005) have questioned whether the study of urban sustainability should actually focus on cities that formally claim to be sustainable. Drawing on numerous political studies of urban sustainability (see Lake, 2000; Portney, 2003), Krueger and Agyeman (2005) claim that much of what counts as actually existing socio-environmental improvements in cities occurs outside of officially sanctioned programmes for sustainable development. Recent criticisms of sustainable urbanism have also drawn attention to its pernicious effects on urban politics (see Swyngedouw, 2010). According to Swyngedouw, the popularisation of relatively weak interpretations of sustainability (largely because of their utility for urban consensus building) actually does more damage than allowing unreformed patterns of neoliberal urban development to continue, as much of what passes for urban sustainability now occupies the ground that alternative environmental politics of the city could occupy (see Bulkeley et al, Chapter Six in this volume). Urban sustainability can thus be seen to foreclose the conditions of possibility under which more radical approaches to urban socio-environmental development could flourish, while helping to maintain a distinctly post-political (and post-democratic) urban system (Swyngedouw, 2010, p 14; see also Mouffe, 2005, and Flint, Chapter Ten, this volume).

Two questions emerge from these opening reflections. First, is sustainable urban development achieving a real change in the nature of the connections between urban social, economic and environmental relations? Second, is sustainable urban development now part of the complex web of barriers that make urban socio-environmental reform so difficult to achieve? It is in the light of these significant questions that I frame this chapter as a form of pre-emptive obituary for sustainable urban development. It is, of course, far too easy to claim the death of something in academic accounts. However, in suggesting the demise of sustainable urbanism I want to achieve two quite specific things. First, I want to chart a series of empirical processes that appear to be threatening the status of the sustainable city as the assumed goal of urban authorities the world over. Second, and more conceptually perhaps, I want to consider what is to be lost and what is to be gained from moving beyond a sustainable urban development paradigm. As with all obituaries, this endeavour is not only a process of unmitigated critique, but is also an assessment of the life, nature and achievements of sustainable urbanism.

This chapter commences with a brief account of origins of sustainable urbanism – an analysis that ultimately claims that sustainable urbanism has actually been with us for much longer than we often think. The following three sections chart a series of processes and challenges that are now threatening the power of sustainable urbanism, including hyper-liberalism, neo-localism and municipal pragmatism. The chapter ends with an assessment of the legacies of that which has been lost, and an indication of how those legacies may help to shape our shared future.

Birth: the origins of sustainable urbanism

While it is difficult to offer a precise date of birth for sustainable urbanism, most scholars will, with a fair degree of confidence, provide an approximate period of origin for the sustainable city (see Whitehead, 2003; Keil and Whitehead, forthcoming). Sustainable urbanism appears, at least ostensibly, to have emerged out of the two interconnected crises in the late 1960s and early 1970s: the first of these crises was ecological, the second urban. The ecological crisis was a product of the culmination of the large and small-scale environmental damage that had been wrought by rapid industrialisation. The urban crisis, on the other hand, had two major components. The first was connected to the ecological crisis and concerned the environmental impacts of rapidly sprawling and heavily polluting cities that had expanded in the so-called 'golden age' of Fordist-Keynesian expansion following the end of the Second World War (Marcotullio and McGranahan, 2007). The second concerned the deteriorating quality of urban life for many urban residents within the rapidly expanding cities of the global South (Marcotullio and McGranahan, 2007). These interconnecting urban concerns were first addressed in a systematic way at the first international conference of the United Nations (UN) Centre for Human Settlements (Habitat) in Vancouver in 1976 (see Keil and Whitehead, forthcoming). The Vancouver Declaration, which emerged from this meeting, is important not because it laid the foundations for the principles of sustainable urbanism (the phrase was never actually used in this conference) but because it embodied the first attempt to try and rein in the worst socio-environmental effects of unregulated urbanism (UNCHS, 1976). But while the desire to produce a more controlled pattern of urbanisation clearly echoes what we would now define as sustainable urban development, it is important to recognise that the Vancouver Declaration, and the early work of the UN Centre for Human Settlements, was actually very different to the contemporary norms of sustainable urbanism (Girardet, 2003, pp 20-2). The outcome of the Vancouver Declaration was essentially an attempt to stop the growth of urban centres by investing in the infrastructures of rural locations (Girardet, 2003, pp 20-2).

The year 1976 is important in the history of sustainable urbanism not because it provided the first blueprints of this paradigm of development, but because it instigated two important processes: a recognition of the dual role of cities as key centres for environmental/ecological regulation and social welfare provision, and an emerging recognition of the importance of addressing the worst socio-environmental impacts of unregulated urban development. Based on these broad foundations, sustainable urbanism is really the product of a series of advances in economics, ecology, planning and architecture during the 1980s (see Rogers and Gumuchdjian, 1997, pp 27–63). These developments were important because rather than simply seeing urban areas as things that must be controlled – if a sustainable balance between economic growth and socio-environmental welfare was to be achieved – they asserted that the spatial form and functioning of cities could actually offer the key to the development of a more sustainable future. Just as ecological science was starting to quantify and qualify the precise environmental impacts of cities, planners, engineers and designers were devising new ways to reduce the ecological demands of urban space and transform the linear metabolisms of cities into self-sustaining circular loops (see Girardet, 2003, pp 32–46). At the centre of these new advances in urban thought was the notion that, if effectively planned and designed, cities could provide highly energy-efficient ways to organise social life and economic activity (see Hall, 2003). Thus the vision of a compact, mixed-use urban setting, replete with low energy technologies, became synonymous with sustainable urbanism, and the twin goals of environmental conservation and enhanced social conviviality (see Rogers and Gumuchdjian, 1997; Girardet, 2003). It is precisely in this context that sustainable urbanism has now become almost synonymous with the planning paradigms of *new urbanism* and *smart growth* and the associated tools of transit-oriented development, urban villages and anti-sprawl zoning laws (Krueger and Gibbs, 2008). As planning systems that emerged in the 1970s and 1980s, these paradigms provided spatial frameworks within which to pursue the *win-win-win* interfaces of economic development, social justice and environmental protection that are prioritised within sustainable development policies more generally.

If sustainable urban development represents a form of spatialised 'fix' (While et al, 2004; see also Chapter Four, this volume) for the broader goals of sustainable development, it is crucial to recognise that the ideas and principles it draws on have a much longer history. The greater efficiency savings that were to be made from carefully planned forms of urban re-concentration were, for example, hallmarks of Le Corbusier's vision of the Radiant City. The closed loops of spatially integrated food-waste-energy production envisaged by sustainable urbanisers are clearly echoes of the garden city plans of Howard and the urban ecological regions envisaged by Mumford and MacKaye (Luccarelli, 1995). The forms of community conviviality pursued within the smart, new urbanisms of sustainable cities also clearly parallel the architectural techniques deployed within Burnham's City Beautiful.

Recognising the varied influences, and urban precursors, to sustainable urbanism does, however, raise the troubling question of what, if anything, is unique about the contemporary pursuit of the sustainable city. I would argue that there are both qualitative and quantitative differences between sustainable urbanism and its ancestor concepts. At a qualitative level – and when applied in its most effective forms – sustainable urbanism is different from many of its planning precursors because rather then seeking to impose big green ideas onto urban communities, it attempts to actively work with existing urban systems in order to achieve more sustainable socio-ecological interchanges (see Jacobs, 1961). To these ends the strong association between sustainable urbanism and local community empowerment is often seen as a key defining characteristic of whether an initiative can be deemed sustainable or not, although, as John Flint argues in this volume (see Chapter Ten), the empowerment of local residents is, in reality, very weak. At a more quantitative level, however, sustainable urbanism is also novel to the extent that it seeks to measure its efficacy across an expanded horizon of time and space. Thus, while in the garden city, and even the urban eco-region, sustainability would have been determined at a relatively local scale, the sustainable city's socio-ecological footprint is increasingly being traced to distant communities and connected to a range of interconnected planetary ecological systems. Perhaps an even more novel dimension of sustainable urbanism is that it urges urban planners and denizens alike to recalibrate their decision making in light of the likely need of future generations within and beyond their own city (Whitehead, forthcoming). While the notion of urban inter-generational justice raises a range of thorny ethical and practical issues (see Barry, 1997), it is arguably the most distinctive feature of sustainable urbanism. Having established the ancestry from which sustainable urbanism has emerged, I now want to move on to consider a series of emerging challenges to its legitimacy as a model of 21st-century urban development.

Death I: hyper-liberalism and experiments in sub-prime urbanism

I begin my analysis of the contemporary decline of sustainable urbanism within the little-studied urban settlement of Mesa. Mesa is a prototypical sun-belt city, located to the East of Phoenix, Arizona (see Figure 2.1). Like many emerging cities in the American southwest, since the 1940s Mesa has developed a distinctive brand of property-led urban expansion (see Molotch, 1976). Basing its economy primarily on the expanded commercialisation of surrounding land, Mesa has grown its population from approximately 7,000 in 1940 to over half a million residents in 2008, making it larger than Washington DC, Cleveland and Miami (see *The Economist*, 2008). Mesa is a classic example of what Harvey Molotch (1976) terms an urban growth machine: a sprawling, low-rise city, with a low density of population, and a high household dependence on the motorcar (see also Davis, 2002). Although Mesa reflects the kind of unregulated, desert urbanism that sustainable urbanists attempt to resist, it is not the contemporary form of Mesa that interests me in this section, but instead the urban authority's plans for the city's future.

Figure 2.1: Map of Mesa

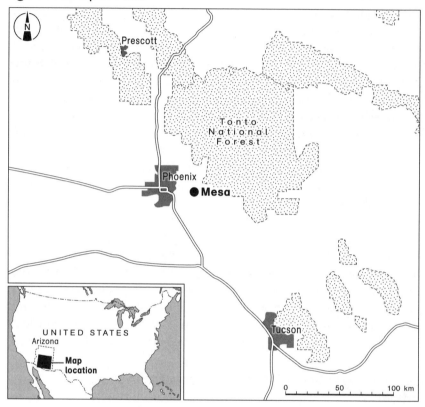

As with many sun-belt cities, the property-based economy of Mesa was severely compromised by the onset of the sub-prime housing crisis in the US. Toxic mortgage debt, repossessions and a lack of available finance for new home buyers served to undermine the economic circuit of capital that Mesa had founded its development on. What is interesting about the sub-prime housing crisis (and associated global 'credit crunch') in terms of sustainable development is that, despite its devastating effects on urban communities throughout the world, it did offer an opportunity to re-think the patterning and logic of urban development, and provide a foothold for the principles of sustainability to take hold (see New Economics Foundation, 2008). According to the New Economics Foundation, the credit crunch offered an opportunity to radically question the unsustainable investment in property that had become the hallmark of so many urban economies and had only been maintained on the basis of the creation of dangerous levels of household debt. In their *Green New Deal* strategy, the New Economics Foundation (2008) envisaged the formation of a new, more sustainable economy, which would be based on investment in green industries and technologies and the creation of so-called *green-collar jobs*. Mesa's response has, however, been very different to this urban *Green New Deal*.

In early December 2008, the city authorities of Mesa annexed 13 square kilometres of desert land in order to provide the basis for a new frontier of urban development. This new segment of credit crunch-busting real estate will be subject, in part at least, to the application of smart urbanist principles. However, in an attempt to give Mesa the competitive edge needed to kick-start its growth machine, the new urban development will also contain a novel focal point: the development will be centred on an airport. According to *The Economist* (2008, p 57): '[R]ather than pushing air traffic to the fringe of the city ... Mesa will build around its runways. It hopes to become ... a city as tied to air traffic as 19th-century cities were to railways'. At least two important points emerge from Mesa's attempt to develop an *aerotropolis*. First is the question of just how sustainable it is to ground urban development around the carbon-intensive transport associated with air travel. Many now argue that air travel needs to become a less, not more, attractive travel option (see Monbiot, 2006). Second, and perhaps of greater concern, is what Mesa's development plans tell us about the rationalities that guide urban planning at the beginning of the 21st century. I would argue that while tempered by the promises of new urbanism, Mesa's search for new outlets for growth is symptomatic of the kinds of hyper-liberal urbanism Mike Davis (2005) uncovered in places like Dubai, Singapore and Las Vegas. As *apotheoses of neoliberalism*, such cities appear to take any steps (whatever the socio-environmental cost) to ensure their continued growth and predominance in an increasingly competitive urban world.

While it is clearly premature to claim that the recent global financial crisis has unleashed an implacable hyper-liberal urban order, it is also apparent that this economic juncture is severely restricting the conditions of possibility for constructing more sustainable cities (see Brenner, 2009). Consequently, whether it is government initiatives to support renewed consumer confidence and spending through the manipulations of various valued-added tax registers, or the lowering of interest rates to promote greater borrowing and mortgage purchases, it appears that the way out of urban recession is one that places economic expansion ahead of its potential environmental consequences.

Death II: urban transition movements and neo-localisation

Totnes is a market town of approximately 7,000 people, located in the English county of Devon (see Figure 2.2). This popular holiday destination may seem like a strange place to be discussing the demise of sustainable urbanism. However, as with the city of Mesa, recent events within this town are challenging the orthodoxies of sustainable urban development. Totnes is significant to this discussion because it is the home of the Transition Initiative Movement (and Transition Town Totnes). The Transition Initiative Movement is a network of communities predominantly located within the UK, Ireland and North America (but increasingly also including other European, South American and Asian communities) that are dedicated to developing locally grounded solutions to the twin threats of climate change and Peak Oil production (see Bailey et al, 2010; Mason and Whitehead, forthcoming; North, 2010). There is now evidence of several hundred Transition culture initiatives operating throughout the world. Inspired by the principles of permaculture and re-localisation, Transition initiatives are essentially dedicated to developing just strategies of *energy descent*, which essentially enable communities to continue to meet their varied needs in a future that is likely to be constrained by high costs for energy and the threats of climate change (see Hopkins, 2008; Hopkins and Lipman, 2009). Although Transition initiatives are formally connected and accredited within a Transition Network, it is clear that they are actually emblematic of a broader series of movements throughout the world, including the Resilience Alliance, the Slow Food Movement, Local Exchange Trading Schemes, the Degrowth movement (*décroissance*) and *Organoponico*, that are looking to construct local systems of trade, food production and service provision in order to counter the high-energy systems of global production and supply that dominate urban economies (see Mason and Whitehead, forthcoming).

Ostensibly there appears to be much that connects sustainable urbanism and the forms of ecologically imbued re-localisation movements that Transition initiatives reflect. They both consider the urban in holistic terms and display a concern for the triple role of the town and cities within environmental protection, securing social justice and supporting economic productivity. There are, however, three key differences between Transition initiatives and sustainable urbanism. These differences can be summarised as approaches to the local, interpretations of economic development and perceptions of the future (see Mason and Whitehead, forthcoming). In relation to localisation, while sustainable urbanism clearly prioritises the importance of creating integrated envelopes of everyday life, where work, play and rest can be achieved in relatively close proximity, it does not encourage the same degree of holistic localisation prioritised in Transition initiatives. Indeed, where Transition initiatives actively work against unnecessary, long-distance trading, sustainable urbanists would see expanded global (fair) trade as part of a city's broader contribution to international development. It is clear that Transition initiatives have a very different approach to questions of economic growth and development than those promoted within the sustainable city. While sustainable urbanists may promote properly framed economic growth (and associated forms of ecological modernisation) as a key basis for addressing broader issues of social justice and poverty alleviation, re-location is in part based on the recognition that economic growth has limits. Consequently, whether it be in the context of the systemic environmental threats associated with climate change, or the thermodynamic limits associated with peak energy production, Transition initiatives assert that urban communities have to face up to the prospect of a contracting sphere of economic production.

Finally, and related to this pessimistic interpretation of economic development, it is clear that the Transition initiatives have a far less optimistic vision of the urban future (in the absence of significant socioeconomic reform) than those encoded within the manifestos of sustainable urban development. Consequently, while sustainable urbanisers talk of the attainment of efficient win–win–win trade-offs between economic development, social justice and environmental protection, Transition initiatives are much more likely to talk

Figure 2.2: Map of Totnes

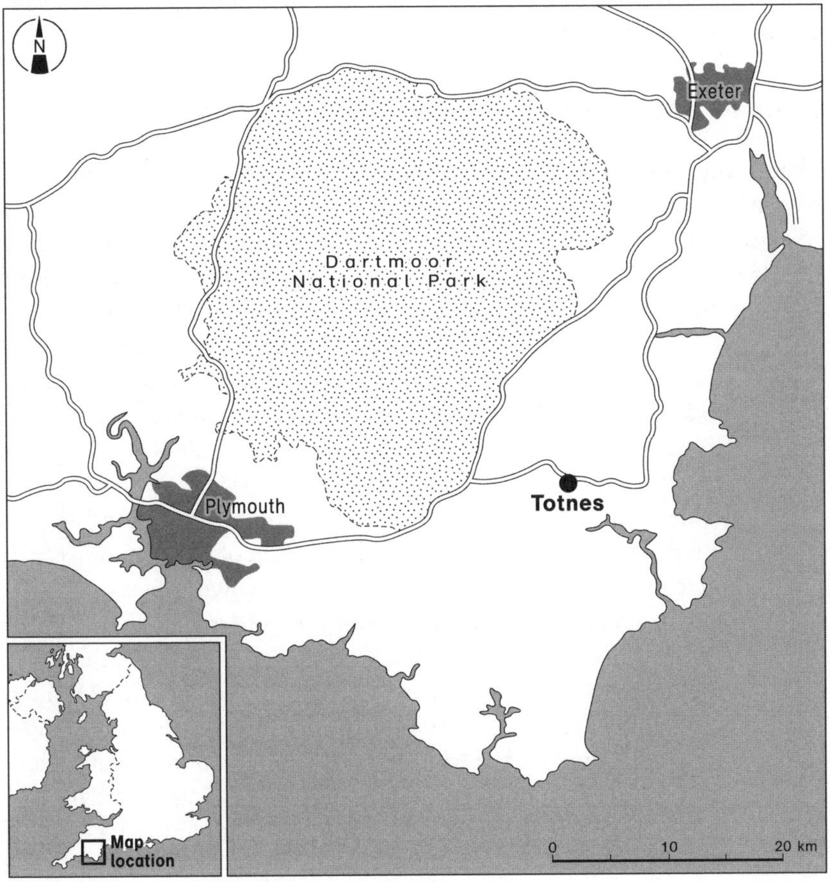

about the need to prepare for the worst. It is precisely in this context that the ecological notion of resilience has effectively replaced the principles of sustainable development at the heart of the Transition Movement. Unlike sustainability, resilience suggests that local communities need to be able to build ways of coping with external shocks, such as those associated with increasing energy costs, or the traumas that climate change could produce (see also Chapter Ten, this volume). Related strategies include, inter alia, the localisation of food and clothing production, the modularisation and diversification of energy supply and the development of an effective range of practical skills and knowledge within the local community in order to support its diverse socioeconomic needs for repair and maintenance.

It is important to recognise that, while the urban experiments being conducted and promoted in Mesa and Totnes challenge the legitimacy of sustainable urbanism, they do so in very different ways. Consequently, if Mesa's plans for a new aerotropolis suggest the increasing irrelevance of urban sustainability in an age of economic decline and growing urban competition, the existence of the Transition Movement suggests that the ideals of sustainable urban development simply do not do enough in an age of ensuing environmental crisis.

Death III: win-lose-lose and the rise of municipal pragmatism

The Meriden Gap is a narrow band of rural land in England separating the West Midlands conurbation (the city of Birmingham and the towns and cities of the Black Country inclusive) from the city of Coventry (see Figure 2.3). If you were to stand in the Meriden Gap you could be forgiven for thinking that it is a relatively innocuous piece of the English countryside. If you were to spend some time in this area, however, you would quickly become aware of the intense controversies associated with this place and how these issues are connected to the rise of a form of municipal pragmatism that appears to threaten the orthodoxies of sustainable urban development (see Whitehead, forthcoming).

The Meriden Gap has become an object of significant political debate within the last decade because of particular aspects of the area. First, it is a key frontier of development for Birmingham's evolving post-industrial urban growth machine. To its immediate west, it is bordered by Birmingham International Airport and the National Convention Centre. As these key hubs of employment of investment have sought to expand, the Meriden Gap has come under increasing development pressure. In addition to these post-industrial growth poles, the Meriden Gap has also come under intense development pressure from the regional housing lobby. Being located in close proximity to the highly desirable residential areas surrounding the town of

Solihull, the Meriden Gap is essentially perceived as prime real estate for high-end housing developments.

Figure 2.3: Map of Meriden

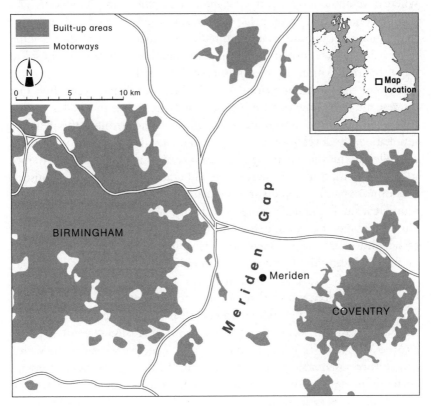

The controversies surrounding the Meriden Gap stem from the fact that, although it represents a key strategic site for the economic future of Birmingham, it is actually part of the West Midlands Green Belt. This is an area of 923 square miles of protected countryside. Established in 1975, it was instigated in order to protect the agricultural land and connected ecological spaces of the region, and to prevent the unregulated expansion of the city of Birmingham (see CPRE-West Midlands, 2007). At one level, of course, the West Midlands Green Belt could be conceived of as an early technology of sustainable urban development. By imposing a strict growth boundary on the city, the West Midlands Green Belt, in part at least, was initially conceived of as a way of intensifying economic development within the city, and encouraged a more compact and efficient blending of living and working places within the city. Increasingly, however, critics have questioned its sustainability credentials. At one level, these critics have argued that by limiting the proximate spread of Birmingham into its most immediate rural hinterland the Green Belt has actually been contributing to increasing journey times to work and the elevated production of air pollution in the region as more and more people live on the other side of the Green Belt, where development is permitted (Whitehead, forthcoming). Concerns have also been raised that green belts, like those in the West Midlands, can lead to the inflation of house prices within the cities that they surround, making it very difficult for low to middle-income families to be able to afford to buy properties within the areas in which they work.

It is not the emerging critiques of the West Midlands Green Belt that interest me here, however. I am more concerned with the strategies that have been put in place to resolve the tensions that surround the desire to simultaneously develop on and protect the Meriden Gap, and what these can tell us about the emerging nature of urban sustainability. In an attempt to find a compromise between the imperatives of affordable housing, economic expansion and environmental conservation a form of pragmatic municipalism is gradually emerging in the West Midlands region (see Chapter Three, this volume, for a further discussion of pragmatism). The broad idea of municipal pragmatism is supported by key environmental groups, including the Campaign for the Conservation of Rural England, West Midlands and planning authorities, including the West Midlands Regional Assembly, who are responsible for producing the key planning strategies in and through which green belt policy is delivered in the area. At the heart of this coalition of pragmatism is the realisation that in places like the Meriden Gap it may be impossible to effectively balance the varied demands of sustainable urban development. To these ends, discussions are currently being convened to establish whether it may be possible to trade green belt development in some areas with the extension of protected areas status in other districts. This approach is actually akin to the natural capital philosophy approach to environmental planning that became popular within statutory agencies in the UK during the 1990s. Such a strategy is pragmatic to the extent that it recognises that certain tracts of the West Midlands Green Belt (particularly those areas that have been subject to intensive farming practices) are not of high ecological value, while other unprotected open spaces (particularly green fragments within the core of the metropolis) support a much broader range of ecological diversity (see Whitehead, forthcoming; see also West Midlands Regional Assembly, 2007; CPRE-West Midlands, 2010).[1]

While elegant in its simplicity, and clearly serving to benefit parties on all sides, I would claim that such brands of municipal pragmatism reflect an important shift away from the core principles of sustainable urban development. Just like the forms of urban sustainability fix articulated by While et al (2004), such strategies involve an open recognition that it is not possible to balance the demands for social justice, economic development and environmental protection in all places, all of the time, as demonstrated by Sarah Dooling's account of Austin, Texas, in Chapter Nine in this volume. While acknowledging the need to move from an idealised *win-win-win* urban development scenario, to one of *win-lose-win*, the *municipal pragmatism* of the West Midlands region also reveals the possible spatial and scalar displacement of social, economic and environmental gains and losses within a city. To these ends, municipal pragmatism does not so much represent a fudging of the principles of sustainable urban development as it does a broadening of the scale at which you determine whether urban sustainability has been achieved.

Resurrection? The future of the sustainable city

Strangely, and despite the pessimistic tone of this chapter so far, its intention has not been to 'bury' sustainable urbanism. Rather the chapter has attempted to lay some of the groundwork for the development of a form of sustainable urbanism that is more worthy of praise than much of what currently uses that name. By exposing some of the very real threats that exist to sustainable urban development we may be both better able to confront the challenges it faces and more keenly aware of what we stand to lose with its potential demise.

If we consider the sub-prime urbanism of Mesa, for example, we find an economic assault on the principles of sustainable urbanism, which essentially asserts that when economic decline takes hold in a city, environmental concerns must recede in the hierarchy of policy priorities. But it is precisely in the context of the purported economic necessity for more growth that sustainable development can become a powerful tool for charting alternative ways out of urban recession. If sustainable development orthodoxies can be dislocated from their arbitrary association with economic models of growth and expansion (see Bernstein, 2000), sustainable urbanism could hold those who have used the current downturn as a basis to pursue economic growth at all costs to account. At one level, it could help remind urban communities that economic growth and economic development are not necessarily the same thing. The principles of urban sustainable development could also be used to reassert the simple realisation that economic development is not incompatible with the attainment of socio-environmental justice: it is only the unfettered, short-term pursuit of economic growth, at any cost, that preclude more progressive metropolitan goals (see Dooling, Chapter Nine, this volume). Urban sustainability can, in this context, help us all remember that there are many different economies that can be built within our cities, which are very different to the narrowly prescribed options we are currently being presented with.

While there is clearly much to admire within the goals and activities of neo-localisation movements such as Transition towns and cities, their emergence also serves as an important reaffirmation of the values that are associated with urban sustainability. While it is perfectly possible to interpret *Transition initiatives* as a species of sustainable urbanism, key goals of sustainable urbanism are compromised within Transition towns (see here Mason and Whitehead, forthcoming). As with many urban movements that are concerned with reducing energy consumption and greenhouse gas emissions, there is a danger within Transition towns that a synoptic focus on these goals can neglect the uneven social impacts that such measures can have (see While et al, 2010). While Transition initiatives do have an explicit concern with so-called 'energy-vulnerable groups' (particularly older people and those on low incomes), they often lack the focus that sustainable urban development places on direct forms of poverty alleviation and wealth redistribution. In a different context, the forms of extreme localism promoted within Transition initiatives works against the forms of international municipalism that underpin sustainable urbanism. Consequently, although neo-localist movements represent powerful responses to the over-extended ecological footprints of cities, they tend to inhibit the development of global empathy, and care-at-distance, that are built out of ethical international trade relations and associated systems of global interaction (see Massey, 2007; Rifkin, 2010).

Finally, in the case of *municipal pragmatism* we are confronted with a movement that navigates the difficulties of meeting the varied goals of sustainable development in specific locations by pursuing a series of socio-environmental trade-offs across urban space. While at its heart sustainable urban development suggests that it should be possible to balance the varied needs of urban life in situ, municipal pragmatism essentially moves these needs around: ensuring that losses in one geographical location are compensated in another. While appealing in political terms, such a strategy raises the ethical conundrum of the unequal distribution of socio-environmental benefits and harm (see Whitehead, forthcoming; Kundu, 2007). By spatially disaggregating the assessment of sustainability-gain throughout an urban region, municipal pragmatism clearly distances itself from the moral commitment of sustainability to ensure geographical equity in the nature of urban development.

It is on the basis of these assessments that this chapter has argued that we have far more to lose than we have to gain from the demise of sustainable urbanism. Despite its obvious corruption within many urban development programmes, it is clear that the presence of the principles of sustainable development within the urban policy process represent a hard-fought victory for those who are eager to see the building of more progressive and just patterns of urbanisation. Rather than starting this discursive battle all over again, armed, perhaps, with a new paradigm of urban eco-development, the principles of urban sustainability could provide a grid of legitimation against which to hold urban authorities and communities who claim to be acting sustainably, to account. We don't need less talk of urban sustainability; we need much, much more.

Key conclusions

- Climate change, the rise of new forms of hyper-liberal urban development, neo-localist urban development strategies and municipal pragmatism are all threatening the power of sustainable urban development as a paradigm of metropolitan planning.
- There is far more to lose than to gain from the demise of sustainable urban development as a key principle of urban planning.
- Adopting more radical interpretations of sustainable urban development could help to shape a more progressive urban planning culture.

Note

[1] Although this is not a strategy that is formally noted in either the Campaign to Protect Rural England – West Midlands and West Midlands Regional Assembly's formal planning statements, it is a process that is openly recognised and discussed by key officials.

Further reading

Krueger, R. and Gibbs, D. (2008) 'Third Wave sustainability: smart growth and regional development in the USA', *Regional Studies*, vol 49, no 9, pp 1263-74.

Portney, K. (2003) *Taking sustainable cities seriously*, Cambridge, MA: The MIT Press.

While, A., Jonas, A.E.G. and Gibbs, D. (2010) 'From sustainable development to carbon control: eco-state restructuring and the politics of urban and regional development', *Transactions of the Institute of Geography and Earth Sciences*, vol 35, no 1, pp 76-93.

References

Bailey, I., Hopkins, R. and Wilson, G. (2010) 'Some things old some things: the spatial representations and politics of change of the peak oil relocalisation movement', *Geoforum*, vol 41, pp 595-605.

Barry, B. (1997) 'Sustainability and intergenerational justice', *Theoria*, vol 45, no 89, pp 43-65.

Bernstein, S. (2000) 'Ideas, social structure and the compromise of liberal environmentalism', *European Journal of International Relations*, vol, 6, no 4, pp 464-512.

Birmingham City Council (2008) *Birmingham 2026 – Our vision for the future: Sustainable community strategy*, Birmingham: Birmingham City Council.

Brenner, N. (2009) 'What is critical urban theory?', *City*, vol 13, no 2-3, pp 195-204.

CPRE-WM (Campaign to Protect Rural England-West Midlands) (2007) *What price West Midlands Green Belts?*, Birmingham: CPRE-WM.

CPRE-WM (2010) *Manifesto for the West Midlands countryside*, Birmingham: CPRE-WM.

Davis, M. (2002) *Dead cities and other tails*, New York: New York Press.

Davis, M. (2005) 'Sinister paradise: does the road to the future end in Dubai?' (www.tomdispatch.com/post/5807/mike_davis_on_a_paradise_built_on_oil).

Economist, The (2008) 'City of the future: a rare opportunity to build an urban centre from scratch', *The Economist*, vol 389, no 8609, pp 56-7.

Girardet, H. (2003) *Creating sustainable cities*, Dartington: Green Books.

Hall, P. (2003) 'The sustainable city in an age of globalization', in L.F. Girard, B. Forte, M. Cerreta, P. De Toro, and F. Forte (eds) *The human sustainable city: Challenges and perspectives from the Habitat Agenda*, Aldershot: Ashgate, pp 55-69.

Hopkins, R. (2008) *The Transition handbook*, Totnes: Green Books.

Hopkins, R. and Lipman, P. (2009) *The Transition Network Ltd: Who we are and what we do*, Totnes: Transition Network Ltd.

Jacobs, J. (1961) *The death and life of the great American cities*, London: Random House.

Keil, R. and Whitehead, M. (forthcoming) 'Cities and the politics of sustainability', in K. Mossberger, and S. Clarke (eds) *The Oxford handbook of urban politics*, Oxford: Oxford University Press.

Krueger, R. and Agyeman, J. (2005) 'Sustainability schizophrenia or "actually existing sustainabilities?" Toward a broader understanding of the politics and promise of local sustainability in the US', *Geoforum*, vol 36, no 4, pp 410-17.

Krueger, R. and Gibbs, D. (2008) 'Third Wave sustainability: smart growth and regional development in the USA', *Regional Studies*, vol 49, no 9, pp 1263-74.

Kundu, A. (2007) 'Dynamics of growth and process of degenerated peripheralization in Delhi: an analysis of socio-economic segmentation and differentiation in micro-environments', in P.J. Marcotullio and G. McGranahan (eds) *Scaling urban environment challenges: From local to global and back*, London: Earthscan, pp 156-78.

Lake, R. (2000) 'Contradictions in the local state: local implementation of the US sustainability agenda in the USA', in N. Low, B. Gleeson, I. Elander and R. Lidskog (eds) *Consuming cities: The urban environment in the global economy after the Rio Declaration*, London: Routledge, pp 70-90.

Luccarelli, M. (1997) *Lewis Mumford and the ecological region: The politics of planning*, New York: Guilford Press.

Marcotullio, P.J. and McGranahan, G. (2007) 'Scaling the urban environmental challenge', in P.J. Marcotullio, and G. McGranahan (eds) *Scaling urban environment challenges: From local to global and back*, London: Earthscan, pp 1-17.

Massey, D. (2007) *World city*, Cambridge: Polity Press.

Mason, K. and Whitehead, M. (forthcoming) 'Transition urbanism and the contested politics of ethical place-making', *Antipode*.

Molotch, H. (1976) 'The city as a growth machine: toward a political economy of place', *The American Journal of Sociology*, vol 82, no 2, pp 309-32.

Monbiot, G. (2006) *Heat: How to stop the planet burning*, London: Penguin, Allen Lane.

Mouffe, C. (2005) *On the political*, New York: Routledge.

New Economics Foundation (2008) *Green New Deal*, London: New Economics Foundation.

North, P. (2010) 'Eco-localization as a progressive response to peak oil and climate change – a sympathetic critique', *Geoforum*, vol 41, pp 585-94.

Portney, K. (2003) *Taking sustainable cities seriously*, Cambridge, MA: The MIT Press.

Rifkin, J. (2010) *The empathic civilization: The race to global consciousness in a world in crisis*, Cambridge: Polity Press.

Rogers, R. and Gumuchdjian, P. (1997) *Cities for a small planet*, London: Faber & Faber.

Swyngedouw, E. (2010) 'Apocalypse forever? Post-political populism and the spectre of climate change theory', *Culture & Society*, vol 27, no 2/3, pp 213-32.

UNCHS (United Nations Conference on Human Settlements) (1976) *The Vancouver Declaration on Human Settlements*, Habitat: UNCHS.

West Midlands Regional Assembly (2007) *West Midlands Regional Spatial Strategy: Phase Two Revision – Draft*, Birmingham: West Midlands Regional Assembly.

While, A., Jonas, A.E.G. and Gibbs, D.C. (2004) 'The environment and the entrepreneurial city: searching for the urban "sustainability fix" in Leeds and Manchester', *International Journal of Urban and Regional Research*, vol 28, no 3, pp 549-69.

While, A., Jonas, A.E.G. and Gibbs, D. (2010) 'From sustainable development to carbon control: eco-state restructuring and the politics of urban and regional development', *Transactions of the Institute of Geography and Earth Sciences*, vol 35, no 1, pp 76-93.

Whitehead, M. (2003) '(Re)analysing the sustainable city: nature, urbanization and the regulation of socio-environmental relations in the UK', *Urban Studies*, vol 40, no 7, pp 1183-206.

Whitehead, M. (forthcoming) 'Urban economic development and environmental sustainability', in R. Paddison and T.A. Hutton (eds) *Cities and economic change*, London: Sage Publications.

three

Sustainable communities and English spatial policy

Allan Cochrane

Introduction

This chapter explores some of the ways in which, in the first decade of the 21st century, the notion of sustainable communities was used to frame a quite distinctive spatial development policy for England, even in the absence of any explicitly stated overall national plan. It considers the rise of sustainability as a language of governance, before moving on to a case study of the Sustainable Communities Plan (initially sponsored by the Office of the Deputy Prime Minister), both in terms of its implications for the different regions of England and as a plan for the South East of England in particular (see also Chapter Eleven, this volume). It highlights the extent to which contemporary planning has both been predicated on assumptions of uneven development and served to reinforce the process, within and between England's regions. Although the Sustainable Communities Plan itself no longer has any political salience, the issues raised by it remain important: because of the implicit spatial understandings which underpinned it; because of the claims it made to environmental sensitivity; and because of the way in which it set out to integrate economic and social priorities in the development of market-based policies oriented towards housing development and the making up of new communities. At least in the South East, the pressures to which it was a response have not disappeared.

Sustainability and sustainable communities

Some words have a privileged place in the language of public policy. Academic debates around their conceptualisation jostle with a range of policy practices in the context of a wider set of popular understandings (see, for example, Cochrane and Talbot, 2008; and Mooney and Neal, 2009, for a discussion of the constellations that have gathered around the notions of 'security' and 'community'). In the last few decades 'sustainability' seems to have joined the list, with all the tensions, uncertainties and possibilities that implies, apparently taken for granted as a policy ambition but with its precise meaning contested or at least uncertain.

Despite the warnings expressed by some (see, for example, Jackson, 2009) who set out to challenge conventional growth narratives, the promise of 'sustainability' or sustainable development is that, as also highlighted by Mark Whitehead in this volume (Chapter Two), somehow economic growth and environmental renewal can be brought together, to complement each other, and in its strongest version, the claim is sometimes even made that the two are mutually dependent. The arguments are supported by a range of consultants (see, for example, TCPA, 2007) and underpinned by a belief in the possibility of 'ecological modernisation' (even if there are constant concerns that the process will not be followed through consistently by policy makers; see, for example, Gouldson and Murphy, 1997; Mol et al, 2009) and reflected in the (by now ubiquitous) virtuous 'triangle' setting out to link environment, economy and society as expressed in the *European spatial development perspective* and elsewhere (Council of Ministers Responsible for Spatial Planning, 1999; see, for example, Campbell, 1996, for a critique of the triangle). As Joe Ravetz puts it, 'Sustainability is the watchword for the new millennium, and a guiding theme for all human activity. It is also a never-ending quest for "having our cake and eating it" – not only economic growth with social justice, but environmental protection into the bargain' (Ravetz, 2000, p 3); a quest that is powerfully critiqued by Sarah Dooling in this volume (Chapter Nine).

If these are the grander ambitions and visions, however, rather more pragmatically, it is also important to explore some of the ways in which sustainable development and sustainability have come to be defined through the politics and practices of public policy. With that in mind, this chapter focuses on the experience of the Sustainable Communities Plan (ODPM, 2003, 2005b), particularly as it was taken forward in the South East of England in the first decade of this century.

Any consideration of the Sustainable Communities Plan is by now largely a historical exercise, despite the short-term survival of some of the institutions associated with it. The economic crisis which hit the housing market and the financial sector after 2008 fundamentally undermined some of the assumptions which the plan took for granted, and the election of the Cameron government in May 2010 effectively drew a line under the policy experiment of state-sponsored growth-driven sustainability. Many of the agencies that once so confidently dominated the world of local and regional development (the regional development agencies and government offices, in particular) as well as the plans and strategies they spawned (including the extensive and weighty regional spatial strategies for which they were responsible) had either already gone by the end of the year or were on their way out.

But it is precisely because it can now be seen through a historical lens that some of the ways in which 'sustainability' was mobilised in that period can be explored more directly. The ways in which the plan brought together a range of policy objectives framed by a series of geographical, or at any rate spatial, imaginaries, makes it possible to explore emergent geographies of social policy in practice (the spatialisation of social policy) at a particular moment, as part of an attempt to understand and explain the complicated and complex political dance associated with 'the governance of economic development in England in the post-devolution UK', set out and described by Andy Pike and John Tomaney (Pike and Tomaney, 2009).

Nor should it be concluded that 'sustainability' has somehow disappeared from political discourse with the effective demise of the Sustainable Communities Plan. On the contrary, it remains a stated priority across party lines as well as retaining a more popular resonance (see Swyngedouw, 2007, 2009, for a discussion of the extent to which it might be considered evidence of a 'post-political' moment), so a renewed iteration of some sort of sustainability politics driven by a changed set of political priorities can be expected. And the broader policy drivers (relating to housing supply on the one hand and ecological imperatives on the other) to which this version of sustainability was a response have not disappeared. This means that a review of this particular moment in the policy history of 'sustainability' is also likely to be helpful in analysing the ways in which that history develops.

Lost in space

Until recently, even in the absence of any formal national plan or, apparently, any explicit national planning framework, some underlying principles and assumptions have been clear enough. Although the existence of significant regional inequalities was recognised, the policy assumption was that these could best be resolved through initiatives taken at the regional level (preferably led by business-oriented coalitions or agencies, since the aim was to generate increased regional competiveness) (see Fothergill, 2005). It was this understanding that underpinned New Labour's creation of the regional development agencies in the late 1990s as well as later proposals to remove them from democratic scrutiny through the abolition of regional assemblies (HM Treasury et al, 2007). Since 2010, following the election of a new national government, the regional development agencies themselves are due to be replaced by more locally – possibly city-region – based enterprise partnerships, with a similar focus but covering a differently defined territory.

If the broad framework was based around the mantra of regional self-help and transformation, it was nevertheless located within a quite specific national imaginary, which can be summarised relatively simply. London and the South East is England's growth region ('an advanced industrial super-region', according to the South East of England Economic Development Agency, 2006, p 4), and the national economy's success depends on its success; it was, therefore said to be important that ways were found to sustain the region's growth (see Chapter Eleven, this volume, for a further discussion). The central emphasis for the South East emphasised competitiveness and growth (expressed in the boosterist language of the South East of England Economic Development Agency in the strap-line 'Working for England's World Class Region'), stressing what was seen to be the region's key role in underpinning the UK's economic prosperity. As Simon Marvin, Alan Harding and Brian Robson (2006) noted, there was (and probably still is) an 'implicit' (and active) regional strategy which tends to benefit what they call the 'London super-region'. In the other English regions the challenge was to find ways of fostering self-sustaining growth, based on the achievement of improved competiveness and the building of increased business confidence (see also Burch et al, 2009, who suggest that the process is internally contradictory, and Pike and Tomaney, 2009, who stress its complexity and fragmented nature).

In the absence of any regionalised industrial policy of the sort pursued by Labour in the 1970s, the clearest spatial expression of these broad understandings was to be found in their translation into policies directed at the housing market, which was identified both as potential constraint and potential source of dynamism. In London and the South East the challenge was identified as being to find ways of providing sufficient housing for key workers to sustain growth (see, for example, Barker, 2004; ODPM, 2005a), developing strategies for the making of (new) sustainable communities on the edge of the region. In parts of the Midlands and the North, by contrast, the task was defined as being to find ways of stimulating housing markets – fostering urban renewal through the remaking of those markets in inner areas. It was this that was in turn expected to make the process self-sustaining (or 'sustainable') as house prices rose and residential property became tradeable once more (see, for example, ODPM, 2005a, 2005b; see Allen, 2008 and Minton, 2009, pp 83-104, for a critique of housing market renewal strategies).

The language of the Office of the Deputy Prime Minister's[1] Sustainable Communities Plan (*Sustainable communities: Building for the future*) (ODPM, 2003), and the programmes and policy summits that flowed from it (see, for example, ODPM, 2005b, which set out a five-year implementation plan), brought together two apparently incontestable good things (sustainability and community) to make up a still more positive whole, a policy hybrid in which the warm connotations of each worked to reinforce the values of the other (see Raco, 2009, for a discussion of New Labour's approach). This was a vision which was capable of underpinning the spatial division of labour identified above, because it offered a means of framing the quite distinct forms of urban policy being developed for the South East and the North of England by incorporating a broad understanding which promised the delivery (by different means in each area) of 'places where people want to live and work, now and in the future. They meet the diverse needs of existing and future residents, are sensitive to their environment, and contribute to a high quality of life. They are safe and inclusive, well planned, built and run, and offer equality of opportunity and good services for all' (ODPM, 2005b, p 56).

Formally, in what was – in retrospect – a remarkable political sleight of hand, all this turned out to make it possible to link the needs, concerns and priorities of the cities of the 'Northern Way' and of the 'Core Cities' Network with the rather different needs of the South East, even if in practice, a central emphasis of policy – as expressed in the Sustainable Communities Plan itself – was on the possibilities and challenges represented by developments in the Greater South East. In line with the broad approach to regional development identified above, in the cities of the North, the expectation was that regional and local authorities would take the initiative and develop plans, but in London and the South East a major programme was launched under the aegis of national government. The 'Sustainable Communities' agenda was organised around plans to develop four new Growth Areas in and around the South East of England – in Ashford, the Thames Gateway, Milton Keynes and the South Midlands and the London-Stansted-Cambridge-Peterborough corridor. Although spending in the Thames Gateway (particularly following the award of the 2012 Olympics to London in 2005) far exceeded anything that might be expected in the other Growth Areas, in each of them a network of (what were called) local delivery vehicles and partnership bodies was created, working across scales, levels of government and public and private sectors (see Allen and Cochrane, 2010).

As I have argued elsewhere (see, for example, Cochrane, 2006; Allen and Cochrane, 2011), building on the conclusions of the Barker Report (Barker, 2004), commissioned by the Treasury and the Office of the Deputy Prime Minister, in the South East this was a plan for housing growth to support the provision of 'affordable housing' for 'key workers' in order to enable wider economic growth. It drew on the dominant policy framework for urban development and regeneration in England, which was based on the assumption of market-driven economic growth.

Despite the incorporation of social and environmental issues through discourses of 'sustainability', in practice the emphasis was placed on finding ways of 'sustaining' economic growth, and in this context that meant a focus on the achievement of housing targets. And the emphasis on housing supply was also reflected in a series of targets set for the broader region and its local authorities by government, which ultimately encouraged a rather bizarre bidding war as the targets proposed in the plan developed by the South East of England Regional Assembly were first raised following Examination in Public and then raised further by the Secretary of State, at just the point when the building industry was withdrawing from new house construction, when it was becoming clear that relying on the market (even with extensive state support) was unlikely to deliver what had been imagined (see, for example, South East of England Regional Assembly, 2006; Government Office for the South East, 2008, 2009).

Spatialising social policy

The model which largely defined 'sustainability' in economic terms and focused on the danger of labour shortages in key areas is closely related to a longer tradition that links spatial and social policies quite directly, through the provision of housing for those identified as 'key workers' (see, for example, Raco, 2007, for an overview of the social and political geographies of key worker policy since 1945). In this case, the emphasis was on those 'key workers' (including nurses, teachers and other public sector employees) whose incomes were insufficient to compete effectively in a localised regional housing market where 'affordable' housing was in short supply.

Implicitly this assumes that these 'key workers' will commute from their 'affordable' homes on the edge of the region to employment at its core. But the wider vision goes further (in tension, if not contradiction, with this priority) to look for ways of linking economic growth and associated housing development with the building of 'balanced' communities (that is, communities within which jobs, housing and services are in balance, and which are not simply suburban dormitory towns; see Flint's coverage of this issue in this volume, Chapter Ten). If not quite ecological modernisation, what was being offered here was a form of modernisation in which housing, economy and better social relations were somehow brought together, in an anglicised version of the US model of new urbanism. The borrowings from new urbanism were quite explicit (at least at first) because of the extent to which they pointed to the possibility of building better 'communities' through particular forms of development or urban design (see, for example, New Urbanism, 2005; Norquist, 2005; Talen, 2005), even if, in practice, Britain's major house builders – the supposed partners in the delivery of sustainable communities – proved reluctant to adopt the model to any significant extent, as Chris Pickvance also argues in this volume (Chapter Eight).

Social policy, spatial policy and economic policy were combined (in principle at least) in initiatives focused on places rather than individuals or disadvantaged groups, in the hope (if not confident expectation) that this would generate a positive cycle of social well-being. Sarah Dooling's chapter in this volume (Chapter Nine) examines the implications for disadvantaged groups arising from these rationales. This was a place-based approach, rather than an area-based one, and, indeed the term 'sustainable places' soon took over from 'sustainable communities' on the Homes and Communities Agency website and in other initiatives such as 'Total Place', which promised to integrate public and community service provision in place (HM Treasury and Department for Communities and Local Government, 2010).

In the context of British urban policy, although formally unacknowledged, the shift away from 'urban renaissance' towards a commitment to building 'sustainable communities' was clearly a significant one, not least because of its rather different spatial expression (see Cochrane, 2007; also Chapter Ten, this volume). In the case of the Thames Gateway (ODPM, 2004), it might be argued that there are continuities with previous rounds of urban policy, because the area incorporates spaces of industrial decline and urban dereliction. But even here the expectation is that new housing will be built and new communities generated, and the whole notion of the Gateway is premised on the need to understand the ways in which London stretches out into Essex, Kent and beyond (see, for example, Cohen and Rustin, 2008; see also Chapter Four, this volume).

The previous emphasis on regenerating existing communities (for example, associated with neighbourhood renewal and the New Deal for Communities) was no longer dominant (see Lawless 2006, 2007, for discussions of urban area-based initiatives and the New Deal for Communities). Instead, policy was increasingly concerned with wider geographical areas and emphasised the potential for successful growth, rather than the solution of urban 'problems' whether concentrated in particular neighbourhoods, in the inner cities or in cities more generally (ODPM, 2003, 2005a, 2005b). In response to this shift the authors of the 1999 Urban Task Force report which launched the 'renaissance' project revisited their recommendations six years on to reassert a commitment to 'brownfield' development (with the dissenting voice of Peter Hall), which fitted uneasily with the aspects of the new approach that had ambitions to build balanced communities outside the inner cities (Urban Task Force, 1999, 2005).

The implications of the strategy went beyond a simple shift in spatial focus, however, because making up new communities required more than simply enabling development in specified areas. If the traditional, and by now rejected, social policy model (that of the Beveridge-Keynes welfare state) saw the job of the state as being to provide the social infrastructure necessary to counter the imperfections of the market (that is, by providing forms of social welfare), now its job was quite explicitly reinterpreted as being to provide the infrastructural support (including social support) that was needed to achieve and sustain economic competitiveness. This did not mean that forms of social support were deemed unnecessary. On the contrary, they were necessary foundations on which the economy – the private, entrepreneurial economy – would be enabled to flourish. That is what provided the context for the building of sustainable communities, themselves in part sustainable because of the economic contribution they made.

While supporting a neoliberal version of market-based growth, this was a form of postwelfarism fundamentally reliant on significant action and even expenditure by a range of state and quasi-state agencies, as Harriet Bulkeley, Mike Hodson and Simon Marvin also identify in their chapter (Chapter Six). Local (and sub-regional) partnerships are overwhelmingly focused on finding ways of gaining access to additional sources of state funding, including forms of infrastructure which can be seen to be delivering collective provision. This goes beyond straightforward regulation to include direct involvement in the 'market', and in the case of Milton Keynes (targeted for a doubling of population in the next two decades), for example, the land market was effectively shaped by the active management of the state.

In some respects the strategies being pursued and policies being fostered through the Sustainable Communities Plan did have strong Keynesian echoes. The expectation was that the new housing developments would be underpinned by significant investment in key social and transport infrastructure of one sort or another – again in the case of Milton Keynes, for example, this included adding a spur line to ensure that intercity trains would continue to stop in the city, as well as widening the M1 and adding a new exit, alongside more traditional (but nevertheless costly) plans for developing new schools and health centres, sponsoring local higher education provision and expanding the hospital (see also Government Office for the South East, 2005, which sets out a programme of infrastructure investment in the region, and Chapter Seven, this volume). There was also a taken-for-granted and widely shared assumption about the need to sustain full employment, with the local partnerships committed to finding ways of attracting business and jobs (see Raco, 2005, for a discussion of the 'hybridity' of approaches associated with the Sustainable Communities Plan and its implementation).

It is in this context that some of the 'environmental' aspects of the Sustainable Communities Plan and its implementation become apparent, because of the new emphasis on making cities attractive to visitors and businesses, as well as the reclamation of derelict places for more productive uses. Aidan While, Andy Jonas and David Gibbs sum up the argument in noting that even 'investment in energy and waste management schemes not only offers incentives in terms of a green image, but also cost savings for residents and businesses' (While et al, 2004, p 550; see also Raco, 2005). This is not a new rhetoric since it was, for example, also heavily mobilised in the promotion and planning of Milton Keynes, in the making of the new town and the activities of the Development Corporation in the 1970s and 1980s (see, for example, Bendixson and Platt, 1992; Clapson, 2004), but in the context of the Sustainable Communities Plan was taken up more broadly by agencies throughout the Growth Areas (and expressed, for example, in what turned out to be the South East of England Economic Development Agency's valedictory Regional Economic Strategy for 2006-16, with its emphasis on what was called 'smart growth' and 'sustainable prosperity' with a focus on quality of life) (South East of England Economic Development Agency, 2006).

Alongside the distorted echoes of the Keynesianism welfare state, reframed so that collective provision is more explicitly imagined as one of the drivers of place-based economic competiveness, the echoes of Ebenezer Howard (similarly distorted) are also hard to ignore. The expectation was that it would be possible to extract a surplus from private housing developers to fund community facilities, schools and transport infrastructure (see, for example, Cochrane and Etherington, 2007; Edwards, 2008), whether through Section 106 agreements or along other lines (for example, in the form of a so-called roof tax to be levied on developers for each house constructed). The ever expanding housing market was identified as a never ending source of value to be tapped, with the state playing the necessary (coordinating) role to ensure that the individual priorities of the developers could be translated into a more positive set of collective outcomes for sustainable communities and the workforce that would live in them (see Chapter Eight, this volume).

Sustainable communities as drivers of uneven development

The spatial strategy embodied in the plan was predicated on the maintenance of existing patters of uneven development in England (see Massey, 2007, and Chapter Eleven, this volume, for a discussion of London's role and positioning within this process). Rather than attempting to challenge the process of uneven development, in other words, attention was directed towards finding ways of sustaining it, ensuring that unequal growth between England's regions was underpinned by government policy and state-backed infrastructural investment. But the plan also had implications within the region, in two significant ways.

First, however much it was sanitised by the language of sustainability (and balance), the strategy carried with it drivers of inequality and uneven development within the region as well as beyond it. This was even recognised in the official documents of regional planning. Within the administratively defined South East, the existence of a coastal arc of economic decline (South East of England Economic Development Agency, 2006, pp 34-6; South East of England Regional Assembly, 2006) was identified, perhaps in contrast to the Western Crescent (Hall et al, 1987) or the Oxford to Cambridge Arc, with its promise of a domesticated silicon valley (Miles, 2008). Although, of course, no direct reference was made to the possibility that there might be any tension between the growth agenda, the uneven nature of growth in the region and the reproduction of such inequalities, it was hard to ignore. In practice, however, the emphasis on the building of new communities to the north and east of London simply reinforced the existing divisions, with a legacy of continued decline for the areas that had benefited in an earlier cycle of Fordist growth (see Allen et al, 1998, pp 70-3).

But the nature of uneven development in the South East is more complex than this simple division between areas of growth and decline might suggest, however significant (and long-standing) the 'south-south' division may be (South East Economic Development Strategy, 1987; Bruegel, 1992). The South East is also a suburban space par excellence, which means that as well as reflecting the growth drivers, there is a strong set of anti-growth coalitions (see, for example, Charlesworth and Cochrane, 1994; Murdoch and Marsden, 1994). Those living relatively privileged lives do not want to see them challenged by the pressures of development, and are committed (as the Regional Economic Strategy implies and the initial draft of the South East Plan developed by the South East of England Regional Assembly reflected) to maintaining their quality of life (South East of England Economic Development Agency, 2006; South East of England Regional Assembly, 2006). It is this that makes them, as Peter Hall and others recognised so long ago (Hall et al, 1973), such staunch defenders of the green belt.

That, too, helps to explain the ways in which the Growth Areas were defined in the plans. They were specifically and clearly located beyond the commuter belts – for example, starting to the north of South Buckinghamshire, outside the so-called 'rural' areas, and not straying into commuterland to the south of London. The spatial imagery changed across the decade, with the identification of a more complex pattern of diamonds and hubs producing a network, rather than a set of almost unbounded Growth Areas that seemed to occupy a large swathe of the outer South East – within plans for the 'official' South East, 21 or 22 hubs and 8 'diamonds for investment and growth' (which incorporate 11 of the hubs) were identified (South East of England Economic Development Agency, 2006). The new patterns both managed to suggest the need to support growth in places outside those areas, while continuing to protect the traditional suburbs as well as the new rural commuting spaces.

Realism, utopianism and sustainable communities

Urban policy, even in its regionalised form, is overwhelmingly presented as realistic and pragmatic rather than a form of politics (Cochrane, 2007, and Chapter Two, this volume). In this context sustainability was the banner around which it was promised that a realistic and pragmatic approach to environment and economic growth can be constructed. But this remained a sustainability in which the emphasis was placed on the economic – support for economic growth was seen to offer a means of solving a series of social and environmental problems. Sustainability was mobilised in ways that were capable of sanitising the development process and framing private initiative within some sort of social/environmental vision. However, as Jacques Rancière reminds us, 'realism' too is a utopian politics (Rancière, 1995, p 15), and that is particularly clear here.

The core principles underlying the Sustainable Communities Plan were based on finding some way of mobilising market-based institutions (and particularly house builders) to deliver the right sort of development supported by the provision of the necessary social and economic infrastructure (part funded out of the surpluses they could be expected to generate). Even in a context where the promise of growth might have been more realistic, the assumptions of unproblematic development were questionable, but today the utopianism of basing policy around the potential of market development is all too apparent. Such policies depended on the market actually delivering, on the coming together of housing and social infrastructure, on the integration of environmental and development agendas. Those assumptions were always problematic (see, for example, Colenutt, 2009b), but the collapse of the growth agenda in the face of a market-induced crisis has confirmed the utopianism of the project particularly starkly (see Flint's account of neighbourhood regeneration in Chapter Ten, this volume, and Mike Raco's discussion of some of the implications of seeking to pursue a growth agenda – and deliver sustainable communities – without growth in Raco, 2009).

The assumptions under which the Sustainable Communities Plan was originally developed have been overtaken by the harsher realities of the housing market, even in the previously favoured areas of the South East (Parkinson et al, 2009, show how the crisis has affected strategies for regeneration and renewal elsewhere in England). In both contexts, the institutions may still be there, the professionals still there, the committees and forums still meeting, but their ability to negotiate effectively is substantially undermined. The Sustainable Communities Plan generated a series of locally based but nationally and regionally connected spaces in which new institutional frameworks were developed. These local and regional arrangements, and the burgeoning class of consultants and lobbyists that sustained them, are now under strain as the recession in the economy and the property market fans out into all areas of regional economic development (Allen and Cochrane, 2007; Colenutt, 2009a).

Yet the underlying drivers that led government to develop strategies for housing market renewal and the building of sustainable communities have not disappeared. In particular, the backlog of unmet housing needs remains severe and continues to create challenges, even if the housing market is presently unable to meet them. The challenge is to find ways of meeting these needs in ways that do not themselves generate new or reinforce old forms of inequality.

The model reflected in the Sustainable Communities Plan was one that delivered (and was intended to deliver) spatially distinctive outcomes. It acknowledged the existence of uneven development and worked with it in ways that generated continuing unequal growth, even if the hope may have been that localised initiatives outside the South East might somehow encourage the emergence of new growth points. In some respects the plan was quite explicit about its spatial agenda, but this was masked by the fragmented arrangements that were fostered as part of it. There was no forum within which broader concerns might be explored, no framework within which concerns about the active production of spatial inequality might be placed. For all the localisation and decentralisation, in practice this made any democratic or popular engagement with the process difficult, if not impossible – debate was not only increasingly located within self-selecting partnership bodies but it was (in any case) also limited to identifying ways in which different localities (regions and sub-regions; cities and city-regions) might position themselves in a competitive policy and economic environment.

It is, of course, important to celebrate the possibilities of local initiative and acknowledge the possibilities of local political mobilising, but the experience of the Sustainable Communities Plan also highlights the need to be able to work, think and plan more widely. The plan itself incorporated a set of spatial understandings, a vision of (and for) England and the relationships between its regions, but this was implicit rather than explicit. The emphasis on finding ways of working with markets not only turned out to be misplaced (in the sense that the aims of the plan could not be achieved) but also made it difficult for alternative visions to emerge that might have begun to challenge the process by which the spatial inequalities that characterise England were reproduced and reinforced (see, for example, Dorling et al, 2007 and Chapters Two and Six, this volume). The challenge is, in other words, to develop an approach to the making of sustainable communities which incorporates them in a wider strategy that repositions sustainability as part of a drive towards forms of, what Ed Soja (2010) has called, spatial justice beyond the neighbourhood and beyond the (South East) region as well as within it, and does so in a context in which – as Jackson, 2009, emphasises – the delivery of prosperity through economic growth along the old lines is no longer to be expected or, indeed, pursued.

Key conclusions

- Over the last decade, the national spatial strategy for England has been an implicit one, with the priority of ensuring the continued growth of the South East as national economic driver; in practice, sustainability was redefined in economic terms, and found an expression in plans for 'sustainable communities' capable of housing the workers needed to sustain economic growth.
- The underlying belief was that environmental and social sustainability could only be achieved if economic growth was sustained. This was always a questionable assumption but the reality of economic crisis has highlighted its utopian nature.
- Instead of a reliance on the market to deliver the desired outcomes on a piecemeal basis, region by region, locality by locality, it may instead be necessary to develop an explicit national strategy directly focused on issues of spatial justice.

Note

[1] The responsibilities of John Prescott's Office of the Deputy Prime Minister have, of course, since been divided up between a range of ministries.

Further reading

Jackson, T. (2009) *Prosperity without growth: Economics for a finite planet*, London: Earthscan.

Raco, M. (2007) *Building sustainable communities. Spatial policy and labour mobility in post-war Britain*, Bristol: The Policy Press.

Soja, E. (2010) *Seeking spatial justice*, Minneapolis, MN: University of Minnesota Press.

References

Allen, C. (2008) *Housing market renewal and social class*, London: Routledge.

Allen, J. and Cochrane, A. (2007) 'Beyond the territorial fix: regional assemblages, politics and power', *Regional Studies*, vol 41, no 9, pp 1161-75.

Allen, J. and Cochrane, A. (2010) 'Assemblages of state power: topological shifts in the organization of government and politics', *Antipode*, vol 42, no 5, pp 1071-89.

Allen, J., Massey, D. and Cochrane, A. (1998) *Rethinking the region*, London: Routledge.

Barker, K. (2004) *Review of housing policy. Delivering stability: Securing our future housing needs. Final report* (Barker Report), Norwich: The Stationery Office.

Bendixson, T. and Platt, J. (1992) *Milton Keynes: Image and reality*, Cambridge: Granta.

Bruegel, I. (ed) (1992) *The rest of the South East: A region in the making?*, Basildon: South East of England Economic Development Strategy.

Burch, M., Harding, A. and Rees, J. (2009) 'Having it both ways: explaining the contradiction in English spatial policy', *International Journal of Public Service Management*, vol 22, no 7, pp 587-604.

Campbell, S. (1996) 'Green cities, growing cities, just cities? Urban planning and the contradictions of sustainable development', *Journal of the American Planning Association*, vol 62, no 3, pp 296-312.

Charlesworth, J. and Cochrane, A. (1994) 'Tales of the suburbs: the local politics of growth in the South East of England', *Urban Studies*, vol 31, no 10, pp 1723-38.

Clapson, M. (2004) *A social history of Milton Keynes. Middle England/edge city*, London: Frank Cass.

Cochrane, A. (2006) 'Devolving the heartland: making up a new social policy for the "South East"', *Critical Social Policy*, vol 26, no 3, pp 685-96.

Cochrane, A. (2007) *Understanding urban policy: A critical approach*, Oxford: Blackwell.

Cochrane, A and Etherington, D. (2007) 'Managing local labour markets and making up new spaces of welfare', *Environment and Planning A*, vol 39, no 12, pp 2958-74.

Cochrane, A. and Talbot, D. (eds) (2008) *Security: Welfare, crime and society*, Maidenhead: Open University Press.

Cohen, P. and Rustin, M. (eds) (2008) *London's turning. The making of Thames Gateway*, Aldershot: Ashgate.

Colenutt, R. (ed) (2009a) *Sustainable urban growth*, Northampton: University of Northampton.

Colenutt, R. (2009b) 'Winners and losers from urban growth in South East England', in L. Porter and K. Shaw (eds) *Whose urban renaissance?*, London: Routledge, pp 60-70.

Council of Ministers Responsible for Spatial Planning (1999) *European spatial development perspective*, Luxembourg: Office for the Official Publications of the European Communities.

Dorling, D., Rigby, J., Wheeler, B., Ballas, D., Thomas, B., Fahmy, E., Gordon, D. and Lupton, R. (2007) *Poverty, wealth and place in Britain, 1968 to 2005*, Bristol: The Policy Press.

Edwards, M. (2008) 'Blue sky over Bluewater?', in P. Cohen and M. Rustin (eds) *London's turning. Thames Gateway: Prospects and legacies*, Aldershot: Ashgate, pp 283-92.

Fothergill, S. (2005) 'A new regional policy for Britain', *Regional Studies*, vol 39, no 5, pp 659-67.

Gouldson, A.P. and Murphy, J. (1997) 'Ecological modernisation: restructuring industrial economies', The Political Quarterly, vol 68, issue B, pp 74-86.

Government Office for the South East (2005) Infrastructure in the South East, Guildford: Government Office for the South East.

Government Office for the South East (2008) Secretary of State's proposed change to South East Plan, Consultation portal (http://gose.limehouse. co.uk/portal/rss/pcc/consult), accessed April 2009.

Government Office for the South East (2009) The South East Plan. Regional spatial strategy for the South East of England, London: The Stationery Office.

Hall, P. with Gracey, H., Drewett, R. and Thomas, R. (1973) The containment of urban England, London: George Allen & Unwin.

Hall, P., Breheny, M., McQuaid, R. and Hart, D. (1987) Western sunrise: The genesis and growth of Britain's major high tech corridor, London: Allen & Unwin.

HM Treasury and Department for Communities and Local Government (2010) Total place: A whole area approach to public services, London: HM Treasury.

HM Treasury, Department for Business Enterprise and Regulatory Reform, Department for Communities and Local Government (2007) Review of sub-national economic development and regeneration, London: HM Treasury.

Jackson, T. (2009) Prosperity without growth: Economics for a finite planet, London: Earthscan.

Lawless, P. (2006) 'Area-based urban interventions: rationale and outcomes: the New Deal for Communities programme in England', Urban Studies, vol 43, no 11, pp 1991-2001.

Lawless, P. (2007) 'Continuing dilemmas for area-based urban regeneration: evidence from the New Deal for Communities programme in England', People, Place and Policy Online, vol 1, no 1, pp 14-21.

Marvin, S., Harding, A. and Robson, B. (2006) A framework for city-regions, Working Paper 4, The role of city-regions in regional economic development policy, London: Office of the Deputy Prime Minister.

Massey, D. (2007) World city, Cambridge: Polity Press.

Miles, N. (2008) 'The Oxford to Cambridge Arc. Struggles in partnership' (A short play in three acts), Paper presented to OECD Workshop on Partnerships for Development and Innovation, Trento, Italy (www.oecd.org/ dataoecd/26/8/40049628.pdf).

Minton, A. (2009) Ground control. Fear and happiness in the twenty-first-century city, London: Penguin.

Mol, A.P.J., Sonnenfeld, D.A. and Spaargaren, G. (eds) (2009) The ecological modernisation reader: Environmental reform in theory and practice, London: Routledge.

Mooney, G. and Neal, S. (eds) (2009) Community: Welfare, crime and society, Maidenhead: Open University Press.

Murdoch, J. and Marsden, T. (1994) Reconstituting rurality, London: UCL Press.

New Urbanism (2005) *New urbanism. Creating livable sustainable communities* (www.newurbanism.org/pages/416429/index.htm).

Norquist, J. (2005) 'How to avoid the pitfalls of the American way', *Society Guardian*, 19 January, pp 10-11.

ODPM (Office of the Deputy Prime Minister) (2003) *Sustainable communities: Building for the future*, London: ODPM.

ODPM (2004) *Thames Gateway*, London: ODPM.

ODPM (2005a) *Sustainable communities: Homes for all*, London: ODPM.

ODPM (2005b) *Sustainable communities: People, places and prosperity. A five-year plan from the Office of the Deputy Prime Minister*, Cm 6425, London: The Stationery Office.

Parkinson, M., Ball, M., Blake, N. and Key, T. (2009) *The credit crunch and regeneration: Impact and implications*, London: Department for Communities and Local Government.

Pike, A. and Tomaney, J. (2009) 'The state and uneven development: the governance of economic development in England in the post-devolution UK', *Cambridge Journal of Regions, Economy and Society*, vol 2, no 1, pp 1-22.

Raco, M. (2005) 'Sustainable development, rolled-out neoliberalism and sustainable communities', *Antipode*, vol 37, no 2, pp 324-47.

Raco, M. (2007) *Building sustainable communities. Spatial policy and labour mobility in post-war Britain*, Bristol: The Policy Press.

Raco, M. (2009) 'A growth agenda without growth: English spatial policy, sustainable communities, and the death of the neo-liberal project?', *Geojournal*, First Online DOI 10.1007/s10708-009-9327-0.

Rancière, J. (1995) *On the shores of politics*, Verso: London [page references to 2007 edition].

Ravetz, J. with the Sustainable City-Region Working Group chaired by P. Roberts (2000) *City-Region 2020. Integrated planning for sustainable environment*, London: Earthscan.

Soja, E. (2010) *Seeking spatial justice*, Minneapolis, MN: University of Minnesota Press.

South East Economic Development Strategy (1987) *South-south divide*, Stevenage: South East Economic Development Strategy.

South East of England Economic Development Agency (2006) *The regional economic strategy 2006-2016. A framework for sustainable prosperity*, Guildford: South East of England Economic Development Agency.

South East of England Regional Assembly (2006) *A clear vision for the South East. The South East Plan core document. Draft plan for submission to government*, Guildford: South East of England Regional Assembly.

Swyngedouw, E. (2007) '"Impossible sustainability" and the post-political condition', in R. Krueger and D. Gibbs (eds) *The sustainable development paradox: Urban political ecology in the US and Europe*, New York: Guilford Press, pp 13-40.

Swyngedouw, E. (2009) 'The antimonies of the postpolitical city: in search of a democratic politics of environmental production', *International Journal of Urban and Regional Research*, vol 33, no 3, pp 601-20.

Talen, E. (2005) *New urbanism and American planning. The conflict of cultures*, London: Routledge.

TCPA (Town and Country Planning Association) (2007) *Best practice in urban extensions and new settlements*, London: TCPA.

Urban Task Force (1999) *Towards an urban renaissance. Final Report of the Urban Task Force*, chaired by Lord Rogers of Riverside, London: E. and F.N. Spon.

Urban Task Force (2005) *Towards a stronger urban renaissance. An independent report by members of the Urban Task Force*, chaired by Lord Rogers of Riverside (www.urbantaskforce.org).

While, A., Jonas, A. and Gibbs, D. (2004) 'The environment and the entrepreneurial city: searching for the urban "sustainability fix" in Leeds and Manchester', *International Journal of Urban and Regional Research*, vol 28, no 3, pp 549-69.

four

Constructions of the carbon city

Will Eadson

Introduction

A century after Svante Arrhenius (1896) first presented his 'hot house theory', the creation of the Kyoto Protocol of the United Nations Framework Convention on Climate Change (UNFCCC) in 1997 was a landmark point in the recognition of climate change as a political concern. The Protocol included binding emissions reduction targets for 37 industrialised nations, which included the UK as part of a European Union (EU) bloc of 15 member states. This marked the point at which climate change policy first became a serious policy issue for nation states. It was a clear sign that a shift had taken place from policy interventions that focused on the science of climate change, to 'science for policy' (Agrawala, 1998).

While the Kyoto Protocol was concerned with the umbrella terms of climate change mitigation and adaptation, it was distinctive in that it focused on emissions reductions, and specifically that it required signatory states to begin to effectively *account* for national emissions levels. This in turn developed the need for effective 'carbon management' systems: the need for governing processes to both account for and then instigate action to reduce carbon emissions (or remove them from the books through other means).

Yet it was not until the mid-2000s that attitudes towards the role of state action on climate change began to change. After nearly a decade of relative inaction following the Kyoto summit in 1997, governments at all levels were seemingly beginning to take heed of the urgent need for action on carbon reduction – and reduced oil dependence – as well as adapting to the likely consequences of climate change. In 2007 the first national binding commitment to emissions budgeting was introduced in the UK Climate Change Bill, which accompanied political rhetoric regarding a new emphasis on spatial and individual carbon budgeting, emissions trading regimes and the search for a new international settlement on carbon reduction post-Kyoto.

Among this new-found seriousness about climate change a host of issues old and new were beginning to emerge or receive new levels of scrutiny. Many of these brought new dimensions to existing debates, such as re-invigorated tensions between state and market, or the organisation of responsibilities between individuals and collective or state bodies. It also brought added dimensions to discussions of how to effect changes in human behaviour, including the methods that governing actors could employ to do so and the time horizons within which such changes needed to take place.

Central to these deliberations were uncertainties about the best form of governmental and spatial organisation for such efforts. This included consideration of geographic scales at which policy would be best organised and implemented, the relationship between different scales of governing, and the role of different forms of network governance across and between cities, regions and nations. Alongside these quandaries of government came more fundamental questions about the 're-imagining' of spaces as 'carbon spaces', including questions of how the idea of such spaces would fit with existing political spatial 'fixes'. Within this, the question of how to effectively compartmentalise space for purposes of carbon accounting is a particularly interesting issue, as it throws human searches for order up against the fundamentally disordered 'seething mass' of nature.

Following initial understandings of the nation state as a 'carbon space' under the Kyoto Protocol, the new emphasis on 'carbon control' (While, 2008) within the nation-state requires a further stage of spatial re-imagining and calculation in order to draw sub-national actors into the logic of carbon management. Of particular interest here is the emergence of different attempts to calculate the city as a carbon space.

This chapter investigates some of the emergent and potential politics of these experiments with carbon calculation in cities. The analysis draws on ideas relating to the 'sociology of accounting' (Miller, 1994; Mennicken, 2002; Power, 2004; Kalthoff, 2005) to understand the way in which calculable spaces are constructed. This follows a call from While (2010) for attention to be paid to the 'urban calculus of carbon control'.

As Bulkeley, Hodson and Marvin's chapter shows (Chapter Six, this volume), calculation has different sites of control, depending in part on who the calculator is. While many city governments have begun their own experimental calculations, there have also been experiments with governing cities at a distance through carbon reduction targets. This chapter will touch on both of these, but the centralisation of spatial emissions calculation is perhaps of greater significance in the long term: it binds cities into a particular set of territorial governing logics and throws up a range of questions about future uneven spatial development, that is, potential and emerging 'carbon inequalities' both within and between cities, or cities and their hinterlands. Carbon reduction targets in the now defunct local area agreements (LAAs) in the UK are an example of how such forms of governing are beginning to emerge, and will provide the main focus of the empirical discussion within this chapter. Data is drawn from 59 interviews with local, regional and national policy actors and stakeholders, carried out between 2007 and 2009. As with Dooling's contribution in this volume (see Chapter Nine), the analysis shows that spatial calculations of carbon produce a range of activities and actors deemed to be 'inside' and 'outside' the city. Similarly, short-term targets have been inevitably linked to short-term and piecemeal action. This brings questions about the extent to which the calculations under consideration in this chapter have a constructive place within long-term transition planning for cities, with a need for wholesale long-term behavioural and technological changes. It also brings forth wider thoughts about the relationship between the state and cities. In particular, which spaces and which activities are deemed as local or extra-local, or within or without state control.

Carbon control

While (2008, 2010; While et al, 2010) has started to open up some of the debates relating to the spatio-political implications of a shift in urban environmental politics towards a specific concern with 'carbon control'. While explores the rise of a low carbon polity as an emerging, and increasingly dominant discourse within states, so much so that 'the management of carbon flows, and especially carbon emissions, could be said to be rapidly supplanting sustainable development as the central goal of ongoing processes of eco-state restructuring' (While, 2008, p 1). This sees a concern for carbon reduction not just as simply the key issue within sustainable development discourses (Bulkeley, 2006), but also as marking a new era of ecological restructuring of states (Meadowcroft, 2005).

A significant part of this turn is the spatial calculation of carbon, which marks a new emphasis on governmental regulation of spaces through monitoring economic circulations through an extra-economic lens. This therefore moves to a narrower, instrumental form of environmental management than approaches take in relation to the more broadly defined sustainable development. These calculations also form a basis for efforts to create carbon markets, through carbon offsetting and trading schemes, leading to a commodification of carbon (Castree, 2008). Bumpus and Liverman (2008; see also Liverman, 2004), for example, discuss the role of carbon offset schemes in providing opportunities for 'accumulation by decarbonisation' (see also Callon, 2009). This focus on carbon reduction, While argues, is 'linked to, but abstracted from a sense of natural limits' (2008, p 3): in other words the wider issues of ecological crisis and the complex science surrounding climate change are restructured so as to be politically legible and technically manageable. This could also be couched in terms of critiques of liberal democracy and non-human space. Climate change forces recognition of the physical limits of space, but because of liberal democracy's entanglement with the capitalist market logic, it is abstracted to the point that it can fit in with existing economic discourses. A number thus becomes reified as a way of bringing about action; somehow as more effective than the central fear that the biosphere is likely to alter to the point that lives are at risk if no action on carbon emissions is taken.

Within this context, as carbon reduction pressures do begin to bite, cities will have to undergo a change in their calculative practices: they will need to start seeing the city as a space of carbon flows. This includes making or re-making connections between what have been seen as separate economic and extra-economic spheres of urban politics (While, 2010). It also has potential ramifications for how the city is governed, both by its own authorities and from a distance. This leads to questions about how the city should be understood: where does the carbon city 'begin' and 'end'? And where does it fit within existing spatial or scalar governing fixes?

Calculative practices of governing

Governing through calculation is an intrinsic part of many governmental practices. More widely even, Crosby (1997) attributes the success of 'western imperialism' throughout the second millennium AD to the ability to effectively master the skills of calculating space and time, then implementing these to create order in both human and non-human elements. Spatial and organisational calculation has become a central point of governmental logics in the 'search for order'. Calculation and accounting were crucial in the development of the exchange mechanisms that allowed capitalism to flourish.

The use of accounting techniques has particular benefits to those who seek to govern space. Not only do calculations of space help to order the process of governing, they also construct ordered spaces that can be more effectively managed. Furthermore, in making and enforcing decisions, policy makers can point to the 'objective expertise' implicit in the calculations made (Miller, 1994). Perhaps most usefully, 'accounting makes comparable activities and processes whose physical characteristics and geographical location may bear no resemblance whatsoever' (Miller, 1994, p 246).

Calculations also act as 'relays' for governing practices, by getting others to calculate their own actions and those of yet others. Calculative practices implement seemingly narrow and fixed understandings of particular sets of activities, while at the same time giving governed entities the 'freedom' to make their own choices about how best to achieve the goals outlined within the calculations. In this sense, such practices are a useful tool for governing at a distance.

Calculable spaces are, however, fundamentally constructed spaces. Boundaries have to be drawn, 'insiders' and 'outsiders' delineated and variables must be 'made the same' in order to create a rationalised object of calculation (Rutland and Aylett, 2008). These programmes must then be tied together in such a way as to create an effective 'black box' (Latour, 1999) that others will find difficult to re-open or challenge. Calculating cities as carbon spaces necessitates that a range of translations are made. These can be split into four programmes: the construction of a calculative currency; the construction of a calculable object; implementation of calculations on the object; and implementation of calculations within the object.

The construction of a calculative currency includes making different sets of greenhouse gases (GHGs), human activities and spaces 'the same'. From this point, the object of the carbon city must be constructed in order to create a manageable or calculable space. This involves scalar and territorial decisions about what constitutes the boundaries to the city – which may not be spatially contiguous in a cartographic sense – alongside questions about the form and extent of powers that may be exercised by city governments and the level of change that should be aimed for.

The construction of a calculable object is a crucial stage in the creation of calculative governing technologies, as it fixes a range of unavoidably political or moral decisions within the frame of seemingly neutral calculation. This – if constructed well – becomes hard to challenge. Understanding the methods and practices of these calculations are as politically important as the 'human' elements of negotiation and implementation: as Mackenzie (2009, p 442) states, 'the specifics ... matter'.

As Miller (1994, p 257) notes, however, 'the technologies of accounting often intersect poorly with the specifics of the "real"' and the politics of these calculations come into greater relief when the abstracted numbers make their way 'back to ground' via mediation through different governing and governed actors. As such, it is important that attention is paid to the implementation of such calculations. This requires a further set of translations, as calculations are mediated between actors before a calculable target is agreed on. As witnessed during international climate negotiations at Kyoto and more recently in Copenhagen and Cancún, this number may bear little resemblance to previous calculations. This draws attention to the extent to which different policy actors are able to mobilise resources to advance their own goals, which includes interaction between city and national governments as well as between competing sets of interests within cities. A final set of translations take place as the agreed target is brought back to ground through the calculation of reductions through different specific actions, and the implementation of these actions.

Calculation and carbon management

A number of works that explore the tensions and politics behind emissions monitoring and related calculative practices internationally and nationally have been published in recent years. These expose, for example, the Kyoto mechanism not only as politicised in its eventual implementation (Barrett,

1998), but also in creation of an all-encompassing 'greenhouse gas' currency (Mackenzie, 2009) and the construction of the 'object' of the global climate ecosystem (Demeritt, 2001).

Demeritt (2001) notes that even the notion of a global 'space' of carbon provides a deeply partial picture of climate change. Approaching climate as a global system works as an analytical abstraction, but in doing so, masks the spatial intricacies of the effects of climate change. Similarly, Demeritt argues that the 'global' approach has a certain level of political utility. Constructing climate change as a global problem potentially divorces the accumulation of gases in the atmosphere from the sites of production. Therefore, 'luxury' emissions in developed countries are seen in the same terms as 'survival' emissions from agriculture in developing nations (Demeritt, 2001, p 313).

This latter argument does not entirely stand up to scrutiny, as there is awareness and discussion among political, academic and campaigning communities of the moral dimension of climate change, even if this is not reflected fully in policy making. However, calculating climate as a global system does have an effect on calculation of carbon emissions and targets. This approach leads to a fundamentally top-down calculation of carbon, which leads to sub-global calculations as disaggregations of the 'global'.

At the same time, carbon is particularly difficult to scale or territorialise. If it is not properly represented as a uniformly global phenomenon, then neither is it easily compartmentalised into discrete spatial areas. And, while carbon and other GHGs can be 'made the same' through a series of translations, the activities that produce them are very different. Instead of tackling this, policy solutions have tended to be mapped onto existing territorial entities. This is potentially useful in terms of inserting 'connective strands' between carbon management goals and other policy concerns, but also creates new sets of issues in attempting to make carbon flows 'fit' into, for example, a predetermined local authority space.

Constructions of the carbon city

Less attention has been given to constructing the city as a carbon space, as the spatial calculation of carbon is only just beginning to impact on calculative regimes for cities as states begin to recognise the need to 'make climate change visible' (Castree, 2010) 'beyond' the nation-state.

At the same time, cities across Europe and North America have experimented with constructing different forms of the carbon city through calculation. Rutland and Aylett (2008) report on Portland, Oregon, as one of the first cities to attempt to monitor and reduce carbon emissions. The city committed to a 20 per cent carbon reduction target (baseline 1990), but at the time there existed no established method for 'rendering visible' local emissions and the city government had to engage in a process of constructing the object of 'local energy consumption'. The resulting framework reflected a range of political concerns about the role of local government, 'and in fact major emissions that might be considered 'local' were left unmeasured (and so ungoverned)' (Rutland and Aylett, 2008, p 628). In other words, 'local' became 'what local government felt they could influence'.

Similar issues come to the fore in other locally led attempts to calculate the carbon city. In the UK, for example, Manchester city-region commissioned a 'mini-Stern' report in 2007 (Deloitte, 2008), which followed on from Lord Stern's review of the economics of climate change (2006). While the Stern report focused on the international economic cost of climate change, the approach taken in Manchester did not measure climate change as a threat in itself. Instead, the city-region was placed within the context of national and international policy, the resulting analysis being framed around the cost to the city-region if they did not comply with or react to changing EU and UK regulations. This construction of the carbon city is not one of a proactive city taking a moral lead on carbon management. Instead it is framed within narrow logics of economic threats and opportunities for Manchester, an attempt to forge a new point of competitive advantage for the city.

Both of these examples raise questions regarding how best to view the carbon city within a multi-level policy context. This is particularly important in the UK, where the nation-state remains largely centralised and continues to follow a predominantly unitary system of governance, despite experiments in recent decades with regionalisation and localism. The UK – or more specifically, England – was also the first site of compulsory emissions monitoring for local authorities, alongside the introduction of a 'quasi-authoritative' regime of voluntary reduction targets through LAAs. This provides an example of calculating the carbon city 'at a distance', and gives rise to a range of further issues regarding the construction and implementation of spatial calculations.

Local area agreements

The nationwide roll-out of LAAs in England in 2008 involved local authorities, with their local strategic partnerships (LSPs), negotiating with Government Offices for the Regions (GORs) – acting on behalf of the Secretary of State for Communities and Local Government, to up to 35 targets from a list of 198 potential indicators. No indicators were mandatory in LAAs, although they did require approval from both the GOR and, ultimately the Secretary of State. All local authorities were monitored through the linked comprehensive area assessment (CAA) regardless of the targets included in LAAs.

The 2008 CAA and LAAs included for the first time a range of climate change related indicators, including NI (National Indicator) 186, which measured local authority-wide carbon emissions, the first example of mandatory spatial emissions reporting in the UK. This indicator was the top priority within the Department for Environment, Food and Rural Affairs (Defra) for inclusion in LAAs (Government Office Yorkshire and the Humber, 2008). Following the creation of the Conservative–Liberal Democrat Coalition government in May 2010, LAAs and CAAs were abolished. Nonetheless, local emissions targets or budgets remain on the agenda, and can be expected to return in some guise: for instance, both Coalition partners signed up to the idea of local authority carbon budgets prior to the 2010 General Election (Friends of the Earth, 2010).

A report was produced by AEA Technology and Defra (2008) to assist with the implementation of NI 186. This included definition of the indicator in terms of the 'calculative currency' as well as a number of clarifications about the 'object' of the indicator: for instance, which emissions sources would be included, suggestions of the types of actions that might be taken to reduce emissions and suggested targets for each local authority area. It is also worth noting at this point that, because LAAs were focused on local authorities, London was split into its constituent boroughs, and so is excluded from the discussion below, which will focus largely on the implications of NI 186 for England's eight 'core cities': Birmingham, Bristol, Leeds, Liverpool, Manchester, Newcastle upon Tyne, Nottingham and Sheffield. The politics of calculating the city through NI 186 are considered in two ways: first, as a set of issues faced by local authorities in general, with the core cities providing examples of these issues; and second, some specific implications of these calculations for understanding cities as spaces in relation to other types of sub-national, national and international space.

Constructing the calculative currency

The 'currency' of NI 186 was quite clearly defined. The indicator was based purely on carbon emissions on a 2005 baseline, and did not include other GHGs. Respondents felt that this limited the potential role of local authorities in reducing emissions. As one local authority officer noted:

> 'It doesn't include emissions from waste. Waste is potentially an area were we could have most impact, and so it seems strange that it won't be included in the indicator.'

Under this indicator, the carbon city is therefore almost exclusively concerned with reducing emissions from combustion of fossil fuels. Other forms of waste become less important, except where they can be used to reduce reliance on other fuels (by redirecting landfill waste to combined heat and power plants, for example).

The currency was the same for all local authorities in England. Each local area was measured under the same criteria, so large cities such as Birmingham and Sheffield were measured in the same way as small towns within their city-regions, such as Rotherham and Barnsley, or the rural communities of Cornwall and North Yorkshire. This has implications for the construction of the object of the city, as discussed below.

The value of this currency was less clear, however. Targets were not linked to any 'cap and trade' mechanisms, and no funding was directly allocated to achievement of them. Nor was there any sense that failure to meet targets would be met with authoritative censure. Nonetheless, the implementation of a top-down indicator that would be centrally monitored for all local authorities, regardless of whether they agreed a target as part of their LAA, meant that it held some weight: most local authorities adopted the Defra emissions monitoring as their unit of currency for measuring success or otherwise on carbon reduction.

Constructing the calculable object

In constructing the calculable object, first and foremost, NI 186 created the carbon city as an object of centralised control, to be governed from a distance. The city government, along with local stakeholders through LSPs, then had the 'freedom' to determine their own methods for reducing emissions within the scope of the newly created object of the carbon city. In some ways this definition of the carbon city potentially looks different from the city as imagined by conventional urban planning; in others it has been shaped in such a way as to map more easily onto pre-existing governing architecture. NI 186 shaped the construction of the carbon city as an object of calculation through three main facets: the methodology used, the emission sources included and the monitoring process.

Cities limited

The methodology for calculating a city's carbon emissions is important in defining the carbon city. It can have a significant effect on both the ambition and scope of policy. A range of alternative approaches may be taken to calculating city-level carbon emissions. For example, a standard approach in the past has been to use a 'production' approach. Such an approach defines the carbon city as responsible for all emissions produced within its boundaries by individuals, businesses and other organisations. A consumption-based approach would focus on a much broader suite of emissions sources, based not on what is produced within the city, but on the emissions embedded within the consumption of goods and services.

NI 186 takes a 'point source' or 'end user' approach, a hybrid methodology that captures elements of production and consumption.

The 'point source' approach essentially allocates production-related emissions to individuals and small to medium organisations, but removes those that are deemed 'extra-local'. Some of these emissions that are 'beyond the city' were captured by other regulatory mechanisms. For example, the EU Emissions Trading Scheme captured large energy producers. Energy production is an interesting case. In essence, energy production was deemed to be a national or international issue, not one for the city. Instead the city was given responsibility for energy consumption through monitoring domestic and commercial energy use. The role of local authorities was therefore to reduce energy demand, with the emphasis on the individual user. This may seem a practical separation of responsibilities, but could also be problematic in the long term: separation of responsibility for demand and supply could lead to piecemeal and inefficient solutions. For example, attempts to implement decentralised, domestic heat and power solutions are of little benefit if energy suppliers do not implement 'smart grids' to make these technologies of practical use.

Another emissions source deemed separate from local authorities was intercity transport. Once more, the argument behind this is that motorways, railways and aeroplanes are 'beyond the city'. This argument potentially leads to a city that can continue to base economic growth on high-emissions air travel, or rely on labour that commutes by car or train from urban hinterlands without having to consider the consequences for carbon emissions.

Finally, emissions embedded in goods and services, other than direct energy consumption, are not included at all. This may be difficult to measure, especially as a top-down indicator, as it would include developing estimates of the carbon cost of everything bought and sold within a city. However, using a methodology that could even partially capture consumption – such methodologies do exist (see Arup, 2007) – would encourage an understanding of cities as entities that are fundamentally tied in to regional, national and international carbon flows. This would no doubt create a greater challenge for cities to engage with the real carbon cost of their activities, but would also potentially lead to more innovative and interesting carbon management solutions.

The point source approach to emissions is, on the other hand, potentially the narrowest possible interpretation of the carbon city. It sees the city as a detached unit made up only of micro processes: the individual boiler, the car journey from home to school, mowing the lawn. These are undoubtedly important, as changes to small actions can add up to large savings. But is the city only a sum of its micro-parts? And if so, this also begs the question, why not use a mechanism that places direct responsibility on the individual to make such changes?

The uncontrollable city

Part of the argument for the point source approach is to give local authorities only responsibility for those areas that they have some level of control over. Yet, Defra's analysis (AEA Technology and Defra, 2008) for the indicator belies this. The analysis document includes a list of 51 potential actions to reduce local emissions, of which only seven are listed as 'purely local' measures. Nineteen are listed as 'purely national' measures, with the remainder categorised as 'national with local influence'. The seven 'purely local' measures include some quite minor actions, such as encouraging better vehicle maintenance and driver training. Again the actual influence of the city 'on its own' is deemed to be relatively small. Indeed, in AEA Technology and Defra's analysis of what reductions individual authorities may be expected to make, 'purely local' emissions are not even calculated in suggested emissions reductions for most local authorities.

At the bottom of this list, however, is one measure that goes unmentioned within the rest of the analysis, is not assigned any value in terms of potential for carbon reduction and is not calculated as part of suggested local authority emissions. This is 'measures that can be used to reduce sprawl'. The role of urban design or of the entire issue of spatial planning in cities is reduced to one, unattributed action. Where the city is seen as having some level of control over something that is scaled beyond individual people or organisations, it is deemed of little importance. On the whole, the city is seen in this indicator as a marginal space within state calculations of carbon transitions.

The incalculable city

In turning to the monitoring process for NI 186, the marginal city also becomes in many senses the incalculable city. This is borne out in four ways: the source, control, availability and adaptability of data.

First of all, as noted, the object of the carbon city was determined through an entirely top-down process: it was very much an object to be controlled and defined. This meant a complete absence of local knowledge about what different types of actions might be possible in different places, and the levels of reductions these might achieve. It also meant that the city was defined purely as its local authority area: there was not room – in this part of the process at least – for any wider geographical interpretations of a city-region, for example.[1]

A second issue related to the role of city authorities in monitoring the targets. On this issue local actors were no more than silent intermediaries for central government. All monitoring was to be carried out by AEA Technology and the Department of Energy and Climate Change (DECC):

"that's a job for us; it's centrally done, and really that's the only way it's possible to do it at the moment" (central government policy executive). This was partly pragmatic, but also shows the lack of control that local actors had over the process. No easily utilisable tool was available to local authorities or regional actors to monitor changes to their own emissions, which made it difficult to challenge the monitoring data, particularly for those authorities with less capacity to do so (see below).

The third issue relates to the availability of data over time. All data for the indicator had a two- to three-year time lag. In 2008, when targets were being negotiated, local authorities only had the data for 2005; 2008 data was not released until 2010, and 2011 data – the data required for measuring final achievement on the target – is unlikely to be available until 2013. This meant that the local authorities were, in the words of an officer, "just putting our finger in the air really, and saying 'does that seem about right?'".

Finally, the data takes no account of possible changes to economic conditions. As one local authority officer argued:

'How can it really be measured? For instance if one big business closes in the area – say xxxxxx down the road – and this causes our emissions to fall, is that then us doing our job? Is that a success?... There are a number of anomalies in the measurement.'

This issue will be returned to below in discussion of the implementation of calculations and their impact on cities.

Implementing the calculation as targets for cities

Of 150 LAAs agreed in 2008, 87 per cent (130) included at least one carbon reduction target. This included 100 LAAs that agreed to a NI 186 target. Table 4.1, below, shows the key descriptive statistics for the targets agreed. In terms of England's 'core cities', six of eight cities adopted the target, with the two non-adopters taking up targets for the local authority's own operations (see Table 4.2).

In all, local authorities pledged to cut emissions by 26.4 mega-tonnes, equal to a 5.7 per cent reduction of total UK carbon emissions as measured through the indicator, or a 4.7 per cent reduction in the UK's total 'Kyoto' carbon emissions in 2005. This would have provided quite a boost to the UK's carbon accounts and such a reduction through implementation of NI 186 would appear to be quite an achievement.

A look at England's core cities – the eight largest cities outside London – helps to bring light to a range of different issues that arose in the negotiation of NI 186 targets, and some specific considerations regarding medium to large cities. Table 4.2 shows the eight cities, with their respective targets.

Table 4.1: NI 186 targets for CO_2 reductions in 'take-up' LAAs (%)

Year	Carbon reduction target 2008-11				
	Mean	Median	Max	Min	Standard Deviation
2008-11 (n=95)	10.5	11.0	15.0	1.0	2.2
2008-09 (n=87)	3.7	3.4	11.8	0.0	2.0
2009-10 (n=86)	3.2	3.3	7.0	0.0	1.2
2010-11 (n=86)	3.7	3.7	11.0	0.6	1.5

Note: Targets based on baseline year of 2005

Table 4.2: Core cities' NI 186 targets (%)

Core cities	Target
Newcastle upon Tyne	13.4
Nottingham	12.6
Manchester	11.1
Sheffield	1
Birmingham	6.9
Bristol	1.0
Liverpool	No target
Leeds	No target

As can be seen, a range of targets were agreed, as well as two cities that opted out of NI 186 in their LAA. The reasons behind the differences across the different cities bring light to one issue in particular: access to knowledge, data and evidence in the negotiation process. It was clear that some local authorities were more 'carbon aware' than others and each of the core cities could be included in this categorisation. As a result, some of these authorities were able to manipulate figures and make a case for a target different to that prescribed by central government. Bristol is the most striking example of this: it was able to make a case for just a one per cent CO_2 reduction over the three years of the LAA. Government figures (AEA Technology and Defra, 2008) suggested that it should have been able to achieve a 13.1 per cent reduction *without* including any local measures. Similarly, Leeds and Liverpool opted out of the indicator, respondents suggesting that this was because they were able to show that, "the flaws in the methodology just meant that it was almost pointless as a local target" (local authority officer).

Authorities with greater knowledge of carbon accounting techniques also engaged in a more subtle process of manipulation. A number of local authorities took the opportunity to manipulate the process by 'front-loading' their target so that the 2008-09 year has the highest projected carbon reduction, including, as it does, any reductions made in the years

2005-08. The LAAs with higher reductions in their first year were then able to commit to much smaller commitments over the final two years of the programme – the mean target for these LAAs was only 0.5 per cent higher than other agreements (see Table 4.3).

Table 4.3: Front-loaded LAAs compared to whole population (%)

	Mean target	
	Whole population	Front-loaded
2008-11	10.5	11.0
2008-09	3.7	6.2
2009-10	3.2	2.4
2010-11	3.7	2.5

Newcastle upon Tyne offer a particularly stark example of this. The city agreed to a 13.4 per cent target over the three years, but pledged to make an 8 per cent reduction in the 'first' year (2008–09). When data for 2008 was released, it showed that Newcastle made a reduction in emissions of almost 7 per cent between 2005 and 2008, meaning that their actual target for year one of the LAA was just 1 per cent. Table 4.4 shows how this time lag affected the level of targets that cities actually signed up to.

Table 4.4: Target achievements in core cities, 2005-08 (%)

Core cities	Target	Achieved 2005-08	'Actual' target
Newcastle upon Tyne	13.4	6.9	6.5
Nottingham	12.6	10.3	2.3
Manchester	11.1	5.9	5.2
Sheffield	10.0	7.2	2.8
Birmingham	6.9	4.7	2.2
Bristol	1.0	10.3	−9.3
Liverpool	No target	4.5	n/a
Leeds	No target	9	n/a

As can be seen, targets were reduced to relatively small levels once the years 2005–08 were taken into account, making them look politically expedient without potentially requiring large efforts to achieve them. Bristol even had an allowance of a 9 per cent increase in emissions over the three-year period.

Implications for local politics: transitions or stop-gaps?

Because respondents were not clear as to how they would be rewarded or censured for their progress on meeting targets, there was a lack of incentive for local authorities to meet their specific goals, as long as most priorities were met. As such, respondents felt that this would mean that NI 186 could drop towards the bottom of priorities as local authorities focused on more politically achievable goals that met dominant economic and social policy lines. GOR officers recognised this, but argued that their role as 'authoritative seducers' came to the fore here in making sure that local authorities remained "on the ball" (GOR officer, South West) with NI 186. It is clear that each of the core cities were beginning to take carbon management seriously, and even those that had not taken up NI 186 had developed climate change strategies by 2010. This brings into question the extent to which the indicator was a catalyst in itself in getting cities to act on climate change, although it may be argued that as part of a suite of other national and international measures aimed at local authorities, such as the Carbon Reduction Commitment for large energy users and renewable energy targets, it helped to push carbon management as a distinctly local agenda.

Analysis of the core cities' approaches to achieving their emissions targets gives some indication of the implications of LAA targets for local politics. Some progressive solutions were sought. For instance, most strategies have some focus on fuel poverty and 'affordable warmth', which had social as well as environmental benefits. The majority of short-term actions in fact centre on domestic energy use. This perhaps reflects an aim to "get the low hanging fruit first" (local authority officer), an understandable and laudable aim in itself. The short-term nature of LAAs means, however, that they have been inevitably linked to short-term actions. Similarly, the focus on domestic and – in some cases – transport-related actions, heightens the sense that there is little evidence within strategies that the need to reduce carbon emissions is having any impact on wider economic logics and decision making. In other words, city governments are not yet facing up to some of the more challenging questions that climate change asks of how cities operate. The 'mini-Stern' reports being carried out by cities suggest that the economy was beginning considered, albeit separately to LAAs, but largely in terms of how to respond in an entrepreneurial manner to emerging climate change regulation.

This brings about questions regarding the extent to which the calculations under consideration in this chapter have a constructive place within long-term transition planning for cities, where a need for wholesale long-term behavioural and technological changes is required. Measurement of the indicator in procedural terms, as well as on a quantitative basis, may therefore have been more effective in promoting long-term change.

Unbound cities, unplugged regional hinterlands?

An equally important issue relates to the spatial implications of NI 186 and the relationship between cities and their urban and rural hinterlands. First, the implementation process suggests a clear difference in 'carbon capabilities' between the core cities, alongside a small number of other local authorities, and many smaller authorities that were less well attuned to carbon management debates.

This was not helped by the fact that national and regional representatives failed to achieve a level playing field in the negotiation of emissions targets. The rationale behind emissions reduction scenarios, produced by AEA Technology on behalf of Defra, is in itself something that in excess of one third of local authority respondents were unaware of. As such, they were automatically disadvantaged in terms of agreeing to a target: they did not know what the target referred to. In many local authorities they "were just really thinking, well that sounds about right, that's similar to the national target, okay" (local authority officer). Similarly, many of the smaller 'carbon naïve' authorities did not possess the resources to effectively negotiate on targets: again, showing a failure by regional organisations to provide adequate support.

The position for authorities that did not adopt NI 186 was similar. As noted, some opted out of the target because they had recognised some of the inherent faults with the methodology, and instead took up NI 185 or a '185+' indicator, which expanded the influence of local authorities to include schools, hospitals and emergency services. Others – mostly smaller authorities – had opted out because carbon management was not yet on the agenda for the authority: most commonly this was described by respondents as being a result of unwillingness from elected members to take this on. It was not clear exactly how they had resisted pressure from GORs to take up NI 186. One possibility was that some authorities were simply more truculent, and perhaps more detached from regional and national policy actors than others. In other words, maybe the 'pushing' from GORs could only be effective from those who already had some level of engagement with the policy actors involved.

One respondent particularly emphasised the fact that data has not been made readily available to local authorities, either through Defra or GORs flagging up where data might be found, suggesting that GORs acted as 'gate keepers and lock keepers' of information:

'I mean I had to do a lot of digging: Defra haven't published a lot of this data. There's an extra layer of data that they didn't put on the website that I had to get from AEA. But an extremely important layer of data. There's only one colleague in [the region] who's recognised that lack of data and has requested to know how I did it. Which leads me to believe, or guess, that there's no other authorities in [the region] that have really nailed down what this indicator means. Because you can't from the level of data on the website.' (local authority officer)

This was something also acknowledged as a problem by respondents within central government departments.

A second issue relating to the relationship between cities and smaller authorities is bound within the logic of the object of the carbon city as discussed above. By measuring cities using the same criteria as other areas – per capita carbon emissions – the indicator places equal responsibility on all local authorities. This is borne out in the levels of reductions proposed by Defra prior to negotiating targets: the mean target proposed for core cities was 12.1 per cent per capita emissions reduction compared to 12.2 for the whole population. This is, in fact, inequitable. Cities both produce more emissions in total than other authorities, and rely on small towns and rural areas to maintain their economies.

The core cities in England are shown therefore to be essentially 'unbound', while many local authorities within their city-regions are left 'unplugged'. This works both in terms of local authorities' ability to effectively deal with carbon knowledges and thus their ability to politically operate with regional, national and international constrictions, but also in terms of cities being 'free' of responsibility for the carbon implications of their dependence on their city-regions – as a start – as well as carbon flows that often stretch around the world.

Conclusions

This chapter has opened up debates about calculating the carbon city through analysis of top-down attempts to implement carbon reduction targets and monitoring in England. By analysing the construction of the object of the carbon city, a range of issues arose regarding how the city should be viewed in terms of their responsibilities for carbon reduction. These may be distilled into two main sets of debates: questions about the carbon city as a governable space and about the city as space in itself.

Cities as governable spaces

The implementation of NI 186 targets and monitoring draw out questions about how the carbon city can, or should, be governed. From the perspective of central government, targets provide a key means for controlling local government and shaping their actions to meet governmental objectives. Top-down targets and monitoring such as those implemented through LAAs are potentially important. They create an opportunity for cities to be measured against one another, as well as against smaller cities and towns. All are seen to be operating under the same conditions. It ensures that not only innovative or experimental cities and towns begin to think about carbon management, while leaving some leeway for different places to approach carbon reduction in their own way. But there are downsides to this approach. First, the object of the city seen through NI 186 sees the city as a technical object to be dealt with through technocratic measures. There is little room for real systemic change to cities in any of the approaches outlined here. Importantly there is no space for 'local' knowledges of low carbon transitions.

Second, the carbon city is seen as no different from the carbon town or rurality. There are spatial elements to this, which I will return to in a moment, but there are also questions about where cities should sit within multi-level governance frameworks. England's eight core cities form the Core Cities Network, and many of these are also involved in international networks such as the International Council for Local Environment Initiatives' Cities for Climate Protection (see Bulkeley and Betsill, 2003). In many ways they operate nationally and transnationally as governing authorities. As noted earlier, the EU Emissions Trading Scheme regulates large emitters in various industries, and the UK's Carbon Reduction Commitment involves committing large energy users to take measures to reduce their emissions. If national and supra-national governing actors seem keen to 'scale' the level at which different types of emissions are regulated, perhaps there is a case for doing the same to different spatial entities. As such, large cities in Europe, for example, may be better governed through an EU carbon reduction scheme, with a national or regional focus on smaller authorities aimed at enabling them to more effectively come to terms with carbon management.

Third, and moving back to 'experimental' city-led calculations, Manchester's mini-Stern sees low carbon transition largely as a means to tap into new markets for the city-region: a narrow 'smart' growth-oriented approach to carbon reduction. This retains the city as a site of entrepreneurial competition, the site of regional or national economic growth. The fact that the cities of Liverpool and Leeds are also engaging in similar activities suggests that this view is one shared by others, and that the chance to reconsider ideas about growth, about how to organise our cities, or how to live a more ecologically sensitive existence is not being taken. In Ulrich Beck's (1998) terms, the risk city perpetuated, with new, potentially unknown, ecological risks hiding unbidden around the corner.

Beyond the city as a focal point?

Emphasis on the city as the focus of sustainable development agendas, or – more narrowly – low carbon transitions, becomes problematic when we delve into some of the issues at heart. If cities are calculated as stand-alone objects, this does not encourage long-term transitions towards developing more locally resilient economies, with cities tied in materially to urban and rural hinterlands. And if these stand-alone objects also have crucial infrastructural points removed from them – such as energy and transport grids – then they will not be encouraged to develop new planning solutions to create new de-centralised sources of energy or reduce demand for transit between cities.

The city is also a site of relative power in many cases, albeit concentrated in a small number of hands. Western cities, even those still suffering from previous rounds of economic restructuring, will not be the worst affected by either mitigative or adaptive pressures. As illustrated above, they will also have greater political and administrative capacity to manipulate or resist central governmental pressure to implement stringent targets. And they will be the best placed to benefit from emerging 'low carbon markets'. Again, it is the urban and rural hinterlands of cities that are potentially left out of new modes of carbon accumulation, are unable to effectively deal with the array of knowledge required to engage with low carbon agendas proactively and are unplugged from regional, national and international networks that may enable them to do so. The questions raised by While (2008, with Jonas and Gibbs, 2010) regarding spatial carbon inequalities become all the more prescient.

Finally, the city is essentially the pinnacle of what humans create through spatial calculation. On the whole this is based around a notion that humans can overcome nature: the modernist project of humans becoming 'Gods in their own right'. Less attention to the city as a focal point and more on the various geographically diffuse material and behavioural networks that they provide points of confluence for may result in a better understanding of how to untangle and solve the various social, environmental and economic crises they sit at the centre of.

Key conclusions

- Targets provide an important means through which central government can seek to control local authorities. Emissions targets in LAAs were seen as a first step towards creating the conditions for local carbon emissions reductions.
- These focused on technocratic measures that gave little space for genuine room for locally led systematic change, in particular by controlling the types of evidence and knowledge that were deemed acceptable.
- Analysis of the implementation of targets brought light to a group of 'unbound' cities that were able to effectively negotiate and manipulate evidence in the target-setting process.
- Both the construction of the 'carbon object' and the negotiation of targets in this process brings forth questions about how to define the 'local' in the context of climate change, and whether all local areas should be 'made the same' within national or supra-national target-setting regimes.

Note

[1] The implementation of multi-area agreements later in 2008 and 2009 did allow groups of authorities to adopt indicators, which could potentially include NI 186.

Further reading

Bulkeley, H. and Betsill, M. (2003) *Cities and climate change*, New York: Routledge.

Miller, P. (1994) 'Accounting and objectivity: the invention of calculable selves and calculable spaces', in A. Megill (ed) *Rethinking objectivity*, Durham, NC and London: Duke University Press, pp 239-64.

While, A., Jonas, A.E.G. and Gibbs, D. (2010) 'From sustainable development to carbon control: eco-state restructuring and the politics of urban and regional development', *Transactions of the Institute of British Geographers*, vol 35, no 1, pp 76-93.

References

AEA Technology and Defra (Department for Environment, Food and Rural Affairs) (2008) *Analysis to support climate change indicators for local authorities* (www.decc.gov.uk/assets/decc/Statistics/nationalindicators/1_20100421 135745_e_@@@_analysisclimatechangeindicatorslas.pdf).

Agrawala, S. (1998) 'Context and early origins of the Intergovernmental Panel on Climate Change', *Climatic Change*, vol 39, no 4, pp 605-20.

Arrhenius, S. (1896) 'On the influence of carbonic acid in the air upon the temperature of the ground', *Philosophical Magazine and Journal of Science*, vol 5, no 41, pp 237-76.

Arup (2007) *Regional strategies and climate change*, Wakefield: YHA.

Barrett, S. (1998) 'Political economy of the Kyoto Protocol', *Oxford Review of Economic Policy*, vol 41, no 4, pp 20-39.

Beck, U. (1998) 'From industrial society to the risk society: questions of survival, social structure and ecological enlightenment', in J.S. Dryzek and D. Schlosberg (eds) *Debating the earth: The environmental politics reader* (2nd edn), Oxford: Oxford University Press, pp 327-48.

Bulkeley, H. (2006) 'A changing climate for spatial planning?', *Planning Theory and Practice*, vol 7, no 2, pp 203-14.

Bulkeley, H. and Betsill, M. (2003) *Cities and climate change*, New York: Routledge.

Bumpus, A. and Liverman, D. (2008) 'Accumulation by decarbonisation and the governance of carbon offsets', *Economic Geography*, vol 84, no 2, pp 127-55.

Callon, M. (2009) 'Civilizing markets: carbon trading between *in vitro* and *in vivo* experiments', *Accounting, Organizations and Society*, vol 34, no 2-3, pp 535-48.

Castree, N. (2008) 'Neo-liberalising nature 1: the logics of de- and re-regulation', *Environment and Planning A*, vol 40, no 1, pp 131-52.

Castree, N. (2010) 'The politics of climate change by Anthony Giddens', *Sociological Review*, vol 58, no 5, pp 156-62.

Crosby, A.W. (1997) *The measure of reality: Quantification and western society, 1250-1600*, Cambridge: Cambridge University Press.

Deloitte (2008) *'Mini-Stern' for Manchester* (www.deloitte.com/assets/Dcom-UnitedKingdom/Local%20Assets/Documents/UK_GPS_MiniStern.pdf).

Demeritt, D. (2001) 'The construction of global warming and the politics of science', *Annals of the Association of American Geographers*, vol 91, no 2, pp 307-37.

Friends of the Earth (2010) *Local carbon budgets*, Briefing (www.foe.co.uk/resource/briefings/mp_local_carbon_budgets.pdf).

Government Office Yorkshire and the Humber (2008) NI 185 and 186, Unpublished presentation.

Kalthoff, H. (2005) 'Practices of calculation: economic representations and risk management', *Theory, Culture and Society*, vol 22, no 2, pp 69-97.

Latour, B. (1999) *Pandora's hope: Essays on the reality of science studies*, London: Harvard University Press.

Liverman, D.M. (2004) 'Who governs, at what scale and at what price? Geography, environmental governance and the commodification of nature', *Annals of the Association of American Geographers*, vol 94, no 4, pp 734-8.

Mackenzie, D. (2009) 'Making things the same: gases emissions rights and the politics of carbon markets', *Accounting, Organizations and Society*, vol 34, no 3-4, pp 440-55.

Meadowcroft, J. (2005) 'From welfare state to eco-state', in J. Barry, and R. Eckersley (eds) *The state and the global ecological crisis*, Cambridge, MA: The MIT Press, pp 3-24.

Mennicken, A. (2002) 'Bringing calculation back in: sociological studies in accounting', *Economic Sociology*, vol 3, no 3, pp 17-28.

Miller, P. (1994) 'Accounting and objectivity: the invention of calculable selves and calculable spaces', in A. Megill (ed) *Rethinking objectivity*, Durham, NC and London: Duke University Press.

Power, M. (2004) 'Counting, control and calculation: reflections on measuring and management', *Human Relations*, vol 57, no 6, pp 765-83.

Rutland, T. and Aylett, A. (2008) 'The work of policy: actor networks, governmentality, and local action on climate change in Portland, Oregon', *Environment and Planning D: Society and Space*, vol 26, no 4, pp 627-46.

Stern, N (2006) *The Stern Review on the economics of climate change*, London: HM Treasury (http://webarchive.nationalarchives.gov.uk/+/http://www.hm-treasury.gov.uk/sternreview_index.htm).

While, A. (2008) 'Climate change and planning: carbon control and spatial regulation', *Town Planning Review*, vol 79, no 1, pp vii-xiii.

While, A. (2010) 'The carbon calculus and transitions in urban politics and urban political theory', in H. Bulkeley, M. Hodson, and S. Marvin (eds) *Cities and low carbon transitions*, London: Routledge, pp 42-53.

While, A., Jonas, A.E.G. and Gibbs, D. (2010) 'From sustainable development to carbon control: eco-state restructuring and the politics of urban and regional development', *Transactions of the Institute of British Geographers*, vol 35, no 1, pp 76-93.

Section 2

Building the sustainable city: policy fields, current issues and themes

five

The property industry and the construction of urban spaces: crisis or opportunity?

Tim Dixon

Introduction

This chapter explores the current shape and form of the UK property industry and its new approaches to urban regeneration in an era of change, focusing on both commercial and residential development.

The chapter begins by examining the key players in the property development and investment processes, and examines current patterns of land and property ownership and how this has changed over the last 50 years. Key property market indicators are examined and the causes of the credit crunch and its implications for the property industry are reviewed. The chapter then examines the variety of development and investment vehicles available (for example, public–private partnerships [PPPs], or a contractual arrangement between a public sector body and a private sector entity, and joint ventures), and how these are framed in the context of the wider UK economy and the current legislative landscape. The key drivers for such vehicles are also analysed, focusing on the growth of the corporate responsibility and sustainability agendas, and how these have also influenced and shaped the rise of a 'responsible property investment' movement both in the UK and in the US.

Based on the author's own research work and other relevant research, a number of systems and frameworks for measuring the impact of urban regeneration are also discussed. The chapter concludes by examining, in the light of the current recession, the ways in which the UK property development and regeneration industry may evolve in the next decade and beyond.

Background and context

Property development and urban regeneration

'Property development' and 'urban regeneration' are two rather different, although linked, approaches to the transformation of the built environment in urban areas in the UK. In strictly legal terms, 'development' is defined in the UK by statute in the Town and Country Planning Act 1990, Section 55(1), as 'the carrying out of building, engineering, mining or other operations in, on, over or under land, or the making of any material change in the use of any buildings or other land'.[1] Alternatively, for Havard (2008), property development is taken to be a process 'that involves the transformation of property from one state to another' (p 2), and for Wilkinson and Reed (2008, p 17), a process that 'involves changing or intensifying the use of land to produce buildings for occupation'. If the private sector is involved in such activity then profit or an enhanced return on capital is the primary motive, although this may not be the case if the development is a public sector-driven project (Guy, 1994; Havard, 2008). There is frequently therefore a strong economic/profit-driven emphasis in the use of the term, 'property development'.

However, at a broader level, recent policy initiatives in the UK have sought to highlight the distinction between 'economic development' and 'regeneration' (CLG, 2008a). Specifically, while development is seen as focusing on profit and commercially viable in its focus, regeneration should also incorporate elements of social and economic diversity to benefit existing communities (IPF, 2009). In the UK the government has defined regeneration as a set of activities which reverse economic, social and physical decline in areas where the market will not resolve this without government support (CLG, 2009). In this context the British Urban Regeneration Association (BURA) definition (Roberts, 2000, p 17) of 'urban regeneration' is also helpful:

> Regeneration is comprehensive and integrated vision and action which leads to the resolution of urban problems and which seeks to bring about a lasting improvement in the economic, physical, social and environmental condition of an area that has been subject to change.

Urban regeneration is therefore seen as being about delivering increased economic inclusion and ensuring that economic development improves the lives of those living in the most deprived areas (although see Chapters Three and Ten, this volume, for a critique). In other words, regeneration is essentially a 'subset' of a broader economic development, which itself includes 'property development'.

The history of urban regeneration in the UK is also characterised by a number of distinctive phases during the 30 years since the seminal White Paper *Policy for the inner cities* (DoE, 1977). Moreover, the period before this was also a time of shifting emphasis (see Figure 5.1).

Following the emphasis on physical redevelopment and social welfare in the 1940s-1950s and 1960s respectively, by the 1970s there had a been a shift away from a welfare emphasis towards economic prosperity, driven largely by criticisms of existing policy and a desire to move towards a more mixed approach in tackling urban issues through partnerships (IPF, 2009).

Figure 5.1: Evolution of urban regeneration policy

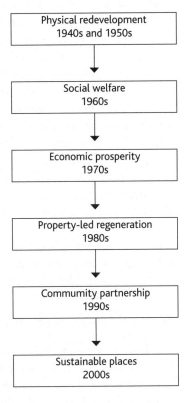

Further changes followed. By the 1980s, and with the advent of the Thatcher Conservative government, a bigger role was played by the private sector in a world of 'de-regulation' and 'privatism', at the expense of the public sector. Essentially a period of property-led regeneration, this borrowed heavily from US policy with an emphasis on 'flagship' projects (Blackman, 1995).

However, by the 1990s, and following the emergence of recession, it was clear that this approach was unbalanced and limited, and so policy swung towards the placing of greater emphasis on partnership-based structures and economic prosperity, through, for example, such initiatives as City Challenge. There was thus a greater role again for local communities, and local residents and businesses were expected to play a greater role in tackling urban deprivation problems within their areas. This was continued through the Blair Labour government's focus on the New Deal for Communities (IPF, 2009).

More recently, sustainability has become a key focus for UK government policy with an emphasis on social, economic and environmental well-being, or what is often referred to in academic literature as the 'triple bottom line' approach to sustainable development (Elkington, 1997; see Chapters Two and Three, this volume, for a further discussion). This attempts to achieve development that promotes economic growth, but maintains social inclusion and minimises environmental impact (Dixon, 2007; Dixon and Adams, 2008).

In turn this has been underpinned by policy guidance (*Securing the future*), which seeks to set a new framework goal for sustainable development (HM Government, 2005), and revisions to national planning guidance which aim to strengthen the focus of sustainable development principles within the wider UK planning system (for example, *Planning Policy Statement 1: Delivering sustainable development* [CLG, 2005] and *Planning Policy Statement 23: Planning and pollution control* [CLG, 2004]). Nonetheless this period has also included a substantial number of property-led regeneration projects, the sustainability of which has been questioned (Dixon et al, 2007a).

This has, however, also coincided with a period when significant investment gaps in urban regeneration have been highlighted as a key issue for European Union (EU) states, including the UK (ULI, 2009; Colantonio and Dixon, 2010). This has also been starkly highlighted with the collapse of the US sub-prime mortgage market (also discussed by Mark Whitehead in Chapter Two, this volume), and the related turbulence in lending markets worldwide, which have exacerbated a downwards trend in land and property asset prices. It is still too early to say what the long-term consequences of the current recession will be, but recent research in the UK suggests that the effects have already fed through into investment, development and occupational demand, and the potential slowdown is seen as being deeper and more severe than the 1990s recession, posing a significant threat to the long-term viability of some regeneration projects in the UK and elsewhere (GLA Economics, 2008; All Party Urban Development Group, 2009; Dixon, 2009; Parkinson, 2009a, 2009b).

Property development industry and key actors

It is clear that urban regeneration in the UK has relied on a strong property development focus. We have also seen the development of a variety of different conceptual models to understand the role of the property development industry and which are broadly based on event sequence models, agency models, production-based approaches and institutional models (see, for example, Gore and Nicholson, 1991; Healey, 1991; Ball, 1998; Guy and Henneberry, 2002). Alternative approaches (see, for example, Wilkinson and Reed, 2008; Havard, 2008) have adopted more descriptive and less theoretical approaches to identify different types of property development activity and to frame key actors in the property development process.

In this context the property development industry comprises the following key players (Havard, 2008; Dixon, 2009):

- financial institutions, including pension companies and insurance funds;
- private sector developers, including house builders, commercial developers (who may be developer investors, who seek to hold the property long term or developer traders, who seek to sell once the development is completed);
- public sector, including local authorities and central government;
- landowners, including the traditional landed estates (for example, Grosvenor).

Moreover, players within the industry focus on commercial property and residential property to varying degrees and are driven by a variety of ambitions. The UK property industry is therefore characterised by both its scale and its complexity. In the remainder of this chapter therefore the key trends which are shaping the UK property development industry, and its engagement with the wider urban regeneration agenda, is examined in more detail, before concluding with an examination of future trends in the industry in the context of the recent recession.

Structural change in the UK property industry: the role of the financial institutions and the private sector

In such a complex industry it is difficult to provide a comprehensive account of the variety of trends impacting on its shape and nature, or indeed on all the players. What is significant, however, is that financial institutions are major players in the commercial investment market, and therefore by implication the commercial development market, and this power base is founded on substantial ownership of urban land and property which has evolved over the last 50 years.

Understanding patterns of urban land and property ownership is important not only because the size and configuration of land holdings affects urban morphology through new development, regeneration and refurbishment of existing land and property, but also because historically, the timing of land sales affects the nature and shape of urban development by reflecting contemporaneous architectural and planning styles (Kivell, 1993; Dixon, 2009). Land ownership also confers economic and social power and wealth on owners who can also potentially exert influence on urban planning policies and outcomes (Massey and Catalano, 1978; Kivell, 1993). Moreover, land ownership is a keystone of national and local economies and may be seen as an important link between the production sector (in terms of the property development and investment sector) and the consumption sector (in terms of occupiers of land and property). Finally, land ownership reflects societal values, given that ownership is a social construct and that urban areas impact on the environment (Kivell, 1993).

Since the earlier domination of the great landed estates during the 19th century, in the postwar era the financial institutions (life insurance and pension funds) have come to strengthen their grip on the commercial property investment landscape, driven by a complex web of interconnecting and related economic, political and social factors (Scott, 1996; Harris, 2005). The predominance of the financial institutions was also re-enforced by the emergence of standardised ownership structures, with the 'institutional lease', based around 21- or 25-year leases with three-yearly or five-yearly 'upwards only rent reviews' (UORR) being the most common way of formalising the commercial property landlord–tenant relationship (Dixon, 2009). Today these institutions own about 30 per cent of UK commercial investment property, by value (IPF, 2007) (see Figure 5.2).

Figure 5.2: UK 'core urban' commercial property ownership by value

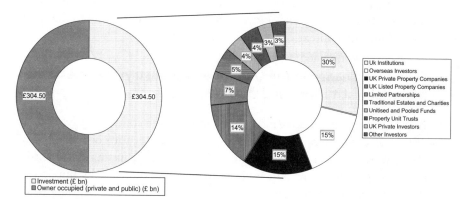

The financial institutions (alongside banks and overseas investors) are very important players in the commercial property market because they directly influence a high proportion of the funding of new development to satisfy investment and occupier-led demand (Harvard, 2008).

Moreover, it is important to recognise that the market for commercial urban land and property traded between these groups is made up of several interlinked markets (Keogh, 1994; Ball et al, 1998; Dixon, 2009). First, there is a 'user market' that comprises property owned by commercial property users (offices, retail and industrial), or rented from financial institutions or property companies, with the principal forms of land ownership being freehold or leasehold. Second, there is also a market in property as a 'financial asset' owned and traded by property investors (which includes financial institutions and property companies). Third, there is a 'property development market' where new property is developed for ownership by investors and developers. Finally, the user and development markets are connected to an 'urban land market' in which new development or redevelopment can take place.

Despite the important role of financial institutions, however, private developers and house builders, and indeed the public sector (including housing associations), also play a substantial role in the development and regeneration of urban areas, as examined by Chris Pickvance in Chapter Eight, this volume. In the UK residential market, private house builders and direct developers (the latter, for example, where there is a 'mixed use' scheme which may combine commercial and residential development) continue to dominate, although the public sector is also a key player in an increasing number of 'joint venture', or PPP schemes, which may themselves focus on regeneration projects.

Even before the recent recession began to bite, however, the UK house building industry had come under close scrutiny for its failure to deliver the number of homes required to meet future demand. Indeed, it was this perceived lack of long-term supply and responsiveness to demand that led to the Barker Review in 2003 and its final report in 2004 (Dixon and Adams, 2008). Ultimately the Barker Review's conclusions led to the introduction of a package of reforms, including changes to the planning system, new regulations, new funding systems and various tax breaks and incentives designed to boost the capacity and output of private and affordable housing (Pretty and Hackett, 2009).

However, two further reports by Calcutt (2007) and the Office of Fair Trading (OFT) (2008) put the UK house building sector under further scrutiny. Ostensibly a review of the house building industry as a 'business', the Calcutt Review also examined how the industry was engaging with the wider sustainability agenda as the government sought to introduce zero carbon measures for residential property. Interestingly, however, the review also suggested that the 'current trader' model of the house building industry was at risk. Essentially a highly concentrated and consolidated industry with the majority of housing built by 'volume' house builders (some 43 companies have a combined market share of 71 per cent; Wellings, 2001, cited in Adams, 2008), the current model is traditionally based on a cycle of land acquisition, development and sale. However, the Calcutt Review suggested that alternative models of delivery (for example, based on 'investment' and 'self-build' models together with greater involvement of registered social landlords, commercial developers or even overseas companies) could offer alternative and viable business models for the sector (Calcutt, 2007).

In contrast, the OFT study was designed to investigate whether competition was behind the sluggish supply-side response to rising prices in the UK house building industry. Despite intensive research and evidence gathering, however, the study found no such problems and perhaps more controversially still, no evidence that land banking (or owning large amounts of land with planning permission on which no building had yet started) was a substantive issue in the private sector (OFT, 2008).

However, when the recession first started to hit the UK in the second half of 2007 it became clear that the current trader model for housing was indeed failing to deliver. As Figure 5.3 shows, in 2008 only 150,000 houses were built by the private sector, the lowest total since 1993. Moreover, in the downturn house prices also fell substantially, albeit with a slight recovery during late 2009. Essentially the housing market was paying the price for a sudden collapse in the UK mortgage market brought on by the collapse of the US sub-prime mortgage market, reduced consumer confidence and high levels of debt (GLA Economics, 2008; Pretty and Hackett, 2009). Moreover, the fall in the viability of developing land brought about by the house price collapse also led to an even larger fall in land values. This also had repercussions for affordable housing provision which had been underpinned by Section 106 contributions from the private sector but which now came under increasing pressure.

Similarly institutional involvement in development activity was also curtailed as tighter credit restrictions operated and the previously bravado assumptions regarding rental growth, voids and rent-free periods (and which had underpinned the 'bubble' in capital and rental values between 2001 and 2007) were trimmed back within financial appraisals. By 2009 therefore there was a much bleaker landscape for both financial institutions, private house builders and the banks that had lent to them, so much so that the government's target of building 240,000 new homes by 2016 was looking

Figure 5.3: UK permanent dwellings completed, 1949–2008

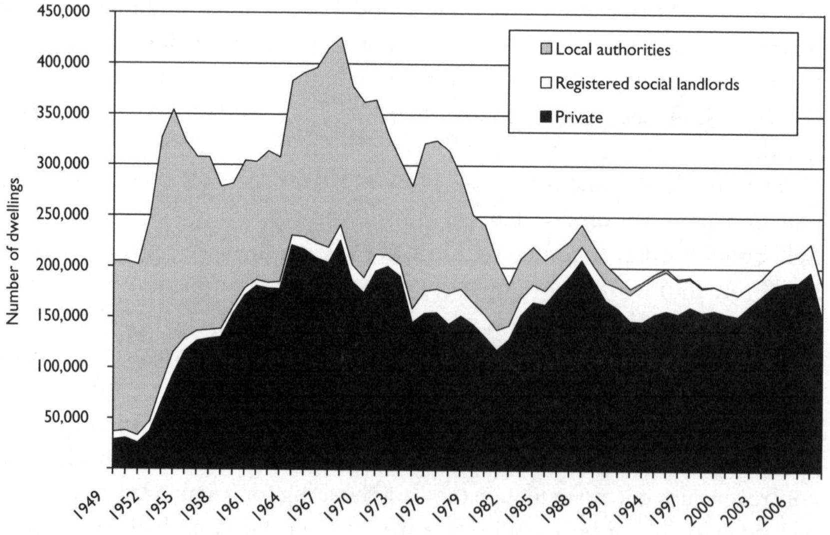

Source: CLG data

increasingly unrealistic, and many urban regeneration projects had stalled (Parkinson, 2009a, 2009b).

Despite this, it should also be remembered that the UK commercial (and residential) property market, in contrast to a number of Northern European countries, has been especially prone to long-term 'boom and bust' cycles with subsequent destabilising economic effects (Harvey, 1985; Scott and Judge, 2000). For example, the 1974 property crash led to a severe banking crisis, with a further crash in 1990 after the boom years of the late 1980s. This cyclical pattern in property has been closely related to similar cycles in bank lending on property within the context of wider macroeconomic policy (Scott, 1996; Harris, 2005). However, property cycles (which can last for 15-20 years) are also associated with changes in the demand for property, because of growing economic activity generally, or because of changes in commercial or social behaviour (Guy, 1994). In that sense the recent recession is nothing new.

New drivers for change: sustainability and responsible investment

Despite the current recession, however, it is clear that the emergence of the UK 'sustainability agenda', driven partly by legislation, but also by a strong desire to enhance shareholder value by aligning with a parallel corporate responsibility (or CR) agenda, is increasingly influencing and directing both financial institutions and private house builders when it comes to engaging with the urban regeneration agenda. In this sense, therefore, perhaps the emerging landscape reflects both 'policy push' and 'opportunity pull' (POST, 1998).

An example of this is the strong emphasis on brownfield land development and regeneration by private house builders (Dixon, 2007). In 2008, for example, some 80 per cent of new housing development was built on such land (CLG, 2010) compared with 76 per cent in 2006, although given the recent fall in UK house building activity, the total number of brownfield completions has been relatively flat (Dixon, 2009).

This focus on brownfield development reflects both a policy driver (through, for example, *Planning Policy Statement 3: Housing* [CLG, 2011][2]), and an increasing engagement by house builders with the CR agenda. CR is essentially an umbrella term which embraces the theory and practice of how a business manages its relationship with society (Blowfield and Murray, 2008), and in this sense the institutions themselves are demanding increasing levels of CR from the house builder sector (Calcutt, 2007). As Osmani and O'Reilly (2009) note, the importance attached to CR was strongly illustrated in the World Wildlife Fund (WWF) (2007) report, entitled *Building a sustainable future*, where a survey of 20 of the UK largest housing developers revealed that 70 per cent report publicly on their approach to sustainability, and 65 per cent have a corporate sustainability policy in place. Consequently, CR has the potential to be a powerful driver for zero carbon homes, as companies strive to improve their environmental performance, although Adams et al (2008) suggest that house builders have paid more attention to improving the sustainability of the production process rather than the product, and in many instances rhetoric still fails to match reality (Dixon, 2007).

However, the goal of zero carbon homes produces fresh challenges (particularly in view of increased costs and perceived regulatory burdens) for an industry in recession (Osmani and O'Reilly, 2009). The *Code for sustainable homes* (CLG, 2006a), which sets a target of all new homes to be zero carbon by 2016, for example, is seen by some (see, for example, Pretty and Hackett, 2009) as another addition to the list of burdens that house builders already face (for example, new building regulations, housing density provision and housing-related infrastructure).

Despite this, and in a more positive vein, it is also apparent that financial institutions have begun to engage with the sustainability agenda in a similar way through the channel of 'responsible investment' (RI). The World Economic Forum define this as (2005, p 7):

> Most commonly understood to mean investing in a manner that takes into account the impact of investments on wider society and the natural environment, both today and in the future.

RI increases in importance for financial institutions and others potentially investing in urban regeneration projects should be seen in the context of other trends towards a broader diversification of investment portfolios to spread risk (including the diversification role of real estate), and the emergence of the related concept of 'responsible property investment' (or RPI) (Rapson et al, 2007).

Historically, prime real estate has tended to dominate as a sub-category of real estate in the majority of institutional investors' portfolios, but increasingly the performance of urban regeneration real estate markets is being closely examined by such investors. Previous research has shown that there is immense potential in urban regeneration areas, which often coincide with inner-city locations (Porter, 1995), and in the UK, recent real estate performance measures have also highlighted the sound financial returns that can be made through engagement in urban regeneration (IPD, 2009). As a result, combined with the clear benefits for CR and sustainability (often focusing on brownfield developments) offered by these locations, there has also been a real interest in understanding how private sector finance can best be attracted into investing in urban regeneration locations.

The quest for diversification has undoubtedly also led to institutions allocating funding to RI-based investments. This has also led to the development of the concept of RPI. Pivo and McNamara (2005, p 129), for example, defined RPI as:

> Maximizing the positive effects and minimising the negative effects of property ownership, management and development on society and the natural environment in a way that is consistent with investor goals and fiduciary responsibility.

This definition has been made more precise through the work of the United Nations Environment Programme Finance Initiative (UNEP FI) (2007), that suggests that RPI:

> ... is an approach to property investing that recognizes environmental and social considerations along with more conventional financial objectives. It goes beyond minimum legal requirements, to improving the environmental or social performance of property, through strategies such as urban revitalization, or the conservation of natural resources.

In this sense RPI can be implemented throughout the property lifecycle, as shown by the following examples (UNEP FI, 2007):

- developing or acquiring properties designed with environmentally and socially positive attributes (for example, low-income housing or green buildings);
- refurbishing properties to improve their performance (for example, energy efficiency or disability upgrades);
- managing properties in beneficial ways (for example, fair labour practices for service workers or using environmentally friendly cleaning products);
- demolishing properties in a conscientious manner (for example, re-using recovered materials on site for new development).

This view of 'responsibility' is predicated on the fact that not only is the built environment a major contributor to carbon emissions and pollutants (RICS, 2007), but also that the social and economic impacts of property investment strategies need to be considered (Pivo, 2005). There is also therefore a strong link between RPI and the concept of sustainable development (Pivo and McNamara, 2005; Rapson et al, 2007).

Development of new urban regeneration vehicles

There is no doubt that construction activity, and particularly house building activity, has been badly hit by the recession in the UK, particularly in northern cities, as the downturn has impacted on the buy-to-let market as well as owner-occupied housing (Dolphin, 2009). In many instances this has led to a chronic oversupply of apartments and low value properties in many city centres (Deloitte, 2009). This carries potential risks for the most deprived areas with further uncertainty over recovery potentially leading to further economic weakness (Parkinson, 2009a, pp 32-3):

> Residential-led regeneration schemes located in less prosperous/
> peripheral economies, particularly where the majority of potential
> buyers are those relying on gaining finance through the "sub-prime"
> mortgage market, have been hit. These are now the least attractive
> schemes to developers.

In comparison, despite the recession, the Investment Property Databank (IPD) Regeneration Index, which focuses on commercial property, has revealed a 'surprisingly resilient' regeneration sector, particularly at an individual sector level, and shows that long-term incentives for investment in regeneration have not been impaired by the market downturn (IPD, 2009). For example, while regeneration returns of −22.6 per cent in 2008 have correlated closely with the downturn in the wider property market with returns of −22.1 per cent, office and industrial properties still outperformed the UK average (IPD, 2009).

Nonetheless, many regeneration projects are being hit hard by the recession and lending to the real estate sector has also fallen dramatically, following the rapid growth of the past decade, which had been founded on sharply increasing commercial property prices. Recent statistics show a 40 per cent fall in prices since June 2007, with a resultant impact on net lending, which although initially slow to react, has also fallen by more than 50 per cent since the same date (see Figure 5.4). Recent analysis (Bank of England, 2009) suggests in the current fragile market that further downward pressure on prices would be exerted if banks sought to sell distressed assets.

Prior to the recession, demand and supply-side restrictions have frequently led to the lack of appropriate finance for urban regeneration or an increasing 'investment gap' (Clark, 2007; ULI, 2009). The involvement of the private sector has, however, been encouraged by new ways of thinking within government as to how to deal with the public sector's asset base in the UK (Sorrell and Hothi, 2007). Reviews such as the Lyons (2004) report and Gershon (2004) report, for example, have supported the UK government's view that it needs to devolve £30 billion of assets in public ownership by

2030. There is now therefore a complex array of investment vehicles for urban regeneration that form part of a wider PPP concept. Examples include (IPF, 2006; CLG, 2007; Sorrell and Hothi, 2007):

• limited partnerships and unit trust models (classified through their legal status); and
• outsourcing and joint venture models (classified through their asset management status).

Figure 5.4: Contributions to growth in lending to UK real estate sectors, 1998–2009

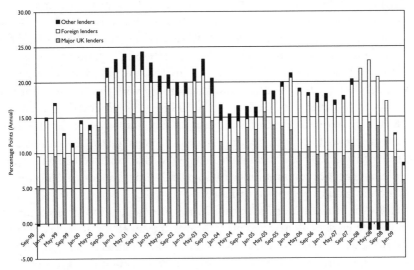

Source: Bank of England data

More recently, within the EU and its member states there has also been much discussion as to how to lever private sector investment into urban regeneration projects (Clark, 2007; ULI, 2009). The concept of an 'urban development fund', or UDF, is core to this. Essentially a UDF is a fund that invests in PPPs and other projects included in an integrated plan for sustainable urban development and provides the key implementation tool for JESSICA initiatives (Joint European Support for Sustainable Investment in City Areas) within the EU (King Sturge, 2009a, 2009b).

Finally, in the UK, alternative funding mechanisms to grant funding (or 'gap' funding) are also being explored in the wake of the recession and its perceived negative impact on regeneration projects. These alternatives include Accelerated Development Zones (ADZs), which are a UK variant on tax increment financing schemes (TIFs), and are intended to fund infrastructure from future increases in tax revenue created by new development (All Party Urban Development Group, 2009; Deloitte, 2009; Hackett, 2009; IPF, 2009; King Sturge, 2009a, 2009b; ULI, 2009).[3]

Urban regeneration – measuring success?

Aside from the financial and ethical advantages of investing in urban regeneration projects, the intellectual arguments for institutional investment in underserved markets, or inner-city areas (which frequently map onto areas of urban regeneration in the UK) have their roots in the US (Dixon, 2005).

The decline of the manufacturing sector in the UK and the long-term trend towards a service sector economy has also led policy makers in the UK to champion the importance of retailing as a potential creator of jobs, and economic vitality, not only nationally but more locally in local regeneration projects, especially in disadvantaged, inner-city areas (and for the sustainability of lower-income neighbourhoods, as John Flint suggests in this volume, Chapter Ten). The origins for this lie with the work of Michael Porter (1995) and his close relationship with the Initiative for the Competitive Inner City (ICIC) in the US in 1994. Policy themes in the UK have therefore been developed around such initiatives as City Growth Strategies, Inner City 100 and Underserved Markets (Dixon, 2005). A recent report (BiTC, 2009), for example, suggested that retail-led regeneration could benefit local communities through jobs provision, the promotion of economic growth and place making.

However, if institutions investing in urban regeneration projects are to prove their credentials in targeting such areas, they need robust and consistent metrics systems to measure the economic, environmental and social impacts of their investments, and to fully engage with communities. For example, Frankental (2001) suggests that the principles of RI can only have real substance if they are reinforced by changes in company law relating to governance; if their implementation is rewarded by financial markets; if they are related to the goals of social sustainability and with full benchmarking and auditing; if they are open to public scrutiny; if compliance mechanisms are in place; and if they are embedded across the organisation horizontally and vertically. It is frequently the 'social dimension' to RI and RPI, however, that is the most problematic and controversial in terms of measurement (see also Roberts et al, 2007).

Developing metrics systems to assess the impacts of investment in property (and regeneration)-based projects has not been straightforward, therefore. As Pivo and McNamara (2005, p 139) suggest, there is no set of broadly accepted metrics for evaluating the 'commitment of real estate investors to principles of RPI', often arising from the different metrics that are required for different countries and different properties. In related research in the

US, Hagerman et al (2007) suggest (in terms of pension fund investment in urban revitalisation) that the investment returns from community-based investing should include financial, social and environmental outcomes. Financial returns, for example, can easily be measured through risk-adjusted internal rates of return and in investment multiples, assessed against bond indices and property indices. Indeed, Pivo (2005) suggests that social investing does not appear to require concessions in financial performance, and this view is supported in relation to real estate investment in regeneration areas in the UK (IPD, 2009). However, Hagerman et al also suggest (2007, p 62):

> On the social impacts there is no universally accepted industry yardstick to date for testing how well an investment vehicle performs on its targeted social returns.

It is therefore the social dimension to investing (and indeed to sustainability) that still lacks a cutting edge in the institutional investment sector in the context of urban regeneration (Dixon et al, 2007b; Colantonio and Dixon, 2010).

The future: crisis or opportunity?

As this chapter has shown, the property development industry faces key challenges as the UK comes to terms with the recession and looks to move into recovery. Although the profit motive continues to dominate the industry and its engagement with regeneration, there are also signs of greater altruism in the industry. Moreover, although, as we have seen, the property market has encountered cyclical changes before, the depth of the current recession in the UK has raised important challenges for key actors and how future regeneration and development and investment markets will play out. In that sense the next decade and beyond will be important for determining how sustainable our future cities and communities will be (Dixon, 2009; Hackett, 2009; Parkinson, 2009b) and attempting to avert the problems associated with the 'lost decade' of growth experienced in Japan in the aftermath of the 1992 property 'bubble' (Dixon et al, 2011).

In the relatively short term the credit crunch will have a continuing impact within the UK's property markets, and, by implication, property development and regeneration patterns. In the commercial property market this will affect investment, development and occupational demand, and we may see increasing levels of sale and leaseback as companies seek to convert assets into cash, although a focus on short-term performance is also likely to bring increased volatility in the sector. What we are likely to see, then, in the next few years are continuing levels of 'churn' in the property market and subtle changes in ownership patterns within our urban areas as levels of private and corporate debt increase. Commercial property is likely to become vacant and the viability of regeneration programmes may also be affected in the short term, particularly in areas outside London and the South East. Although the recession offers opportunities to acquire assets at reduced prices, liquidity and confidence in the lending sector is still likely to remain low. For example, typical loan-to-value ratios have fallen from more than 80 per cent pre-credit crunch to about 70 per cent so that commercial developers have to provide around 50 per cent more equity to finance acquisition (IPF, 2009).

Environmental issues are also likely to play a substantial role as climate change impacts in the UK. Institutions will, for example, be less likely to invest in urban areas that are at risk from climate change (that is, floods, droughts, subsistence). A recent UK report funded by Hermes (Austin et al, 2008) suggested that as a result of climate change occupiers of buildings would be more likely to suffer heat stress causing disruption in shops, offices and industrial premises; there would be an associated risk of flooding and flash flooding in urban areas; and that water shortages could be become more common, with ground movement also problematic. Cities such as Southampton, London, Bristol, Cardiff and Cambridge were all seen in the report to be at risk. As a result we might expect to see a changing geographic distribution of property investment and development within the UK in the longer term as investors (both UK and from overseas) move out of riskier locations which may be flood-prone, and into areas relatively immune from the worst effects of climate change. There are also associated insurance risks for both commercial and residential property and consequent impacts on value and ownership patterns in urban areas, as insurance companies seek to reduce exposure to flooding and climate change risk, particularly in flood plain and coastal locations. There is also evidence to suggest that we will see a growing number of 'green leases' in the commercial property market which attempt to formalise landlord and tenant responsibilities in the context of energy and environmental issues associated with the building (Hinnells et al, 2008).

As we saw earlier there are serious doubts as to whether the volume house building model is sustainable and robust enough to deliver the homes that are needed in the UK. Demographic pressures will continue to drive demand for housing, but it is also likely that home ownership itself may no longer dominate policy as it once did. There are already signs that owner-occupation is declining in the UK, for example (Dixon, 2009). Institutional involvement could therefore become much more important in the private rented sector (Daly, 2008), perhaps in partnership with the public sector through the Homes and Communities Agency.

The importance of public sector-led delivery in partnership with the private sector is likely to continue to be a key element of the future property industry landscape in the UK (see Chapter Six, by Harriet Bulkeley, Mike Hodson and Simon Marvin, this volume). After all, the new towns of 20th-century Britain were founded on development corporations which had the powers to acquire, own, manage and dispose of land and property and undertake building operations and provide public utilities, but during the latter period of new town development private sector finance also played a vital role (CLG, 2006b). Unified land control was therefore fundamental to the success of the development corporations.

This also raises the important related question of how development value might be captured in future and how land ownership patterns are viewed in the light of this. The high political risks over addressing this issue directly are seen in the Barker Review's calls for a planning gain supplement (PGS) (Barker, 2003) and their subsequent dismissal by the government in favour of a continuation of Section 106 agreements in conjunction with a new community infrastructure levy.

Other more direct approaches to the land value question have also been proposed. In the absence of any political shock to the system, however, it is unlikely that land in the UK would be nationalised or redistributed in any substantive way in the near future in order to ensure common ownership rights and to address the land value uplift issue. However, the idea of a Land Value Tax (LVT) has been promoted by both centre and left of centre political parties over the last decade (Jones, 2008). Essentially LVT taxes only the market value of land and not the buildings on the land, and from that point of view is seen as a fairer and more equitable system by its proponents than the current system of UK taxes which focus on the property itself (Jones, 2008). The thinking behind the tax is that if buildings or machinery and plants are taxed, people may be dissuaded from using the asset beneficially, and that enterprise and efficiency are penalised as a direct result of the burden of taxation. However, this does not apply to LVT, which is payable regardless of whether or not the land is used or how well it is used, because the supply of land is inelastic, and an added benefit is that the tax revenue created by an increase in land values can be used to underwrite the funding of public infrastructure (Muellbauer, 2005).

This also invites the question as to how land and property ownership patterns could change if the public sector is to become an even more important player in urban land markets. Community land trusts (CLTs) have, for example, been seen as an important vehicle to enable public ownership and community empowerment; they were first developed in Britain and Ireland out of early exercises in practical land reform by the cooperative movement and the Chartists in the 19th century (and subsequently revived in India and in the US). CLTs are local community-controlled organisations set up to own and manage land and other assets in perpetuity for the benefit of the community (for example, affordable housing, workspaces, agricultural facilities, commercial outlets or community facilities; see CLG, 2008b).

The next 10 years and beyond will therefore be challenging for the UK property development and regeneration industry as it seeks to develop and redevelop our urban areas. The structural changes required to achieve sustainable outcomes for these projects parallel those needed in the wider UK economy. As Michael Parkinson has recently concluded (2009b, p 9):

> The past decade has been a good decade for English cities. They have undergone a substantial renaissance underpinned by a successful national economy and buoyant public spending. But those circumstances will not be found in the next decade. Equally, the sectors of the economy that underpinned their renaissance in that cycle may not be the most appropriate for the next cycle. The drivers of much of the renaissance were retail, leisure, residential and financial services. These are primarily consumption or service sector activities, which may not be as robust in the coming years. Places will need to look to higher-value-added production activities based upon innovation and learning, or more sustainable sectors that feed into the national and global low-carbon sustainability agenda.

Key conclusions

- Although the credit crunch has hit regeneration projects hard, the importance of public sector-led delivery in partnership with the private sector is likely to continue to be a key element of the future property industry landscape in the UK.
- There are serious doubts as to whether (i) the volume house building model is sustainable and robust enough to deliver the homes that are needed in the UK; and (ii) owner-occupation will continue to dominate in housing markets.
- Medium- to longer-term changes in the property development and regeneration industry are likely to include a much stronger focus on innovative ownership and financing structures and on environmental issues, the latter of which is founded on an increasingly important CR agenda, as well as legislative change.

Notes

[1] This definition is clarified by the remainder of Section 55 and the inclusion of the Generally Permitted Development Order 1995 and the Use Classes Order 1987.

[2] It should be noted that the new Coalition government in the UK has abolished the 60% target for new housing on brownfield, and that PPS3 now suggests that there is no presumption that brownfield land is necessarily suitable for housing development. The requirement for local authorities to have regard to national minimum density for housing has also been removed and regional housing targets abolished. Part of the consequence of this is the removal of 'private residential gardens' from the definition of brownfield land. In a wider sense the government and some commentators also felt that the 60% target had restricted the development of 'non-brownfield' sites, reducing the supply of land available for housing and commercial development, with the result of higher house prices and higher commercial rents.

[3] The UK Coalition government has also introduced 21 new enterprise zones across England, which will seek to stimulate selected areas of the country through tax breaks, reduced planning restrictions and 'superfast' broadband

Further reading

All Party Urban Development Group (2009) *Regeneration and the recession*, London: All Party Urban Development Group.

Colantonio, A. and Dixon, T. (2010) *Urban regeneration and social sustainability*, Oxford: Wiley-Blackwell.

GLA Economics (2008) *Credit crunch and the property market*, London: GLA Economics.

References

Adams, D. (2008) 'Mapping out the regulatory environment and its interaction with land and property markets', *Energy Policy*, vol 36, no 12, December, pp 4570-4.

Adams, D., Payne, S. and Watkins, C. (2008) 'Corporate social responsibility and the UK housebuilding industry', in M. Murray, and A. Dainty (eds) *Corporate social responsibility in the construction industry*, London: Taylor & Francis.

All Party Urban Development Group (2009) *Regeneration and the recession*, London: All Party Urban Development Group.

Austin, P., Rydin, Y. and Maslin, M. (2008) *Climate change: The risks for property in the UK*, London: University College London Environment Institute.

Ball, M. (1998) 'Institutions in British property research: a review', *Urban Studies*, vol 35, no 9, pp 1501-17.

Ball, M., Lizieri, C. and MacGregor, B. (1998) *The economics of commercial property markets*, London: Routledge.

Bank of England (2009) *Financial stability report*, London: Bank of England.

Barker, K. (2003) *Review of housing supply: Securing our future needs, Interim report – Analysis*, London: HM Treasury.

Barker, K. (2004) *Review of housing supply: Delivering stability: Securing our future housing needs*, London: HM Treasury.

BiTC (Business in the Community) (2009) *Retail-led regeneration: Why it matters to our communities*, London: BiTC.

Blackman, T. (1995) *Urban policy in practice*, London: Routledge.

Blowfield, M. and Murray, A. (2008) *Corporate responsibility: A critical introduction*, Oxford: Oxford University Press.

Calcutt, J. (2007) *The Calcutt Review of housebuilding delivery*, London: Department for Communities and Local Government.

Clark, G. (2007) *Sustainable development finance for city regions*, Greg Clark City Development Finance (www.citiesandregions.com).

CLG (Department for Communities and Local Government) (2004) *Planning Policy Statement 23: Planning and pollution control*, London: CLG.

CLG (2005) *Planning Policy Statement 1: Delivering sustainable development*, London: CLG.

CLG (2006a) *Code for sustainable homes*, London: CLG.

CLG (2006b) *Transferable lessons from the New Towns*, London: CLG.

CLG (2007) *Financing investment in sustainable cities and communities in Europe: The role of the European Investment Bank*, London: CLG.

CLG (2008a) *Transforming places, changing lives: A framework for regeneration*, London: CLG.

CLG (2008b) *Community land trust: Making it happen*, London: CLG.

CLG (2009) *Transforming places, changing lives: Taking forward the regeneration framework*, London: CLG.

CLG (2010) *Land use change statistics (England) 2008: Provisional estimates*, Planning Statistical Release, London: CLG.

Colantonio, A. and Dixon, T. (2010) *Urban regeneration and social sustainability*, Oxford: Wiley-Blackwell.

Daly, J. (2008) *Overcoming barriers to institutional investment in residential property*, GLA Economics Working Paper 29, London: GLA Economics.

Deloitte (2009) *The northern way: Private Investment Commission: Preparing the ground: Private investment in the regions, in the recovery period and beyond*, London: Deloitte.

Dixon, T. (2005) 'The role of retailing in urban regeneration', *Local Economy*, vol 20, no 2, May, pp 168-82.

Dixon, T. (2007) 'The property development industry and sustainable urban brownfield regeneration in England: an analysis of case studies in Thames Gateway and Greater Manchester', *Urban Studies*, vol 44, no 12, pp 2379-400.

Dixon, T. (2009) 'Urban land and property ownership patterns in the UK: trends and forces for change', *Land Policy*, vol 26, Supplement 1, December, pp S43-S53.

Dixon, T. and Adams, D. (2008) 'Housing supply and brownfield regeneration in a post–Barker world: is there enough brownfield land in England and Scotland?', Urban Studies, vol 45, no 1, pp 115-39.

Dixon, T., Raco, M. Catney, P. and Lerner, D.N. (eds) (2007a) *Sustainable brownfield regeneration: Liveable places from problem spaces*, Oxford: Blackwell.

Dixon, T., Colantonio, A. and Shiers, D. (2007b) *Socially responsible investment (SRI), responsible property investment (RPI) and urban regeneration in the UK and Europe: Partnership models and social impact assessment*, Measuring Social Sustainability: Best Practice from Urban Renewal in the EU 2007/02, EIBURS Working Paper Series, September, Oxford: Oxford Brookes University.

DoE (Department of the Environment) (1977) *Policy for the inner cities*, Cmnd 6845, White Paper, London: DoE.

Dolphin, T. (2009) *The impact of the recession on northern city-regions*, Newcastle: IPPR North.

Elkington, J. (1997) *Cannibals with forks: The triple bottom line of 21st century business*, Oxford: Capstone.

Frankental, P. (2001) 'Corporate social responsibility – a PR invention?', *Corporate Communications: An International Journal*, vol 6, no 1, pp 18-23.

Gershon, P. (2004) *Releasing resources to the front line: Independent review of public sector efficiency*, London: HM Treasury.

GLA Economics (2008) *Credit crunch and the property market*, London: GLA Economics.

Gore, T. and Nicholson, D. (1991) 'Models of the land-development process: a critical review', *Environment and Planning A*, vol 23, no 5, pp 705-30.

Guy, C. (1994) *The retail development process: Location, property and planning*, London: Routledge.

Guy, S. and Henneberry, J. (eds) (2002) *Development and developers: Perspectives on property*, London: Blackwell Publishing.

Hackett, P. (ed) (2009) *Regeneration in a downturn: What needs to change?*, London: Smith Institute.

Hagerman, L.A., Clark, G.L. and Hebb, T. (2007) 'Investment intermediaries in economic development: linking public pension funds to urban revitalisation', *Community Development Investment Review*, vol 3, no 1, pp 45-65.

Harris, R. (2005) *Property and the office economy*, London: *Estates Gazette*.

Harvard, T. (2008) *Contemporary property development* (2nd edn), London: RIBA.

Harvey, D. (1985) *The urbanisation of capital*, Oxford: Blackwell.

Healey, P. (1991) 'Models of the development process: a review', *Journal of Property Research*, vol 8, pp 219-38.

Hinnells, M., Bright, S., Langley, A., Woodford, L., Schiellerup, P. and Bosteels, T. (2008) 'The greening of commercial leases', *Journal of Property Finance and Investment*, vol 26, no 6, pp 541-51.

HM Government (2005) *Securing the future: Delivering UK sustainable development strategy*, London: Department for Environment, Food and Rural Affairs.

IPD (Investment Property Databank) (2009) *Urban Regeneration Index*, London: IPD.

IPF (Investment Property Forum) (2006) *Institutional investment in regeneration: Necessary conditions for effective funding*, London: IPF.

IPF (2007) *Understanding commercial property investment*, London: IPF.

IPF (2009) *Urban regeneration: Opportunities for property investment*, London: IPF.

Jones, J. (2008) *Land value for public benefit*, London: Labour Land Campaign.

Keogh, G. (1994) 'Use and investment in British real estate', *Journal of Property Valuation and Finance*, vol 12, no 4, pp 58-72.

King Sturge (2009a) *Short term JESSICA consultancy study: Final report*, Bristol: King Sturge.

King Sturge (2009b) *JESSICA preliminary study for Wales: Final report*, Bristol: King Sturge.

Kivell, P. (1993) *Land and the city: Patterns and processes of urban change*, London: Routledge.

Lyons, M. (2004) *Towards better management of public sector assets: Report to the Chancellor of the Exchequer*, London: HM Treasury.

Massey, D. and Catalano, A. (1978) *Capital and land: Landownership by capital in Great Britain*, London: Arnold.

Muellbauer, J. (2005) 'Property taxation and the economy after the Barker Review', *The Economic Journal*, vol 115, March, pp 99-117.

OFT (Office of Fair Trading) (2008) *Homebuilding in the UK: A market study*, London: OFT.

Osmani, M. and O'Reilly, A. (2009) 'Feasibility of zero carbon homes in England by 2016: a house builder's perspective', *Building and Environment*, vol 44, no 9, pp 1917-24.

Parkinson, M. (2009a) *The credit crunch and regeneration: Impact and implications*, London: Department for Communities and Local Government.

Parkinson, M. (2009b) 'The credit crunch and regeneration', in P. Hackett (ed) *Regeneration in a downturn: What needs to change?*, London: Smith Institute.

Pivo, G. (2005) 'Is there a future for socially responsible property investments?', *Real Estate Issues*, Fall, pp 16-25.

Pivo, G. and McNamara, P. (2005) 'Responsible property investing', *International Real Estate Review*, vol 8, no 1, pp 128-43.

Porter, M. (1995) 'The competitive advantage of the inner city', *Harvard Business Review*, May-June, pp 55-71.

POST (Parliamentary Office of Science and Technology) (1998) *A brown and pleasant land*, London: POST.

Pretty, D. and Hackett, P. (2009) *Mind the gap: Housing supply in a cold climate*, London: Smith Institute.

Rapson, D., Shiers, D. and Roberts, C. (2007) 'Socially responsible property investment (SRPI): an analysis of the relationship between equities SRI and UK property investment activities', *Journal of Property Investment and Finance*, vol 25, no 4, pp 342-58.

RICS (Royal Institute of Chartered Surveyors) (2007) *A green profession? RICS members and the sustainability agenda*, London: RICS.

Roberts, C., Rapson, D. and Shiers, D. (2007) 'Social responsibility: key terms and their uses in property investment', *Journal of Property Investment and Finance*, vol 25, no 4, pp 388-400.

Roberts, P. (2000) 'The evolution, definition and purpose of urban regeneration', in P. Roberts and H. Sykes (eds) *Urban regeneration*, London: Sage Publications, pp 9-36.

Scott, P. (1996) *The property masters: A history of the British commercial property sector*, London: E. & F.N. Spon.

Scott, P. and Judge, G. (2000) 'Cycles and steps in British commercial property values', *Applied Economics*, vol 32, no 10, pp 1287-97.

Sorrell, S., and Hothi, K. (2007) 'Approaching regeneration in partnership: models for private and public sector collaboration', *Journal of Urban Regeneration and Renewal*, vol 1, no 1, June-August, pp 37-43.

ULI (Urban Land Institute) (2009) *Closing the investment gap in Europe's cities*, London: ULI.

UNEP FI (United Nations Environment Programme Finance Initiative) (2007) *Responsible property investment: Property workstream* (www.unepfi.org/ work_streams/property/responsible_property_investment/index.html).

Wellings, F. (2001) *Private housebuilding annual 2001*, London: Credit Lyonnais Securities Europe.

Wilkinson, S. and Reed, R. (2008) *Property development* (5th edn), London: Routledge.

World Economic Forum (2005) *Mainstreaming responsible investment*, Geneva: World Economic Forum.

WWF (2007) *Building a sustainable future*, London: WWF.

six

Emerging strategies of urban reproduction and the pursuit of low carbon cities

Harriet Bulkeley, Mike Hodson and Simon Marvin

Introduction

Over the past decade, national governments, municipal authorities and a range of non-state actors in the UK and across the world have sought to position cities as critical sites for responding to the challenges of reducing greenhouse gas (GHG) emissions and adapting to climate change. In so doing, the sustainable development agenda that dominated urban environmental agendas across the UK in the 1990s (Whitehead, 2003) began to be overwritten by an alternative vision of the sustainable city – one in which addressing climate change reigned supreme. In the process, not only have climate politics been significantly rearticulated across the global–local divide, but so too have strategies for the reproduction and regeneration of the UK's urban communities.

In this chapter we critically explore the interconnection between the emerging climate change agenda and cities (see also Chapter Four, this volume). In particular we are interested in what roles and strategies it is assumed cities will play and adopt in the pursuit of low carbon transitions by urban authorities as well as those envisioned by the national state. The critical question which we seek to address is: are cities assumed to be sites where multiple partners can utilise knowledge, capability and networks to 'accelerate' national low carbon policy priorities? Alternatively, are cities conceived as sites that can prevent or even slow the implementation of national carbon reduction targets?

First, we focus on the emergence of a new 'low carbon' urban politics in the UK, examining the strategies and tactics deployed by national governments, local authorities and other actors to place climate change in the city. Here we chart the way in which a space has emerged that has made possible a high degree of innovation and experimentation in the way that urban responses are conceived and implemented that are then selectively taken up in national strategic responses. In the second part of the chapter we focus on the articulation of this politics in one key national strategy – the 2009 UK Low Carbon Transition Plan (LCTP) (DECC, 2009). The LCTP explicitly charts how the UK will meet its target of reducing GHG emissions by 34 per cent below 1990 levels by 2020. In the third part of the chapter we subject this plan to critical scrutiny by teasing out the divergent and contradictory roles – explicitly and implicitly – envisaged for cities through a typology of four emerging styles of urban strategy. Our particular interest is in how the national state selectively picks up and then reworks the divergent urban responses and experiments into a more nationally oriented top-down strategy of defined roles for cities. Finally, in the concluding section we reflect on these strategic roles envisioned for cities and speculate about how the strategic and spatially selective take-up of urban responses and their subsequent reworking by the national state shapes our understanding of future urban sustainability. These multiple strategies demonstrate the ambivalence of urban climate politics, articulated through the tensions between seeking to manage carbon 'from the top down' and opening up space for experimentation and alternatives on the one hand, and the ambitions for universal 'transitions' and the specificities of place on the other.

A new urban politics: the rise and rise of climate change

In this section we examine how both cities and national states have become active in sustainable development and the way that these responses have subsequently shaped the style of urban and national responses to climate change issues. We are interested in the different ways in which the urban agenda is conceived in these responses – especially the complexity of the resonances and dissonances between 'top-down' state responses and 'bottom-up' urban responses (see Chapter Two, this volume). Here we particularly focus on the way in which the national state picks up, selectively transforms and passes back down through national policy documents, strategies and revised roles for cities.

Urban restructuring and the emergence of sustainability

Most accounts of urban governance and regeneration in the UK since the mid-1970s predominantly point to the fundamental role played by neoliberal doctrines and the promotion of competition in general and between places in particular. Global flows of goods, services and people were lubricated by the changing roles of national states and international institutions where the predominant ethos was no longer one of territorial equalisation but instead a process of promoting growth by making places more amenable to mobile capital investment. At the same time, the 'rescaling of statehood' (Brenner,

2004) led to the devolution of responsibilities for economic development and social welfare to local authorities and a growing number of quasi-public and private organisations, meaning that cities have had to become more entrepreneurial in attracting (and retaining) mobile capital (Jessop, 2002). These processes in turn required and sought to produce innovation in infrastructure, resource flows and services and created pressures for amenable 'light touch' regulatory frameworks through which environmental issues might be managed.

Despite the narrow drive for economic competitiveness emerging at the urban level through these processes of economic restructuring, the reconfiguration of state-based authority and the privatisation of urban infrastructures, a distinct urban environmental politics, primarily predicated on issues of sustainable development, also began to emerge during this period (Whitehead, 2003; Bulkeley, 2005). While et al (2010, p 77) suggest that this is symptomatic of a broader process of 'eco-state restructuring' defined as 'the ongoing reorganisation of state powers, capacities, regulation and territorial structures around institutional pathways and strategic projects which are (at least from the vantage of state interests at a given moment in time) viewed as less environmentally damaging than previous trajectories'. The importance of eco-state restructuring for urban development during the 1990s is evident in, among other examples, reforms to the planning system that sought to integrate sustainability (Owens, 1994; Davoudi, 2000; Owens and Cowell, 2002).

Yet the rise to prominence of sustainable development has also taken place beyond the strategic intervention of the nation-state, driven by the actions of municipal authorities, community groups, Non-governmental organisations (NGOs) and the European Union (EU). For example, the emergence and development of Local Agenda 21 took place largely through partnerships between local authorities and the EU, while numerous community groups sought to organise protests against the development of infrastructure projects in the name of sustainability. These responses have both sought to support neoliberal political and economic projects and also to offer alternative approaches to development (Bulkeley, 2005). Consequently, rather than conceiving of urban environmental governance as emanating solely from the nation-state, the multiple actors, institutions and processes involved suggest that it should be viewed as a multi-level phenomenon, within which the nature of both the urban and sustainability are contested, and the outcomes ambivalent.

Towards a low carbon urban politics

As part of the emergence of an urban environmental politics during the 1990s, selected cities and non- or quasi-state actors (environmental groups, charities, public–private partnerships etc) in the UK began to turn their attention to the issue of climate change. With the first report of the Intergovernmental Panel on Climate Change in 1990 and the subsequent agreement of the United Nations Framework Convention on Climate Change in 1992, the issue rapidly rose to prominence on political and public agendas. In 1994, a group of 16 local authorities in the UK, including the urban authorities of Newcastle and Leicester, formally constituted the nascent 'Energie-Cités' network as an association of European municipalities whose membership now includes over a hundred participants (Kern and Bulkeley, 2009). Following a campaign by Friends of the Earth to persuade local authorities to pledge to address climate change by signing a Climate Resolution, the International Council for Local Environmental Initiatives (ICLEI) Cities for Climate Protection programme (CCP) recruited 11 UK local authorities[1] and, after a protracted process of negotiation with national government, a pilot UK-based CCP programme was launched with 24 members[2] (Bulkeley and Betsill, 2003). Initially climate change was dominated by a few pioneering cities and political champions, organised through two transnational municipal networks within which (European) cooperation was emphasised, and characterised by a marked disinterest from central government (Bulkeley and Betsill, 2003, 2005; Bulkeley and Kern, 2006; Kern and Bulkeley, 2009).

At the local authority level, climate change has now become a mainstream issue in the UK. The creation of the Nottingham Declaration in 2000, a voluntary agreement by local authorities to develop climate change mitigation and adaptation plans, represented something of a turning point (EST, 2010). Launched at a conference in Nottingham by the local authority, the Declaration provided a means for galvanising responses beyond the early pioneers. While signatories to the declaration were initially slow to come forward, with just one or two councils committing to action every month in the period 2000-05 (Gearty, 2007), by 2005 the Declaration was re-launched with government support and the backing of several national agencies (including the Energy Savings Trust and The Carbon Trust), and in 2010 the majority of English local authorities had committed to action. Following these developments in England, in 2006 all Welsh local authorities signed the Welsh Commitment to Address Climate Change and in 2007 all Scottish local authorities signed the spin-off Scottish Climate Change Declaration.[3]

At the same time particular cities have emerged as critical sites for the development of emblematic and exemplary low carbon urban responses to the challenges of climate change, especially London and Manchester. For example, in 2007 the former mayor of London committed the Greater London Authority (GLA) to carbon reduction targets in excess of those adopted by central government after having established the London

Climate Change Agency (LCCA) in 2005, in an attempt to develop a systemic response to climate change. Although the new mayor of London subsequently abolished the LCCA, the GLA continues to play a central role in the C40 network of large world cities developing exemplary and replicable solutions. The C40 was formed in 2005 and is a group of the 'World's largest cities committed to tackling climate change (because) cities and urban areas consume 75 per cent of the world's energy and produce up to 75 per cent of its greenhouse gas emissions' (see www.c40cities.org/). Manchester undertook its own 'mini-Stern' analysis of the economic dimensions of the climate change agenda at city-regional level and followed this up with a commitment to establish a Manchester Climate Change Agency. Manchester was not, however, able to join the C40 network because it did not meet the exacting membership criteria for world cities.

National state responses and territorial implications

During the 2000s climate change became a key strategic issue on the urban agenda in the UK. Mirroring international developments that have witnessed the growth and diffusion of transnational climate networks, the increased politicisation of urban responses to climate change, and recognition on the part of national and international actors, this has mainly been driven from the 'bottom up', by local authorities and NGOs. But subsequently it has also been driven from the 'top down' as the UK government has sought to enrol the urban as a key site in the pursuit of a low carbon economy. Consequently, this new engagement with climate change at the urban scale also has to be seen as a response to the growing priority that the issue has been afforded in national government. The UK's commitment in 2003 to reducing GHG emissions by 60 per cent below 1990 levels by 2050 has been followed by a raft of strategies, initiatives and policies. These include the Climate Change Act (which upgraded the 60 per cent target to 80 per cent), Energy Act 2008, the UK LCTP (DECC, 2009) and the *Low Carbon Industrial Strategy* (LCIS) (BIS/DECC, 2009). Consequently, three features of the policy approach which has been developed to pursue these ambitions have particularly significant implications for urban governance: the development of legally binding targets and carbon budgets; the integration of climate change commitments into the planning system (Smith, 2007; Bulkeley, 2009); and the convergence of climate change and energy policies (Lovell et al, 2009).

The confluence of these national responses, initially emanating from networks of municipal authorities, individual local governments, non-state actors and, crucially, then selectively taken up and incorporated into government strategy, has served to place climate change firmly on urban agendas. As the most recent manifestation of 'eco-state restructuring', While et al (2010, pp 86–7) suggest that 'the coming era of carbon control will alter the strategic context for urban and regional management in ways that go beyond the largely voluntaristic carbon reduction strategies so far pursued by activist authorities' through, for example, the need to comply with new forms of legislation, pressure to invest in low carbon infrastructures, the need to manage low carbon budgets and the opportunities offered by new carbon markets. In the following section, we take a closer look at the UK's most recent and influential policy document, the *Low Carbon Transition Plan* (DECC, 2009) in order to then examine just what the politics of carbon control in the city might entail.

UK *Low Carbon Transition Plan* – making space for the city?

In July 2009, the UK government published its LCTP (DECC, 2009) that detailed how the UK would meet the 2020 and 2050 emissions reduction commitments set out in the Climate Change Act 2008. It is underlain by five stated principles: first, to protect the UK public from the immediate risks of climate change; second, to anticipate that regardless of our future actions there is likely to be climate change and that this needs to be prepared for, particularly in relation to infrastructure and housing; third, that climate change requires a new international agreement on global emissions reduction; fourth, that the UK can play its part by developing a low carbon country in line with the targets set out in the Climate Change Act 2008 and in doing so also address vulnerabilities and promote economic opportunities; and fifth, that addressing climate change requires widespread participation from communities, businesses, individuals and so on (DECC, 2009).

The LCTP is a wide-ranging national-level response to the challenges of climate change which explicitly states that the transition to a low carbon future is an opportunity for economic growth and job creation. In this respect it was published at the same time as the UK LCIS that details a set of critical government interventions in relation to strategic low carbon priorities (BIS/DECC, 2009). The LCTP is not only a transition route map to 2020 for the UK but also operates to prioritise the carbon savings expected across different sectors. The headline effect of this is that it is claimed that by 2020: more than 1.2 million people will be in green jobs; 7 million homes will have benefited from whole house makeovers, and more than 1.5 million households will be supported to produce their own clean energy; around 40 per cent of electricity will be from low carbon sources, from renewable, nuclear and clean coal; and the UK will be importing half the amount of gas that it otherwise would.

The LCTP is a critical document to look at in terms of the role of the city in climate politics as the plan effectively captures and seeks to reproduce the different strands of urban climate responses and in so doing captures the tensions and dynamics of future urban low carbon transitions. It provides a key window through which we can see how the role of cities is being conceived, enacted and contested. This allows us to better understand the relationships between these scales and how and why they are coordinated, in tension or disconnected. The power issues this raises require an examination of the relationships between national priorities and plans and how these interpret and frame urban responses and also the extent to which cities' strategies and national plans and priorities can be better integrated.

Conceptualising cities in low carbon transition plan: a typology

In this section we develop a framework for understanding the roles of cities as conceived in the UK's LCTP. We develop an understanding of the explicit – and where these are absent, the implicit – roles envisaged for cities in the plan. Are cities seen as 'sites' for the implementation of the plan? Or are strategy and action 'co-produced' by the national state and cities? Alternatively, are cities able to 'accelerate' the implementation of the strategy by managing systemic socio-technical change? A typology of the different urban roles envisaged in the LCTP is outlined in Figure 6.1. The typology is a conceptual framework through which we can explore the LCTP's perspective on the role of cities in the implementation of a national low carbon transition. The typology is constructed according to two axes that are designed to provide a way of conceptualising different views of the city.

The vertical axis is primarily concerned with how the national state views cities according to two perspectives. At the top of the axis are national views of an envisioned role for cities in the implementation of national priorities, either in the form of targets and/or technologies. Here the city is conceived as a site that has to comply with national priorities that are set by the national state or its agencies in order to facilitate low carbon transitions. At the bottom there is a national perspective that views cities as sites of response to national policy frameworks. This envisages that cities are potential sites for experiments and innovations in response to incentives offered on a competitive basis by national policy frameworks. In this sense cities can decide to respond to national opportunities by competing for designation and/or resources to be sites for low carbon experiments.

The horizontal axis refers to the degree of territorial selectiveness in national state prioritisation of the urban according to two dimensions. On the left of the axis we refer to spatially universal or standardised responses that are meant to be undertaken in all urban contexts. This, for example, means that all cities are meant to respond to carbon regulation targets and accelerate low carbon transitions through their planning functions. In contrast the right of the axis refers to much more spatially selective responses in specific urban contexts. This means that particular cities are selected – either through strategic prioritisation or competition – as critical sites for the testing and implementation of low carbon infrastructure and economic zones. What this implies is that specific cities adopt particular roles in a low carbon transition.

Figure 6.1: Typology of urban roles in the Low Carbon Transition Plan

Central/top-down perspectives

Eco-targets for sub-nationl governance **National targets cascaded on to sub-national contexts**	Strategic eco-liberalism **Strategic sites for national infrastructure and demonstration**
Implement change in socio-technical systems and carbon budgets **Urban transitions – systemic or project?**	**Locales competing for eco-status in national competitions** **Competitive eco-urbanism?**

Universal/ standardised (left)   *Selective/ specific context* (right)

Existing cities/bottom-up responses

The typology can be used as lens through which we can start to conceptualise a four-fold characterisation of different styles of urban response (and provides an alternative and complementary classification to the urban responses of hyper-liberalism, neo-localism and municipal pragmatism developed by Mark Whitehead in Chapter Two, this volume). Below we discuss each of the styles of urban roles drawn from the LCTP in turn. For each response we set out: a characterisation of the response; outline how it is supposed to work and function; offer emblematic exemplars from the LCTP; assess what it says about the relationships between the national and urban; and identify any key implications.

National eco-targets for urban governance

National eco-targets for urban governance refers to a centralised and standardised approach – where a national framework sets out carbon and energy management targets for urban contexts to support the implementation of national priorities. These are expressed as targets in relation to low carbon transitions as part of national state roles in international carbon reduction agreements. National targets are then cascaded onto cities as a new set of indicators and targets with statutory force that are then layered on to established priorities. Here there is further variability with urban and regionally produced responses in the devolved administrations of Scotland,

Wales and Northern Ireland that may exceed in level and time national UK targets. Consequently, cities in the devolved administrations potentially may have to meet carbon reduction targets based on more challenging assumptions and priorities than those developed for cities in an English context.

The key feature of this style is the allocation of carbon budgets and renewables targets by the national state to all cities as a means of drawing urban authorities and their networks into the operation of programmes to achieve key government goals, such as the overall targets for a 34 per cent emissions cut and an increase of 30 per cent in renewable energy by 2020. For example, the LCTP states that the carbon budget is intended to 'set the pathway' (DECC, 2009, p 36), and the government sets the 'share' of responsibilities to the relevant government bodies. Looking specifically at carbon regulation, the UK Climate Change Act 2008 positioned the UK as the first country in the world to have a legally binding framework for cutting carbon emissions that means, regardless of whether and on what scale there is international action on climate change, the UK must act. This is addressed through five-year carbon budgeting systems – with the first three periods of carbon budgeting operating between 2008-12, 2013-17 and 2018-22. Part of the rationale for the long-term and binding framework is to provide a degree of certainty that creates the necessary but not sufficient conditions for the development of capacity to underpin the transition to a low carbon future. This is achieved by setting legally binding targets, creating powers to address those targets and providing the institutional framework to underpin the achievement of these targets.

The development of legal commitments to reduce GHG emissions and carbon budgets will exert new pressures for carbon regulation on urban local authorities (While, 2007; While et al, 2010). Critically, a new carbon regulation framework with specific targets and indicators will be laid over all cities requiring a more systemic response as they seek to manage carbon emissions. Cities will have to develop knowledge, expertise, capacity and capability to produce effective responses as they seek to balance a carbon regulation framework with their existing economic competitiveness and other priorities.

Strategic eco-localism

Strategic eco-localism is a style represented by a centralised framework that is more spatially selective for implementing technologies and developing emblematic solutions in specific cities to deliver national targets. This refers to those cities that are strategically important, either because they contain significant potential in energy resource terms or because they are strategically important in the development and testing of low carbon responses that may have wider national relevance through their applications and replication in other contexts.

In this case we can identify new state roles that envision cities as sites where local constraints on the development of low carbon transitions need to be overcome to lead to the more rapid development and/or roll-out of particular socio-technical solutions. A key example would be the Infrastructure Planning Commission (IPC) that is designed to accelerate progress of large renewable schemes, nuclear power and other critical national infrastructure through the local planning system. This represents an increased state role in overcoming local objections, prioritising managed change and pushing through responses in particular places through steerage and intervention (Newman, 2009). The LCTP specifically mentions the Severn tidal barrage – which could provide up to 5 per cent of the UK's energy supply – and states that the government is 'investigating these issues, and after public consultation in 2010, will decide whether to support a scheme in the Severn' (DECC, 2009, p 62).

The LCTP also refers to particular places – specifically London and the Thames Gateway – that are seen as having exemplary and emblematic roles in the development of new eco-solutions. For instance, the national government is investing £1.75 million to support the creation of a 'flagship district heating scheme for London in partnership with the London Development Agency' (DECC, 2009, p 121), and is also 'piloting new developments which meet the highest environmental standards on a large scale' in the Thames Gateway eco-region and the London Olympic Park (DECC, 2009, pp 20-1; see Chapter Eleven, this volume, for a case study of London). It is the government's 'ambition' that these responses provide a 'blueprint for sustainable living' through the testing and application of new technologies, low carbon materials and innovative solutions (DECC, 2009, p 92).

Strategic eco-localism is mainly concerned with nationally important spaces as sites for the development of strategically important low carbon infrastructure or the exemplification of low carbon responses. It envisions that the national state has a more active role – working through intermediaries in the case of the IPC or through government departments – in accelerating low carbon transitions. But crucially certain contexts are seen as sites for the implantation of critical technologies while others are seen as sites of experimentation for new technologies and styles of living that may have wider applications in other urban contexts. This certainly privileges London, the Thames Gateway and the Olympic Park as sites for the 'production' of new low carbon solutions.

Urban transitions – systemic or project?

Urban transitions refers to an implicit role where cities are being conceived as contexts for the implementation of low carbon transitions through the application of smart meters, renewables, community renewables and carbon reduction. There is a national expectation of cities utilising their formal planning powers and discretionary capacity for projects to support the implementation of a low carbon transition. While the plan assumes some sort of 'systemic' change, the policy response implied at an urban level is more about the delivery of individual projects in an urban context than the development of capacity to deliver system change at the urban level.

Consequently, this is the most problematic style to exemplify. It is quite piecemeal and envisages a mix of initiatives that have urban implications. These include: financial incentives for the development of renewables; 'streamlining the planning process, supporting innovation, speeding up grid connection and developing UK supply chains ...' (DECC, 2009, p 54; requiring new developments to be located and designed to reduce carbon emissions; as well as 'piloting a community-based approach to delivering green homes in low income areas' (DECC, 2009, p 4).

All these initiatives envision roles for cities and their partners as amenable sites for the implementation of measures associated with new development and the retrofitting of existing development or an extension of existing responsibilities for the fuel poor. But what is missing from this approach is any understanding of the forms of knowledge, capability and social learning that need to be developed at the urban level for this role to be anything other than a relatively passive acceptor of national transitions.

Eco-competitive low carbon urbanism

Eco-competitive urbanism refers to urban responses to national funding opportunities and/or designation through competitions to set up 'test beds' or 'exemplar' opportunities for cities to develop low carbon transitions. There is a long history of competitions for funding for urban regeneration, innovation and economic development funding that is consistent with this approach. When this approach is applied to the low carbon agenda the national state offers: support to cities wanting to develop low carbon technologies; funding for communities to experiment with low carbon living initiatives that may have wider relevance; and competitions for innovation and status as low carbon exemplars. This appears to be a form of competitive low carbon eco-urbanism that is layered over conventional economic competitiveness agendas and policies.

There are four examples of this approach in the LCTP. First, low carbon economic areas (LCEAs) have received particular focus and the first based on tidal and wind technologies in the South West of England was launched in the LCTP. The UK LCIS, published in parallel with the LCTP, identified further LCEAs (BIS/DECC, 2009). A total of nine LCEAs were subsequently designated including two city-based areas – Manchester city centre for a low carbon-built environment and London for urban retrofitting. Second, competitions will also take place at other levels including up to 15 communities selected to participate as 'test hubs' including multiple stakeholders to develop 'community-wide plans for their neighbourhoods and learn how different initiatives – for example in energy and water conservation, or travel – work together in practice' (DECC, 2009, pp 93-4). These are seen as experimental test beds where the government 'can use what we learn to help roll-out of a nationwide plan, potentially helping every city ... make the transition to a sustainable future' (DECC, 2009, pp 93-4). Third, the plan launched a competition for the country's first 'sustainable travel city' by providing £29 million for 'a major urban area to demonstrate how to cut car travel and increase walking, cycling and public transport use' (DECC, 2009, p 135). Although four cities were shortlisted in autumn 2009 with the expectation of two being funded, it was then confirmed in March 2010 that the Department for Transport had cancelled the scheme. Finally a competition to build up to four commercial scale carbon capture and storage demonstration projects was also announced in the plan (DECC, 2009, p 53).

Consequently, this approach envisions a competitive framework for cities and their partners to position themselves as sites for experimentation and learning about low carbon transitions. This seems to imply a more active partnership between the national state and cities in selecting and working towards more specifically defined experimental roles of particular cities in the implementation of low carbon transitions.

Conclusions

In this section we summarise the key findings, review the wider issues raised and identify future research priorities. First, we have reviewed the way in which urban contexts play a discretionary and voluntary role in developing bottom-up and often experimental responses to new ecological and economic pressures shaped by climate change. We have examined the ways in which the national state selectively takes up these urban responses and reworks them into national policy frameworks that then creates a new contextual framework that itself re-shapes the style and content of urban responses. Although these are mediated by regional contexts – not least in the context of the devolved authorities – we find that these national frameworks establish new roles for urban contexts in the conceptualisation and implementation of low carbon transition. We have developed a typology to critically explore the multiplicity of roles envisioned for cities in the LCTP. These range from standardised and universal roles in which new carbon management targets and low carbon infrastructure will be devolved on to cities to roles that are more selective and include national state prioritisation of locales and sites for the implementation of strategically important low carbon technologies as well as national competitions for local experiments and initiatives – both community and industrial policy – for experiments in low carbon transitions.

Second, it is evident that these approaches envision a series of multiple and divergent roles for urban contexts in the achievement of a national low carbon transition that raises wider questions about the roles of cities in a new system of carbon control, regulation and low carbon energy transition (Hodson and Marvin, 2009). Initially, at least, there is evidence of a new set of national targets being laid over the existing urban governance framework for carbon regulation and the production of low carbon energy sources. An emerging system of carbon regulation – through carbon reduction targets in local government estates and buildings and even per capita reduction targets – is likely to be devolved to urban local authorities who will then have to engage in the difficult trade-off between their existing economic and territorial ambitions and the needs for low carbon transition (see While, 2007; While et al, 2010). As research concerning the politics of urban climate change governance has demonstrated, such trade-offs are likely to be highly contested, leading to conflicts within and between existing groups and interests in cities (see Chapter Nine, this volume). This in turn opens up questions about where, how and with what effect resistance to such forms of carbon regulation will emerge. These issues are particularly potent politically, given that at the same time as the national state is developing new regulatory targets that sit over cities, it is also assuming that such units will be active agents and drivers of system changes as all new developments will have to be designed to reduce carbon emissions.

While new national targets for carbon regulation, low carbon energy systems and local roles in the implementation of transitions are being developed, the national state also envisions specific roles for selected urban areas in the implementation of a national low carbon transition. These range from the use of special zones – such as London, Thames Gateway – and eco-towns as exemplars of low carbon urban development (see Hodson and Marvin, 2007, 2010). Yet they also include the national state prioritising certain strategic localities for the implementation of nationally important energy infrastructure such as the Severn Barrage. The establishment of the IPC could also be read as consistent with this approach as the national state develops new regulatory and planning mechanisms to overcome local resistance to low carbon energy infrastructure (see Newman, 2009). The national state has also put in place new forms of place-based competition where regions, cities, local authorities and even communities can complete for funds – often quite limited – to demonstrate or exemplify low carbon transitions. In ways resonant of competitive urban regeneration initiatives, areas can position themselves as sites of experimentation and learning in order to accelerate low carbon transitions. The differing capacity of cities to respond, resist or capitalise on such opportunities, particularly where such initiatives are controversial, will in turn create a varied landscape of climate change response within and between cities.

In addition to these specific concerns, our analysis of the transition envisioned in the LCTP raises wider issues. National government priorities in relation to state spaces and energy in the UK in recent decades have been marked by views that have promoted competition between places and the liberalisation and privatisation of energy markets. In this view the predominant view of the role of the state has been a 'hands off' and 'light touch' one, although in practice this has often seen the state intervening to prioritise places (for example, London) and to make places (for example, old industrial areas) more 'amenable' to foreign direct investment. Pressures in the last two or three years have seen some (albeit limited) questioning of this role of the state and the development of a view that the state can intervene directly to facilitate the transformation of places that were previously told to make themselves adaptable to the whims of global capital. This is beginning to contribute to a collection of national priorities, that while in some cases are still anchored in the old shibboleths of the free market is also rediscovering a more explicitly interventionist role for government in contributing to place-based transformation. The tension is between trying to buttress the existing growth model and to explore new forms of low carbon industrial interventionism.

Finally, in thinking about future research agendas and the mediation of social interests in low carbon urban transitions we would highlight the following issues that are worthy of further research. First, in what different ways are the current confluence of economic and ecological crises and pressures being used to influence low carbon urban transitions? Are they being used to defend or challenge the status quo? Second, to what extent do these crises and pressures contribute to or constrain the possibilities for fundamentally different notions of low carbon urban transitions? Third, in different urban contexts, to what extent is the mediating of low carbon transitions a participatory process, how are these organised and with what consequences? Finally, must low carbon urban transitions emanate from a national or city-regional level? What are the possibilities for grassroots and community initiatives to inform such transitions?

Key conclusions

- Urban responses to climate change developed largely as voluntaristic and bottom-up responses to new pressures and challenges.
- The national state has selectively taken up these responses, re-incorporated them and then cascaded these back onto cities through national priorities and strategies.
- Urban responses and roles are, consequently, complex and variegated and based on the construction of standardised and discretionary roles of cities as sites of production and reception.

Notes

[1] The local authorities involved were: Birmingham City Council, Burnley Borough Council, Cambridgeshire County Council, Eastleigh Borough Council, Exeter City Council, Leicester City Council, Manchester City Council, Newcastle City Council, Sheffield City Council, Swale Borough Council, Swansea City Council.

[2] The local authorities involved with this pilot programme were: Bristol City Council, Bury Metropolitan Borough, Chesterfield Borough Council, Daventry District Council, Hampshire Country Council, Kirklees Metropolitan Borough, Lancashire County Council, Leicester City Council, London Borough of Barnet, London Borough of Camden, London Borough of Hillingdon, London Borough of Southwark, London Borough of Tower Hamlets, Nottingham City Council, Norwich City Council, Nottinghamshire County Council/Newark and Sherwood District (joint bid), Oldham Metropolitan Borough, Oxford City Council, Sandwell Metropolitan Borough, Shropshire County Council, Slough District Council, Suffolk County Council.

[3] See www.wlga.gov.uk/english/climate-change/ and http://climatechange. sustainable-scotland.net/

Further reading

Bulkeley, H. (2010) 'Cities and the governing of climate change', *Annual Review of Environment and Resources*, vol 35, pp 229-53.

Bulkeley, H., Castan Broto, V., Hodson, M. and Marvin, S. (eds) (2010) *Cities and low carbon transitions*, London: Routledge.

Hodson, M. and Marvin, S. (2010) *World cities and climate change*, Maidenhead: Open University Press.

References

BIS (Department for Business Innovation and Skills)/DECC (Department of Energy and Climate Change) (2009) *Low Carbon Industrial Strategy: A vision*, London: HM Government.

Brenner, N. (2004) *New state spaces: Urban governance and the rescaling of statehood*, New York: Oxford University Press.

Bulkeley, H. (2005) 'Reconfiguring environmental governance: towards a politics of scales and networks', *Political Geography*, vol 24, no 4, pp 875-902.

Bulkeley, H. (2009) 'Planning and governance of climate change', in S. Davoudi, J. Crawford and A. Mehmood, A. (eds) *Planning for climate change: Strategies for mitigation and adaptation for spatial planners*, London: Earthscan, pp 284-96.

Bulkeley, H. and Betsill, M.M. (2003) *Cities and climate change: Urban sustainability and global environmental governance*, New York: Routledge.

Bulkeley, H. and Betsill, M.M. (2005) 'Rethinking sustainable cities: multilevel governance and the "urban" politics of climate change', *Environmental Politics*, vol 14, no 1, pp 42-63.

Bulkeley, H. and Kern, K. (2006) 'Local government and climate change governance in the UK and Germany', *Urban Studies*, vol 43, no 12, pp 2237-59.

Davoudi, S. (2000) 'Planning for waste management: changing discourses and institutional relationships', *Progress in Planning*, vol 53, no 3, pp 165-216.

DECC (Department of Energy and Climate Change) (2009) *The UK Low Carbon Transition Plan*, London: HM Government.

EST (Energy Saving Trust) (2010) *The Nottingham Declaration: About the declaration* (www.energysavingtrust.org.uk/nottingham/Nottingham-Declaration/The-Declaration/About-the-Declaration).

Gearty, M. (2007) *The Nottingham Declaration: Symbols, strategy and confidence, A Learning History*, Issue VWS – Report from Workshop No 2 'Innovation for carbon reduction in or connected with local authorities, May, University of Bath (www.bath.ac.uk/carpp/publications/doc_theses_links/pdf/dt_mg_APPDXGNott_case_issue_vws_A5.pdf).

Hodson, M. and Marvin, S. (2007) 'Transforming London/testing London: understanding the role of the national exemplar in constructing "strategic glurbanisation"', *International Journal of Urban and Regional Research*, vol 31, no 2, pp 303-25.

Hodson, M. and Marvin, S. (2009) 'Urban ecological security: a new urban paradigm?', *International Journal of Urban and Regional Research*, vol 33, no 1, pp 193-215.

Hodson, M. and Marvin, S. (2010) 'Urbanism in the anthroprocene: ecological urbanism or premium ecological enclaves?', *City*, vol 14, no 3, pp 298-313.

HM Treasury, (2009) *Budget 2009*. London: HM Treasury.

IPCC (Intergovernmental Panel on Climate Change) (1990) *IPCC first assessment report (FAR)*, Cambridge: Cambridge University Press.

Jessop, B. (2002) *The future of the capitalist state*, London: Polity.

Kern, K. and Bulkeley, H. (2009) 'Cities, Europeanization and multi-level governance: governing climate change through transnational municipal networks', *Journal of Common Market Studies*, vol 47, no 2, pp 309-32.

Lovell, H., Bulkeley, H. and Owens, S. (2009) 'Converging agendas? Energy and climate change policies in the UK', *Environment and Planning C*, vol 27, no 1, pp 90-109.

Newman, P. (2009) 'Markets, experts and depoliticizing decisions on major infrastructure', *Urban Research and Practice*, vol 2, no 2, pp 158-68 (www. informaworld.com/smpp/title~db=all~content=t777186834~tab=issues list~branches=2 - v2).

Owens, S. (1994) 'Land, limits and sustainability: a conceptual framework and some dilemmas for the planning system', *Transactions of the Institute of British Geographers*, vol 19, no 4, pp 439-56.

Owens, S. and Cowell, R. (2002) *Land and limits: Interpreting sustainability in the planning process*, London: Routledge.

Smith, A. (2007) 'Emerging in between: the multi-level governance of renewable energy in the English regions', *Energy Policy*, vol 35, no 12, pp 6266-80.

While, A. (2007) 'Climate change and planning: carbon control and spatial regulation', *Town Planning Review*, vol 79, no 1, pp vii-xiii.

While, A., Jonas, A. and Gibbs, A. (2010) 'From sustainable development to carbon control: eco-state restructuring and the politics of urban and regional development', *Transactions of the Institute of British Geographers*, vol 35, no 1, pp 76-93.

Whitehead, M. (2003) '(Re)Analysing the sustainable city: nature, urbanisation and the regulation of socio-environmental relations in the UK', *Urban Studies*, vol 40, no 7, pp 1183-206.

seven

Transport in a sustainable urban future

Iain Docherty and Jon Shaw

Introduction

Transport is acknowledged as a vital ingredient of any credible strategy for the sustainable city because of the key role it plays in promoting economic development, quality of life and well-being. Yet managing urban transport effectively, given its complex and intersecting economic, environmental and social impacts, is also precisely the kind of 'wicked problem' that policy makers consistently find hard to resolve (Rittel and Webber, 1973; Conklin, 2006; Docherty and Shaw, 2011a; see also Chapter Nine, this volume). Many of the reasons for this are long-standing and emanate in particular from the dominance of the private car in meeting the demand for mobility, which has built up over many decades in the developed world, but which is now being reproduced at a much higher pace in the fast growing cities of the Pacific Rim and elsewhere (Newman and Kenworthy, 1999; Lyons and Loo, 2008). Although it has undoubtedly transformed our patterns of travel and consumption, concerns over the limitations and externalities of private car transport – primarily traffic congestion, environmental degradation and social exclusion – have for many years stimulated various initiatives designed to mitigate these externalities (Feitelson and Verhoef, 2001; Knowles et al, 2008). The conflict between the car, long promoted by neoliberal voices as a potent weapon of the free market and individual liberty, and competing visions of a more 'public' transport system based on collective modes such as the bus and train, and active travel by walking and cycling, has been played out over many years. Nowhere has this conflict been more intense than in cities, as it is here that the problems such as congestion, poor local air quality and mobility deprivation are often at their most intense (Docherty et al, 2008; Cahill, 2010).

Since the aftermath of the previous major global economic crisis in the 1970s, the macro-regulation of transport has been shaped by the rise of neoliberalism and policy themes derived from it, such as the notion of city competitiveness in the 1990s and 2000s (Jessop, 2002; Keeling, 2009), and the impact of three decades of neoliberal-inspired governance continues to shape contemporary debates on what a sustainable future might look like (Jessop, 2002; Docherty et al, 2004; Grengs, 2005; Siemiatycki, 2005; Keeling, 2009). In the late 1970s/1980s, transport was something of a pioneer in implementing the radical new neoliberal political economy. Transport networks and services were successively deregulated and privatised in order to open them up to the rigours of competition and reduce the state's requirement to intervene, both in policy and financial terms. But since the nascent 'environmental turn' of the early 1990s, governance networks have re-engaged more actively with the transport sector, attempting to ameliorate the various problems of car-dominated mobility patterns. After the millennium, intervention has increased further as cities and regions around the world became convinced of the need to improve – drastically in many cases – their transport systems in the pursuit of economic competitiveness in a globalising economy in which cities compete intensely for resources of all kinds. Despite the lack of any properly conclusive evidence base demonstrating the links between transport investment and economic growth (see Banister and Berechman, 2001), the boom years of the 2000s generated huge investment programmes in urban transport, especially in areas such as new light rail and metro networks. These investments not only (at least rhetorically) tackled the resilient issues of environmental and social disbenefits of the car, but were also stylish additions to the urban realm, and were immediately attractive to policy makers across several disciplines from civil engineering to planning and urban design. They were a tangible, visceral example of the new modernity, bringing together sustainable development, international brand image and city marketing in a sleek high technology form (Lawless and Gore, 1999; Kaufmann et al, 2008; Docherty et al, 2009).

In this chapter we start with a consideration of how the debates over the role of the car and related policy perspectives have shaped the development of city transport systems over the last 20 to 30 years. We then explore what the uncertain conditions of the post-financial crisis economy might mean for urban transport and its contribution to the sustainable city of the future. In exploring these themes, we highlight how concerns over the impacts of mass car-based mobility evolved into a wider examination of transport's position at the heart of various sustainability debates throughout the 2000s, and how public transport in particular became a laboratory for broader experiments in marketisation, private sector financing and service delivery that have been subsequently applied across many areas of urban economic and social life (see Chapters Two and Six, this volume, for further examples of cities as sites of policy innovation). It is undoubtedly the case that the financial crisis and subsequent recession have revealed significant weaknesses in many of the assumptions about how transport infrastructure and services would be developed in future, especially in heavily marketised economies such as the UK. Indeed, the process of marketisation, and the restructuring of urban governance that has accompanied the broader response of the state to the challenges of globalisation, add further barriers to action for policy makers seeking to effect change in pursuit of contemporary objectives such as carbon reduction and distributive justice (Marsden and May, 2006; Shaw et al, 2008).

As if this were not enough, the financial crisis and the stern austerity measures being introduced to deal with its aftermath could bring the era of high spending on urban transport – which was a key part of many cities' competitiveness strategies in the 2000s – to a juddering halt. Transport is often one of the first areas of government spending to be axed in times of financial retrenchment, since it is associated with significant capital expenditure, and is rarely as politically toxic as cutting back on investment in health and education. Given that transport infrastructure provision has been increasingly underpinned by private finance that may no longer be readily available, the potential for network development and standards of service provision – already exposed to the harsh economic logic of deregulated operating environments – to decline further becomes very clear indeed. But the prospect of a sustained spending squeeze lasting a decade or more is something altogether new for the sector in modern times, and will likely necessitate very significant realignment of policy objectives for transport. The investment patterns of the last decade have been embedded in a rhetoric focused on growth and competitiveness rather than consolidation, retrenchment and genuine sustainability, and substantial reductions in state expenditure on both capital and revenue support will mean that policies will increasingly have to focus on getting the most from existing infrastructure and services. Rather than development plans being fixated by 'the new', the thorny problem of managing demand will once again come to the fore.

Transport and the reproduction of cities

It is difficult to understate the extent to which transport has determined the shape of today's cities. The underlying morphology on which urban societies, cultures and economies combine to form the cities we inhabit is created by the transport technologies available to each generation that reshapes and reproduces the urban system. From the classical Italian hill town built to celebrate the pedestrian and the meeting place, through the great metropolises of London, Paris, New York and Tokyo that grew along their expanding underground railway networks, to motor cities from Los Angeles to 21st-century Shanghai, each urban place owes much of its character and identity to its transport system. The classic definitions of the city focus on the spatial concentration of economic, social and cultural processes in a node of production, exchange and interaction, the unique local combination of these generating the dense and diverse places we know as cities.

Urban transport, and the policies and governance structures and processes that reproduce it, can be usefully analysed through these two interrelated perspectives of space – the territory across which economic systems extend – and the places formed by complex social and cultural interaction (Hanson, 2004; see also Chapters Three and Four, this volume). This is because each of these perspectives has traditionally implied a different set of objectives and priorities for the development and management of the urban transport system. Those perspectives prioritising economic development focus on the need to supply as much physical mobility as possible in the urban system so that industrial production and key enabling systems such as the labour market can function as efficiently as possible (Glaeser, 2004; Laird et al, 2005). More recently, as many cities have revitalised themselves as centres of the service and consumption economy, these concerns have been translated into policy priorities including the maximisation of urban road and rail network capacity. The aims have been to extend and deepen the diversity and 'thickness' of the labour market, and tackle traffic congestion through infrastructure improvements or – more exceptionally – the introduction of congestion charging to minimise delays and their cost to the economy (see below). The latest incarnation of this approach delves more deeply still into the complex network effects of transport systems by pursuing the additional 'agglomeration economies' claimed to result in the cities with the very densest infrastructure patterns (Graham, 2007; see also Preston, 2008).

The alternative normative view of the role of urban transport systems, to facilitate the city's role as a place of social and cultural creativity, has an equally long heritage. Perhaps the most celebrated work in this regard – although not itself a 'transport' analysis – is Jane Jacobs' (1961) seminal *The death and life of great American cities*, in which the rapid rise to dominance of the car in cities formed and shaped according to earlier transport technologies was identified as a key underlying determinant of their decline in vitality. Half a century on, urban places, from old neighbourhoods to the largest city centres, have been exposed to successive waves of car-oriented development such as out-of-town business parks and shopping centres that have undermined their viability. These experiences have generated a substantial literature, making the connections between the quality of the urban realm, the importance of pedestrian activity in sustaining neighbourhood economies and social networks and how public transport facilitates this (Hass-Klau, 1993; Logan and Molotch, 2007).

The regeneration of major cities has also stimulated renewed interest in the interaction of transport systems and larger urban agglomerations over the last 20 years. Cities have rediscovered the importance of their central cores and other key public places in attracting service sector investment and the kind of 'creative class' (Florida, 2005) that works in high-value sectors, and in contributing to wider ideas of quality of life and well-being.

Figure 7.1 Urban space and the vibrant city

Figure 7.2 Transport and the vibrant city

The potential for better transport to act as a catalyst for this – especially by reducing the impact of traffic and rehabilitating places of aesthetic, historical and/or cultural merit – has never been higher (Gärling and Steg, 2007). Across the world, cities have switched transport investment away from the car towards other modes, particularly urban rail, and there are now many celebrated examples where transport investment has been targeted at re-engineering the city to make it a more vibrant, diverse and socially inclusive place (Haywood and Hebbert, 2008; Shaftoe, 2008).

Transport – a trailblazer for neoliberalism

For the first 70 to 80 years of the 20th century there was a widespread consensus across developed nations that the peculiarities of transport – the high capital cost of infrastructure, the desire to create integrated networks rather than competing freestanding routes and so on – necessitated a strong state involvement in planning and operating transport systems. Spurred on by the insolvency of many private railway companies across Europe, the 'acute and wasteful competition' between many private transport operators (Barker and Robbins, 1974, p 211) and developing analyses of the welfare benefits of effective transport which drew on the spirit of municipalism that had underlain public works in housing and sanitation in 19th-century cities, new institutions and structures of governance emerged to regulate and control transport operations. At the urban scale, London led the way with a series of reforms that culminated in the creation of the London Regional Transport Board (LRTB) in 1933. The LRTB was designed to create a unified transport network for the wider London region, and in so doing support the further extension of the Underground by ensuring it was coordinated, as opposed to in competition, with the bus network (Bagwell, 1988).

Government and municipal control of the management and operation of transport steadily extended through the Second World War until the 1960s, including the notable milestones of the establishment of the Régie Autonome des Transports Parisiens (RATP) in Paris in 1948 and the Metropolitan Transportation Authority (MTA) in New York in 1968, which both amalgamated several bus and rapid transit operations in a new public authority similar to the London model. These and subsequent further governance reforms, including the creation of city-regional transport authorities in many provincial conurbations across Europe, and the significant investment in new public transport infrastructure ongoing throughout the 1960s and early 1970s, had in mind particular social policy objectives. In the US especially, but also increasingly across much of Europe, rapidly rising car ownership and postwar development planning structures were targeted at the 'outmoded' environments and mobility patterns of the dense, public transport-dependent industrial city. These were to be replaced by new edge-of-town locations for housing, employment, retailing, health, education and other public services served almost entirely by road. Such developments led to a 'very uneven' distribution of travel choices between those with and without access to a car (Schaeffer and Sclar, 1975). Extending the reach of governance to control and integrate the public transport network to create a real alternative to the car was paramount.

The second half of the 1970s, however, saw a collapse in transport investment in many countries as governments struggled to adjust to new financial realities and cut public spending quickly to cope with rising levels of debt. The subsequent rise to pre-eminence of the great neoliberal economic experiment in the aftermath of the energy crisis and related recessions is well documented (see, for example, Harvey, 2005), but what is perhaps less widely acknowledged is that transport played a leading role in the roll-out of neoliberal reforms – the 'marketisation transition' (Docherty and Shaw, 2011b) – demonstrating their veracity and impact across various dimensions of regulation and service delivery before their application more generally across the economy (see Headicar, 2009).

Transport was a particularly appropriate laboratory in which to test the 'kind of operating framework or "ideological software"' of neoliberalism (Peck and Tickell, 2002, p 380) because of the growing importance of the state and its social policy objectives in the sector running up to the 1970s' crisis. At the level of high ideology, neoliberals focused early attention on transport since it had become one of the strongest expressions of the 'welfare' state, exemplifying the notions of welfare economics and the public good: the very idea of collective, 'public' transport was anathema to their own ideals of reduced state intervention, the promotion of market forces in order to encourage competition, and normative values of enterprise and individual self-reliance. Instead, transport was to be treated the 'same as any other good, subject to market forces and the rigours of competition' (Sutton, 1988, p 132). The dominance of the private car as it exists today was assured in this period after governments, led by the US and UK, elevated the car from its role as a provider of flexible personal mobility as part of a wider transport system to a symbol of prosperity, individual autonomy and indeed the free market itself (Chatterjee and Dudley, 2011).

Although mass car ownership undoubtedly facilitated structural adjustments in the labour and housing markets and in other economic domains that stimulated enhanced productivity (Meyer and Gomez-Ibanez, 1981; Pucher and Lefevre, 1996), the rapid growth in car use in the 1980s and 1990s also brought a range of negative externalities associated with 'unrestricted mobility' – especially environmental and social costs – to the fore (see Cahill, 2010; Sheller and Urry, 2006). From the neoliberal perspective, the inevitable social consequence of rising car ownership and use – that public transport services would reduce – was an appropriate outcome given that it both stimulated innovation in the services that remained, and (more importantly) reduced the requirement for public subsidy of the transport system. The downside to this marketisation was that public transport networks were reduced in scope, frequency and quality to the extent that vulnerable and disadvantaged groups that depend on them most – for example, the elderly, the young, the unemployed and the infirm – became increasingly 'mobility deprived' (Lucas et al, 2006). The fact that these groups tended to be over-represented in particular urban communities, and that the vicious circle of the decentralisation of economic activity to car-friendly fringe sites further reduced the demand for public transport in urban cores, contributed to the well-documented 'hollowing out' and social polarisation of many cities. This renewed calls for a more interventionist approach by government to safeguard at least some degree of equity in transport provision (Le Grand, 1991; Buchan, 1992; Torrance, 1992).

'New Realism' and beyond

It was against this background of steadily rising car ownership and use, social and neighbourhood decay and the escalating concerns of congestion and pollution that the first robust challenges to the 'great car economy' gained traction. One of the most notable was the development of a policy prescription known as the 'New Realism' (Goodwin et al, 1991) that took as its starting point that it was in cities that the problems of the car were most keenly felt. New Realism put forward both a number of propositions about the structural nature and importance of over-reliance on the car, and also what could be done about it. Most important was the analysis that the demand for mobility would outpace whatever the actual capacity to expand the transport system through investment in new infrastructure might be. As a result of this, increasing traffic congestion and the longer and less reliable journeys it brings about were inevitable, which would first undermine the claimed benefits of the car in terms of its facilitation of enhanced mobility, but also go on to erode quality of life, damage the local and global environment, and (eventually) constrain economic growth.

Many governments took the ideas associated with New Realism to heart (at least rhetorically) in the early 1990s, spurred on by the alignment of two important political trends. The first of these was a cluster of events – including the 1987 United Nations (UN) World Commission on the Environment, the 1989 European Congress of Ministers of Transport and the 1992 Rio Earth Summit – which together represented the coming of age of the environmental movement, the adoption of environmental concerns such as climate change into the mainstream of politics and the key contribution of transport and especially the car to these concerns (see, for example, Baumol and Oates, 1988; Pearce et al, 1989; Ison et al, 2002). The second was budget-related. The UN's 1987 Brundtland Report explored the economic consequences of environmental pollution, noting there had been 'a growing realization ... that it is impossible to separate economic development issues from environment issues ... and environmental degradation can undermine economic development' (World Commission on Environment and Development, 1987, p 3). But it was the short-term economic issue of another deep recession that precipitated real policy change. In the UK, an ambitious programme of road building, championed by the ideologically driven neoliberals of the Thatcher-led Conservative government in 1989 as the 'largest ... since the Romans' (DfT, 2007, para 1.7), was to largely disappear under the aegis of her successor John Major.

In many ways the Major-led Conservative governments (1990-97) created the conditions for a deeper debate about the future direction of transport policy, and the value of 'alternative' approaches such as New Realism to flourish. Although hesitant at first, given the Conservatives' historic commitment to the car, Major's administrations found their way towards a more sustainable approach to transport by adopting the recommendation of the Royal Commission on Environmental Pollution (1994) to raise the price of petrol steadily, with the aim of doubling its cost in real terms in order to reduce road traffic levels. At the same time a limited revival of light rail in several English cities was sponsored, and construction began on the first new Underground line in London since the 1970s (Knowles and White, 2003; Wolmar, 2004). New *Planning policy guidance* on transport was introduced in 1994 (DoE and DoT, 1994) that for the first time sought to limit car-dependent development on the urban fringe and reduce the need for people to travel more generally (Headicar, 2009).

Similar trends were apparent in other countries: in France, the updated *Plans de Déplacements Urbains* (PDUs – Urban Development Plans) legislation from 1996 made it obligatory for each urban area in France with a population exceeding 100,000 to adopt a PDU. These are explicitly designed to reduce the impact of road traffic and improve the quality of public transport, to the extent that France is now a world leader in urban public transport development, with over 20 new tram systems and six new metro systems being built since their introduction (Tricoire, 2007). Even in the US, the most car-dependent nation of all, light rail seems to be enjoying something of a renaissance, with new or extended systems pursued in sprawling western centres such as Seattle, Portland, Denver and Los Angeles.

Competitiveness agenda

A central theme in this book is the profound shift emerging from the 'boom' discourses that positioned revitalised cities as the key knowledge-intensive nodes of a truly globalised economy in the 1990s and 2000s, to the 'bust'

– or at least austerity – debates that increasingly characterise post-financial crisis urban policy. For transport, this has already led to something of a rupture in the seemingly self-reinforcing narrative that placed transport and the 'connectivity' it generates between and within places at the very heart of the notion of urban competitiveness (Docherty et al, 2009). The so-called competitiveness agenda, which attempted to reconcile the seemingly discordant aspirations to maintain or even enhance rates of economic growth while at the same time reducing the impacts of this growth on the environment, impacted on urban transport policy in a number of ways (the tensions between these policy goals are further examined by Whitehead and Cochrane in this volume, Chapters Two and Three respectively).

Many regional economists and city governments have focused on the traditional idea of the urban 'asset set' as the key to growth. This 'asset set' is the bundle of 'physical', 'human' and 'soft' resources – ranging from land and property, the labour pool and its skills base, the governance and regulatory environment, to quality of life factors such as the artistic, sporting and cultural environment – seen as explaining city competitiveness. The challenge for cities in the era of the competitiveness paradigm was therefore commonly framed in terms of improving this 'asset offer' to make them more attractive places for people to live, work and invest in (Begg, 2001). Transport plays an important role in many of these asset sets. As already noted, the transport system 'links people to jobs; delivers products to markets; underpins supply chains and logistics networks; and is the lifeblood of domestic and international trade' (Eddington, 2006, p 11). But it also plays a critical role in defining quality of life in the city, and the extent to which citizens are able to access the cultural and other services that are argued to be of such importance in explaining the relative level of competitiveness between different cities (see, for example, Banister and Berechman, 2000; Porter and Ketels, 2004).

The emergence of the competitiveness paradigm, at a time when the economy was recovering from the early 1990s recession, combined with the environmental and social cases for shifting the balance of investment away from the car – especially in cities, with their heightened exposure to problems such as congestion, local air pollution, community severance and so on. In many places this generated an urban transport policy that remained focused on substantial infrastructure construction, but one in which new roads were replaced (or at least augmented) by new public transport schemes. With more financial resources at their disposal, governments again became re-engaged with transport development, not just in terms of infrastructure construction but also in terms of re-regulating public transport services to achieve better integration between modes and between transport and other areas of public policy such as planning (Hull, 2005; Williams, 2005) and public health (Lopez and Hynes, 2006; Li Ming Wen and Rissel, 2008). This reflected the 'changing connections and inter-relations between social, political and cultural factors' (Painter, 1995, p 276) characterising the shift to more complex patterns of governance in line with the public–private alignment rhetoric of 'the third way' (Giddens, 2000). At the sub-national scale, powerful urban governments with strong leaders and mandates were able to maximise the impact of the investment bubble by applying complementary policies aimed at changing travel behaviour and re-invigorating the urban realm, with the radical greening and road space reduction of key radial roads in Paris (since copied in New York), and London's globally significant Congestion Charge scheme perhaps the best examples.

Thus in the period immediately before the financial crisis, when the city competitiveness paradigm was at its most intense, urban transport was the subject of more policy attention and public investment than it had enjoyed for decades. The mindset of planners and economic development organisations was focused on the notion of competition between places, with cities attempting to out-do one another on the quality and image of their public transport networks as part of their wider strategies to attract investment. The onset of recession would necessitate something of a re-evaluation of these strategies.

After the financial crisis – what kind of (sustainable) future?

In the immediate aftermath of the financial crisis, when states were frantically trying to find policy instruments that might prevent a deep recession from developing into a full-blown depression similar to that experienced in the 1930s, some governments actually increased their spending on urban transport in order to safeguard jobs and the viability of the construction industry. But as the medium-term policy imperative moves from providing financial stimulus to reducing debt levels and ongoing public expenditure, the extent to which such investment will continue is highly uncertain. Past recessions have hit transport hard, not only because governments – especially in the UK – have chosen to reduce public expenditure quickly with transport top of the list for cutbacks, but also because of the secondary economic effects that influence the financial viability of service operations.

As the economy shrinks, the overall tax take declines and the level of public support needed to cover increased social costs, primarily unemployment and other welfare benefits, rises. At the same time, rising unemployment means that fares revenue declines, with public transport operators facing a financial gap long after the economy has begun to grow again since the unemployment rate (and hence reduced travel, especially commuting) tends to lag any return to economic growth by several months. As a result, a vicious circle can be created in which public transport declines, making it harder for newly unemployed people to find alternative jobs, which depresses

141

economy recovery further. If this pattern is followed for any length of time then the consequences can be severe: public transport becomes residualised as private operators can no longer afford to operate services commercially and the state is unable to provide anything more than a minimum 'safety net' service given the financial pressures on it. The end result is the kind of isolation of whole communities and the decline of economic, social and cultural activity that characterised the dying cities that Jane Jacobs (1961) wrote about.

Although any kind of forecasting for a complex area of public policy is difficult enough, the uncertain economic future, coupled with the divergent scenarios for environmental change that are even more apparent after the failure of the Copenhagen Climate Summit, make planning for future urban transport especially problematic. Not least is the question of whether the economic recovery will be robust and resilient enough worldwide for a return to the 'business-as-usual' approach to growth and competitiveness. In the transport sector, the early exchanges in this debate are being played out in terms of how targets already adopted by various governments for carbon reduction in the first half of the 21st century might be met (see, for example, Anable and Shaw, 2007).

Central here is the battle between proponents of 'conventional' notions of economic growth, many of whom now adopt a rhetoric that places climate change as a challenge for technological development to overcome in order to stimulate the next wave of growth, and those who see the scale of the potential crisis as a compelling reason to pose more fundamental questions about how society organises itself. For the first group, the key innovation in transport must be the 'greening' of the car through the widespread adoption of electric vehicles, a process that might (arguably) 'solve' many of the environmental problems of the contemporary car-based 'mobility regime' (Kemp et al, 2011), but one which would entrench the social problems of highly polarised mobility and which does not address the problems associated with congestion (see Chapter Four, this volume, for a further discussion of cities as focal points for transit networks). For the second, more radical group, the development of strategies and tactics designed to reduce and ameliorate carbon emissions is a truly cross-cutting endeavour. Rather than 'just' greening the car, a large-scale reorganisation of the transport system is implied, including all modes in order to achieve gains in other domains including land use planning, public health and community well-being in addition to environmental harm reduction.

If we assume that the impacts of the financial crisis and post-2008 recession are real and long-standing in terms of a diminution in the rate of growth seen in the 'boom' years of the urban competitiveness paradigm, then a number of critical policy questions for transport in cities emerge. Crucial here is whether the very notion of 'sustainability' itself will be reconfigured so that the roles of urban transport systems change significantly. 'Sustainability' is a slippery term, and has been appropriated by different interests to mean different things. As Bill Black noted over a decade ago, the early popular definition of sustainable transport derived directly from the Brundtland Report – that which could 'satisfy current transport and mobility needs without compromising the ability of future generations to meet these needs' – was problematic, since 'there is no limit placed on "future generations" and nothing is sustainable forever' (Black, 1998, p 337). But then, as Wackernagel and Rees (1995, p 64) argued, the 'deliberate vagueness' associated with sustainability is 'a reflection of power politics and political bargaining'. This explains why many governments and others were keen to promote potentially contradictory ideas such as 'sustainable economic growth' and the choice of large infrastructure schemes as the means to address the problems of urban transport in the first place.

Equally, moving away from the rhetoric of 'sustainable growth' towards a more 'deep green' standpoint that elevates the protection of the environment above all other policy considerations is almost impossible in a democratic society: politicians (probably rightly) judge the impact this would have on people's lifestyles as too great an electoral liability. The challenge is therefore to work out how radical change in our consumption of mobility might be achieved in such a way that the opportunities of technological change are grasped, but that their promise of a future zero emissions transport paradise is not converted into an excuse to avoid radical policy reform, pursue alternative approaches such as reducing the need to travel in the first place and/or shy away from tackling resilient transport-related policy problems such as community isolation in the interim.

Although this description of the scale of the challenge might suggest that transport's status as a 'wicked problem' is well deserved, there are many things that can be done to improve the situation. Critically in the context of recession and austerity, these approaches do not require large financial resources. Earlier we noted how the urban transport policy prescriptions of New Realism grew up in the early 1990s against a background of rapidly increasing environmental concern and recession economics, conditions that are not dissimilar to those of today. The original thinking behind New Realism was that first, there needed to be a recognition that the benefits of the car were beginning to be eroded by its externalities, and second, that urban transport policy should be about making cities better places in which to live and work, rather than trying to tweak existing policies so that problems such as congestion and pollution got worse more slowly. Given that the 'crisis of mobility' still exists, and is indeed made worse by the scale of the climate change challenge as contemporary scientific consensus understands it to be, revisiting New Realism might well be the way to begin addressing the urban transport problem in the coming decade.

In practice, although there are myriad different urban contexts, locations and communities with their own distinctive local needs and cultures, the problem of transport in cities remains one of how to maintain the very real economic and social benefits of mobility, which is now dominated by the car, while making real attempts to tackle the social and environmental problems that we have outlined. Part of the reason relatively little of this happened in the 1990s and 2000s was because the scale of economic growth enjoyed over this period meant that expensive, high technology solutions such as new public transport infrastructure were affordable and therefore attractive to policy makers operating in the competitiveness paradigm. But if the post-financial crisis environment turns out to be one of real austerity, then the rhetoric of making the most out of existing infrastructure will have to be made real. This means rediscovering and renewing the concept of accessibility, encouraging land use patterns that reduce the need to travel, and in so doing promoting public transport solutions and non-motorised travel such as walking and cycling.

Perhaps most controversially of all, this future vision is one in which cities will have to focus their finite motorised mobility resources – which may well decline in future if carbon-related or other policy imperatives such as energy security impose substantial constraints on our inherited travel patters – on those journeys that generate the greatest benefits. Defining which journeys deliver more benefits than others is inevitably a political minefield, and is why many attempts to rebalance the distribution of mobility between modes and across space and time have failed thus far. Nevertheless, with the financial and policy imperatives such as they are in the 2010s, the critical question of how mobility demands might be prioritised as important will need to be revisited. In large part, 'alternative' policy prescriptions such as New Realism did not falter because they somehow failed to live up to the trial of implementation; they did so because their focus on a broad range of policy measures, including unpopular elements such as road space rationing, charging and other aspects of behaviour change, did not fit the 'boom' narrative of the period in which they were first tentatively tried out in the latter half of the 1990s and 2000s (Docherty and Shaw, 2011a).

Challenging and politically controversial though such 'sophisticated policy mixes' (Eddington, 2006; Potter, 2007) might be, there are some examples of success that could point to a pathway to an urban transport future with a more holistic approach to mobility management in pursuit of environmental and social as well as economic objectives. One of these is the thorny issue of road user charging, which is a potentially very powerful mechanism to reduce the levels of road traffic, and which can generate substantial revenues that can be used to improve transport infrastructure and services across all modes (Button and Vega, 2008).[1] Although road pricing had been introduced elsewhere before, including in several Scandinavian cities and Singapore

(Button and Vega, 2008), the London Congestion Charge scheme is globally important because of both its scale and the fact that it was implemented in a society that had taken to heart the neoliberal messages of deregulation and individual liberty expressed through the notion of 'the right to travel', especially by car. As Sarah Dooling shows in her chapter (Chapter Nine, this volume), such notions of access and 'rights' to the city can have detrimental impacts on less powerful groups in urban societies.

One of the key lessons of the London scheme is that level of the power and resources enjoyed by city governments is critically important if radical policies are to be successfully introduced (although see Chapter Eleven, this volume, for examples of the limitations of city government). London was able to deliver a policy such as congestion charging because it had very substantial strategic capacity – that is the leadership, the finance, the powers, the technical know-how – to move effectively from policy formulation through to implementation (MacKinnon et al, 2008). Other UK cities that have tried to adopt London's model as a means of controlling traffic levels and generating resources for much improved public transport failed to win public support to proceed because they lacked these attributes and were unable to negotiate these political barriers to actually deliver a shift towards more radical policy directions (Gaunt et al, 2007).

The importance of the system of governance and its ability to coordinate and organise efforts to improve local transport systems should not be underestimated (see also Chapter Six, this volume). It is quite clear that the ability of cities to mobilise their governing networks to plan, implement and manage important policy interventions – such as the provision of good public transport – is highly variable, with many continental European and some North American cities doing much better than their counterparts in the UK in this regard. In part this is because of the vagaries of local political cultures – witness the long-standing debate about the value of elected city mayors, for example (see Elcock and Fenwick, 2007) – but it is also because British cities have remarkably little control over their own finances, and so their capacity to invest in costly assets, such as their public transport networks, is limited (Docherty et al, 2009).

Devolution – the transfer of political power to a lower tier of government – was characterised by UK government as providing the opportunity for 'local solutions to local problems', and the potential for institutions close to the issues at the local and (city-)regional levels to actually implement difficult policy choices that seem beyond current central government is well documented (see, for example, Trench, 2007). Where it has been implemented, devolution has certainly led to some widely supported transport policy innovations, including the London Congestion Charge, the expansion of the railway network in Scotland and the introduction of universal concessionary fares first in Wales and then elsewhere. Taking the idea of devolution further to move the focus of transport policy governance from the city scale to that of the local neighbourhood also opens up important possibilities to move travel behaviour further towards greater sustainability. Policies targeted at the neighbourhood scale, such as the support for 'Smarter Choices' in the UK – a set of policy tools including workplace and school travel plans, personalised travel planning, innovative marketing and ICT-based trip substitution – has been able to bring about quick and important reductions in car use by more than 10 per cent in demonstration towns (DfT, 2005; Sloman et al, 2010). These approaches are important not just for the immediate reductions in car use that they bring about – showing that real modal shift is possible – but also because they play an important part in challenging many current mindsets about transport, which remain fixated by moving as many people as far and as fast as possible.

While we do not argue against the utility of mobility *per se* – travel does indeed broaden the mind – this kind of more sophisticated mobility planning is likely to capture the greatest possible modal share for public transport services, offer attractive alternatives for those who do have a choice of how to travel and improve overall urban social equity by directing the transport system towards enabling easier access to a wide range of personal needs. Given the scarcity of resources, the environmental imperative and the resilience of many urban social problems rooted in a lack of connection between individuals, communities and places of economic and social opportunity, such an approach has many attractions. But to do this would require a shift away from the neoliberal-inspired narrative of transport policy as enabling individual choice in a free market of mobility, back to ideas of public value and management of the transport system as an instrument of welfare. It is on this territory that the urban transport debate of the next decade will be fought.

Key conclusions

- Transport is critical to the physical form of the city, and the opportunities it provides in large part shape the social and economic life of urban places.
- Urban transport has been a laboratory for regulatory change, with the neoliberal era and its focus on promoting the car contributing to profound changes in the organisation of urban life.
- The key policy choice for the future of urban transport is between applying new technologies to try and 'green' the existing mobility system – primarily through the introduction of electric vehicles – and the more radical task of reorganising the city to reduce reliance on motorised transport, and especially the private car.

Note

[1] This is not to say that road user charging is without negative impacts, but discussion of these is beyond the scope of this chapter.

Further reading

Kemp, R., Geels, F. and Dudley, G. (2011, in press) *Automobility in transition? A socio-technical analysis of sustainable transport*, Abingdon: Routledge.

Knowles, R., Shaw, J. and Docherty, I. (eds) (2008) *Transport geographies: Mobilities, flows and spaces*, Oxford: Blackwell.

References

Anable, J. and Shaw, J. (2007) 'Priorities, policies and (time) scales: the delivery of emissions reductions in the UK transport sector', *Area,* vol 39, no 4, pp 443-57.

Bagwell, P. (1988) *The transport revolution* (new edn), London: Routledge.

Banister, D and Berechman, J. (2000) *Transport investment and economic development*, London: UCL Press.

Banister, D. and Berechman, Y. (2001) 'Transport investment and the promotion of economic growth', *Journal of Transport Geography*, vol 9, no 3, pp 209-18.

Barker, T. and Robbins, M. (1974) *A history of London Transport (Volume II)*, London: Allen & Unwin.

Baumol, W. and Oates, W. (1988) *The theory of environmental policy* (2nd edn), Cambridge: Cambridge University Press.

Begg, I. (2001) *Urban competitiveness: Policies for dynamic cities*, Bristol: The Policy Press.

Black, W (1998) 'Sustainability of transport', in B. Hoyle and R. Knowles (eds) *Modern transport geography* (2nd edn), Chichester: Wiley, pp 337-51.

Buchan, K. (1992) 'Enhancing the quality of life', in J. Roberts, J. Clearly, K. Hamilton and J. Hanna (eds) *Travel sickness*, London: Lawrence & Wishart, pp 7-17.

Button, K. and Vega, H. (2008) 'Road user charging', in S. Ison, and T. Rye (eds) *The implementation and effectiveness of transport demand management measures: An international perspective*, Aldershot: Ashgate, pp 29-48.

Cahill, M. (2010) *Transport, environment and society*, Maidenhead: Open University Press.

Chatterjee, K. and Dudley, G. (2011, forthcoming) 'The dynamics of regime change: challenges to the dominance of the private car in the UK', in R. Kemp, F. Geelsand and G. Dudley (eds) *Automobility in transition? A socio-technical analysis of sustainable transport*, Abingdon: Routledge.

Conklin, E. (2006) *Dialogue mapping: Building shared understanding of wicked problems*, Chichester: Wiley.

DfT (Department for Transport) (2005) *Smarter choices: Changing the way we travel*, London: DfT.

DfT (2007) *Towards a sustainable transport system: Supporting economic growth in a low carbon world*, Cmnd 7226. London: DfT.

Docherty, I. and Shaw, J. (2011a) 'The transformation of transport policy in Great Britain? "New Realism" and New Labour's decade of displacement activity', *Environment and Planning A*, vol 43, no 1, pp 224-51..

Docherty, I. and Shaw, J. (2011b, forthcoming) 'The governance of transport policy', in R. Kemp, F. Geelsand and G. Dudley (eds) *Automobility in transition? A socio-technical analysis of sustainable transport*, Abingdon: Routledge.

Docherty, I., Shaw, J. and Gather, M. (2004) 'Changing roles of the state in 21st century transport', *Journal of Transport Geography*, vol 12, no 4, pp 257-64.

Docherty, I., Giuliano, G. and Houston, D. (2008) 'Connected cities', in R. Knowles, J. Shaw and I. Docherty (eds) *Transport geographies: Mobilities, flows and spaces*, Oxford: Blackwell, pp 83-101.

Docherty, I., Shaw, J., Knowles, R. and MacKinnon, D. (2009) 'Connecting for competitiveness: future transport in UK city regions', *Public Money and Management*, vol 29, no 5, pp 321-8.

DoE (Department of the Environment) and DoT (Department of Transport) (1994) *Planning policy guidance 13: Transport*, London: DoE and DoT.

Eddington, R. (2006) *The Eddington transport study: The case for action. Sir Rod Eddington's advice to the government*, London: The Stationery Office.

Elcock, H. and Fenwick, J. (2007) 'Comparing elected mayors', *International Journal of Public Sector Management*, vol 20, no 3, pp 226-38.

Feitelson, E. and Verhoef, E. (eds) (2001) *Transport and environment: In search of sustainable solutions*, Cheltenham: Edward Elgar.

Florida, R. (2005) *Cities and the creative class*, New York: Routledge.

Gärling, T. and Steg, L. (2007) *Threats from car traffic to the quality of urban life: Problems, causes, and solutions*, Oxford: Elsevier.

Gaunt, M., Rye, T. and Allen, S. (2007) 'Public acceptability of road user charging: the case of Edinburgh and the 2005 referendum', *Transport Reviews*, vol, 27, no 1, pp 85-102.

Giddens, A. (2000) *The third way and its critics*, Cambridge: Polity Press.

Glaeser, E. (2004) *Four challenges for Scotland's cities*, Allender Series, Glasgow: University of Strathclyde.

Goodwin, P., Hallett, S., Kenny, P. and Stokes, G. (1991) *Transport: The New Realism*, Oxford: Transport Studies Unit, University of Oxford.

Graham, D. (2007) 'Agglomeration, productivity and transport investment', *Journal of Transport Economics and Policy*, vol 41, no 3, pp 317-34.

Grengs, G. (2005) 'The abandoned social goals of public transit in the neoliberal city of the USA', *City*, vol 9, no 1, pp 51-66.

Hanson, S. (2004) 'The context of urban travel: concepts and recent trends', in S. Hanson and G. Giuliano (eds) *The geography of urban transportation* (3rd edn), New York: Guilford Press, pp 3-29.

Harvey, D. (2005) *A brief history of neoliberalism*, Oxford: University of Oxford Press.

Hass-Klau, C. (1993) 'Impact of pedestrianization and traffic calming on retailing. A review of the evidence from Germany and the UK', *Transport Policy*, vol 1, no 1, pp 21-31.

Haywood, R. and Hebbert, M. (2008) 'Integrating rail and land use development', *Planning Practice and Research*, vol 23, no 3, pp 281-4.

Headicar, P. (2009) *Transport policy and planning in Great Britain*, Abingdon: Routledge.

Hull, A. (2005) 'Integrated transport planning in the UK: from concept to reality', *Journal of Transport Geography*, vol 13, no 4, pp 318-28.

Ison, S., Peake, S. and Wall, S. (2002) *Environmental issues and policies*, Harlow: FT Prentice Hall.

Jacobs, J. (1961) *The death and life of great American cities*, New York: Random House.

Jessop, B. (2002) 'Liberalism, neoliberalism, and urban governance: a state-theoretical perspective', *Antipode*, vol 34, no 3, pp 452-72.

Kaufmann, V., Jemelin, C., Pflieger, G. and Pattaroni, L. (2008) 'Socio-political analysis of French transport policies: the state of the practices', *Transport Policy*, vol 15, no 1, pp 12-22.

Keeling, D. (2009) 'Transportation geography: local challenges, global contexts', *Progress in Human Geography*, vol 33, no 4, pp 516-26.

Kemp, R., Geels, F. and Dudley, G. (2011, forthcoming) *Automobility in transition? A socio-technical analysis of sustainable transport*, Abingdon: Routledge.

Knowles, R. and White, P. (2003) 'Light rail and the London Underground', in I. Docherty and J. Shaw (eds) *A new deal for transport? The UK's struggle with the sustainable transport agenda*, Oxford: Blackwell, pp 135-57.

Knowles, R., Shaw, J. and Docherty, I. (eds) (2008) *Transport geographies: Mobilities, flows and spaces*, Oxford: Blackwell.

Laird, J., Nellthorp, J. and Mackie, P. (2005) 'Network effects and total economic impact in transport appraisal', *Transport Policy*, vol 12, no 6, pp 537-44.

Lawless, P. and Gore, T. (1999) 'Urban regeneration and transport investment: a case study of Sheffield 1992-1996', *Urban Studies*, vol 36, no 3, pp 527-45.

Le Grand, J. (1991) *Equity and choice*, London: HarperCollins.

Logan, J. and Molotch, H. (2007) *Urban fortunes: The political economy of place* (2nd edn), Berkeley, CA: University of California Press.

Lopez, R. and Hynes, P. (2006) 'Obesity, physical activity, and the urban environment: public health research needs', *Environmental Health*, vol 5, no 25, pp 5-25.

Lucas, K., Tyler, S. and Christodoulou, G. (2008) *The value of new transport in deprived areas*, York: Joseph Rowntree Foundation.

Lyons, G. and Loo, B. (2008) 'Transport directions to the future', in R. Knowles, J. Shaw and I. Docherty (eds) *Transport geographies: Mobilities, flows and spaces*, Oxford: Blackwell, pp 215-26.

MacKinnon, D., Shaw, J. and Docherty, I. (2008) *Diverging mobilities? Devolution, transport and policy innovation*, Oxford: Elsevier.

Marsden, G. and May, A. (2006) 'Do institutional arrangements make a difference to transport policy and implementation? Lessons for Britain', *Environment and Planning C*, vol 24, no 5, pp 771-89.

Meyer, J. and Gomez-Ibanez, J. (1981) *Autos, transit and cities*, Cambridge, MA: Harvard University Press.

Li Ming Wen, L. and Rissel, C. (2008) 'Inverse associations between cycling to work, public transport, and overweight and obesity: findings from a population based study in Australia', *Preventive Medicine*, vol 46, no 1, pp 29-32.

Newman, P. and Kenworthy, J. (1999) *Sustainability and cities: Overcoming automobile dependence*, Washington, DC: Island Press.

Painter, J. (1995) 'Regulation theory, post-Fordism and urban politics', in D. Judge, G. Stoker and H. Wolman, (eds) *Theories of urban politics*, London: Sage Publications, pp 276-95.

Pearce, D., Markandya, A. and Barbier, E. (1989) *Blueprint for a green economy*, London: Earthscan.

Peck, J. and Tickell, A. (2002) 'Neoliberalizing space', *Antipode*, vol 34, no 3, pp 380-404.

Porter, M. and Ketels, C. (2004) *UK competitiveness: Moving to the next stage, Framework paper to DTi and ESRC Cities Programme* (www.isc.hbs.edu/econ-natlcomp.htm).

Potter, S. (2007) 'Eddington – another New Realism for transport?', *Town and Country Planning*, vol 76, no 1, pp 24-5.

Preston, J. (2008) 'Is Labour delivering a sustainable railway?', in I. Docherty and J. Shaw (eds) *Traffic jam: Ten years of 'sustainable' transport in the UK*, Bristol: The Policy Press, pp 75-96.

Pucher, J. and Lefevre, C. (1996) *The urban transport crisis in Europe and North America*, London: Macmillan.

Rittel, H. and Webber, M. (1973) 'Dilemmas in a general theory of planning', *Policy Sciences*, vol 4, no 2, pp 155-69.

Royal Commission on Environmental Pollution (1994) *Transport and the environment*, Oxford: University of Oxford Press.

Schaeffer, K and Sclar, E. (1975) *Access for all: Transportation and urban growth*, London: Penguin.

Siemiatycki, M. (2005) 'The making of a mega project in the neoliberal city', *City*, vol 9, no 1, pp 67-83.

Shaftoe, H. (2008) *Convivial urban spaces: Creating effective public places*, London: Earthscan.

Shaw, J., Knowles, R. and Docherty, I. (2008) 'Transport, governance and ownership', in R. Knowles, J. Shaw and I. Docherty (eds) *Transport geographies: Mobilities, flows and spaces*, Oxford: Blackwell, pp 62-80.

Sheller, M. and Urry, J. (2006) 'The new mobilities paradigm', *Environment and Planning A*, vol 38, no 2, pp 207-26.

Sloman, L., Cairns, S., Newson, C., Anable, J., Pridmore, A. and Goodwin, P. (2010) *Effects of Smarter Choices programmes in the sustainable travel towns*, London: Department for Transport (www.dft.gov.uk/pgr/sustainable/smarterchoices/smarterchoiceprogrammes/pdf/effects.pdf).

Sutton, J. (1988) *Transport coordination and social policy*, Aldershot: Avebury.

Torrance, H. (1992) 'Transport for all: equal opportunities in transport policy', in J. Roberts, J. Clearly, K. Hamilton and J. Hanna (eds) *Travel sickness*, London: Lawrence & Wishart, pp 48-56.

Trench, A. (ed) (2007) *Devolution and power in the United Kingdom*, Manchester: Manchester University Press.

Tricoire, J. (2007) *Le Tramway en France (Tramways in France)*, Paris; La Vie Du Rail.

Wackernagel, M. and Rees, W. (1995) *One ecological footprint: Reducing human impact on the earth*, Gabricola, Canada: New Society Publishers.

Williams, K. (2005) *Spatial planning, urban form and sustainable transport*, Aldershot: Ashgate.

Wolmar, C. (2004) *The subterranean railway. How the London Underground was built and how it changed the city forever*, London: Atlantic Books.

World Commission on Environment and Development (1987) *Our common inheritance*, Oxford: University of Oxford Press.

eight

Understanding UK sustainable housing policy

Chris Pickvance

Introduction

The aim of this chapter is to describe and explain the development of UK[1] sustainable housing policy. The chapter examines in turn the definition of sustainable housing, the four main types of UK sustainable housing policy and the main influences that have shaped them (see also Chapter Five, this volume). The chapter argues that sustainable housing policy has focused on technical aspects of housing rather than changing lifestyles or social justice elements (see Chapter Nine, this volume), and has been driven by international target commitments, proactive local authorities and lobbying by stakeholders. However, the economic climate since 2007 has slowed down the impetus towards sustainable housing.

Definition of sustainable housing

The term 'sustainable development' as publicised by the Brundtland Report (WCED, 1987) has three elements: economic, environmental and social.[2] However, the term 'sustainable' is now often used so loosely that it has lost any connection with this definition. For example, only half of the 12 requirements of a sustainable community in the previous UK government's *Sustainable Communities Plan* (ODPM, 2003, p 5) have anything to do with the Brundtland definition. Sustainable housing is used here to mean housing which has a reduced impact on the environment. The omission of a reference to social justice is not because it is not an important goal but because established terms like affordability and social exclusion are adequate to debate it. Using 'sustainable' in this restricted sense avoids overlap and confusion (see Priemus, 2005, who also adopts a narrow definition). Sustainable housing also relates to wider concepts such as sustainable building and the sustainable city.

The idea of reduced impact on the environment conceals a number of complexities.

First, the term 'impact' obscures the many ways in which housing affects (environmental) sustainability. The concept is therefore multidimensional, and most useable measures are likely to capture only some of the impacts concerned. Second, it seems more useful to use the term 'sustainable housing' to refer to housing which has a 'lower then usual' impact on the environment than to use an extreme definition of sustainable housing, for example, the 'zero carbon' house. This means that the term is part of the discourse of 'ecological modernisation' that stresses the compatibility between environmental movement demands and continued economic growth without major changes in lifestyles (Hajer, 1995).

The environmental impact of 'housing' has four sources:

- the location of the dwelling (for example, previously used 'brownfield' sites);
- the construction process (for example, minimising waste and journeys) and raw materials used (for example, timber from renewable sources);
- the dwelling's technical features (for example, dual-flush lavatories, double glazing and condensing boilers, solar panels, rainwater recycling);
- those activities of the household(s) occupying it which take place in the dwelling.

This last point is particularly important as homes use two thirds of the water put into the public supply network, 30 per cent of energy, and are responsible for 24 per cent of greenhouse gas (GHG) emissions (HoCEAC, 2006, Ev 11). The energy used in homes depends on households' lifestyles – for example, what levels of heating and cooling they choose, what electronic equipment they use – and also on 'rebound effects' such as whether people who use energy-saving light bulbs leave them on longer (Parker et al, 2005).

Character of UK sustainable housing policy

The term 'sustainable housing' goes back to the 1990s (Sunikka, 2003). In the UK it was originally purely a social construct (Hannigan, 2006), bringing together a heterogeneous set of policies that affected housing sustainability either directly (Building Regulations, planning policy) or indirectly (energy policy, fuel poverty policy). However, in 2005 the term appeared in the Code for Sustainable Homes (CLG, 2005), and in December 2006 the government announced its '100 per cent zero carbon for new homes by 2016' target. This can be seen as an attempt to provide an overall goal and focus for state intervention in this field.[3] Subsequently, in July 2007, the government published the Housing Green Paper (CLG, 2007a) and *Building a greener future: A policy statement* (CLG, 2007c) that outlined the measures to be used to deliver this policy. So it is now fair to say that sustainable housing is an explicit object of policy.

Current sustainable housing policies may be grouped into four main types: domestic energy-saving measures, sustainability rating schemes, Building Regulations and local governement planning policy. These policies involve different mixes of the three classic forms of state intervention: exhortation, regulation and economic measures, for example, grants or tax relief. Each of these types of policy is now discussed in turn.

Domestic energy-saving measures: an example of exhortation and economic measures

In 1993, post-Rio, the UK government committed itself to reducing CO_2 emissions by 20 per cent by 2010 relative to 1990 levels, and to be in line for a 60 per cent reduction by 2050 (DTI, 2003). In 2007, the UK government committed itself to a 30 per cent reduction of GHGs by 2020 relative to 1990, and a 15 per cent reliance on renewable energy sources by 2020 (DTI, 2007).

The Department of Trade and Industry (DTI) created the Energy Saving Trust (EST) in 1993 to promote household energy efficiency via advice and publicity campaigns and to operate DTI grant schemes. This was part of the Department's aim of stimulating innovation in UK industry. The EST had 160 staff and a budget of £72 million including grants. In 2002 the DTI introduced the Clear Skies and Major Photovoltaics (PV) demonstration programmes. These involved spending of £43 million in grants towards small-scale solar PV projects, solar hot water systems, micro-wind installations, wood stoves and ground-based heat pumps, either at the level of individual households or neighbourhoods. Typically the grants funded 10-50 per cent of a project's cost.

In 2006 these schemes were replaced by the three-year DTI £30 million Low Carbon Buildings programme which offered grants to households for micro-generation, for example, installation of solar PV, wind turbines, small hydro, solar thermal hot water, ground/water/air source heat pumps and bio-energy. The maximum amount paid was 50 per cent of the capital cost, subject to a £15,000 ceiling. In 2007, in the face of strong demand, this ceiling was reduced, and applications were only allowed after planning permission had been obtained. This led to a sharp fall-off in applications. In March 2007 an increase in micro-generation grants for homes from £12 million to £18 million was announced.

Since 2002, under the 'Energy Efficiency Commitment', energy suppliers have been obliged to provide roof and cavity wall insulation, energy-saving light bulbs and more efficient appliances primarily to poorer households to achieve specific total energy-saving targets. In 2008 this scheme was expanded to new categories of household and a 'community energy saving scheme' for improved insulation and other measures in 100 poor districts was added. One criticism of this scheme is that the costs are added to utility costs paid by all consumers, rather than being borne by the energy suppliers.

To help achieve the '100 per cent zero carbon for new homes by 2016' goal the 2007 budget announced a five-year stamp duty Land Tax exemption for zero carbon new homes valued up to £500,000, starting in October 2007.[4] For these purposes 'zero carbon' is defined as houses which over a year are net exporters of home or locally generated power to the national grid. It will therefore encourage energy efficiency and micro-generation. The budget also announced grants to pensioners to install insulation and central heating, and tax relief to householders on income from the sale to the grid of electricity from micro-generation.

In 2008 energy saving and energy were brought together in a new Department of Energy and Climate Change (DECC), although the Department for Environment, Food and Rural Affairs (Defra) retained certain responsibilities. In September 2008 50 per cent off roof and cavity wall insulation for all households was announced, and free provision for 11 million low-income and pensioner households. In 2009 the UK Low Carbon Transition Plan was announced to achieve the 34 per cent cut in 1990 emissions levels by 2020. New policies included ending the sale of conventional light bulbs by 2011, insulating all lofts and cavity walls by 2015 and installing 'smart' electricity meters by 2020. Households will be encouraged to pay for energy-saving measures themselves, or will be offered loans by energy companies; the accent will be 'pay as you save'. In 2009 a 'community-led government supported' initiative was announced for 20 low carbon communities that will receive £10 million for schemes reducing carbon emissions and improved local energy efficiency in 2010–12.

The Energy Act 2008 allowed the government to require electricity companies to achieve renewable energy targets by offering feed-in tariffs, an approach that has been very successful in Spain and Germany.[5] (The 2010/11 renewables target is 11 per cent of all electricity.) In 2010 a major programme of spending on feed-in tariffs was introduced to encourage households and small commercial users to install alternative energy sources such as PV cells, hydro and wind of up to 5MW capacity. A 'generation tariff' will be paid on all electricity produced, and an 'export tariff' on electricity which is exported to the grid, these tariffs being index-linked, guaranteed for 20 years but subject to review. The estimated annual cost is £610 million (averaged over 20 years), and this is expected to fund 744,000 domestic installations as well as commercial schemes (DECC, 2010). Like all the measures under the 'Energy Efficiency Commitment', the cost is borne initially by the energy companies which recoup it by charging higher prices to electricity consumers in general. The cost of the policy is thus borne by consumers not by government. DECC estimates the annual increase on domestic electricity bills at 1.5 per cent averaged over 20 years. This is an interesting innovation in public policy. Instead of government acting directly by raising taxes and spending the money on subsidies to consumers to help achieve the renewable energy target, it has acted indirectly by obliging electricity companies to achieve a renewables target while allowing them to charge higher prices to domestic and industrial consumers. This has the advantage of diverting potential public pressure from government (over taxes) to electricity companies (over prices). The cost of all spending by energy companies on reducing carbon emissions is estimated at £3.36 billion for the three years 2008–11 (HoCEFRAC, 2009, p 36), and the lack of transparency of this spending was pointed out by the House of Commons Environment, Food and Rural Affairs Committee (2009).

The other policy bearing on domestic energy saving is the Home Energy Efficiency Scheme (now called Warm Front), launched in 2000 to eliminate fuel poverty in vulnerable households by 2010 (that is, those spending more than 10 per cent of their income on fuel for heating and containing a child, or elderly, sick or disabled person). Grants of up to £4,000 for insulation or heating measures are paid. The 2000-08 budget was £800 million; 1.1 million households benefited from 2000 to 2005, and the number of people in fuel poverty fell from 4 million in 1996 to 1 million in 2003 (Defra/DTI, 2006). In 2008 the budget was increased by £74 million, but sharp utility price increases in 2008 meant the number of fuel-poor households was expected to rise to 3.5 million households (DECC, 2009, p 98). This is essentially a social policy which indirectly contributes to sustainable housing. The Warm Front programme continues in operation and future plans are to transfer the costs to energy companies who will recoup them from consumers.

Sustainability rating schemes: an example of exhortation and regulation

This heading covers three schemes for rating and promoting housing sustainability: EcoHomes, the Code for Sustainable Homes and Energy Performance Statements. They can be seen as ways of giving sustainable housing an operational meaning.

In 1993, the Building Research Establishment (BRE), a technical agency (formerly governmental, now independent), which undertakes research on building methods and materials, and establishes standards, introduced a set of environmental assessment methods (BRE Environmental Assessment Method, BREEAM) for rating buildings. In the case of houses this was known as the EcoHomes method. The criteria used included: (a) project management (overall management policy, commissioning, site management and procedural issues); (b) energy use (operational energy and carbon dioxide [CO_2] issues); (c) health and well-being (indoor and external issues affecting health and well-being); (d) pollution (air and water pollution issues); (e) transport (transport-related CO_2 and location-related factors); (f) land use (greenfield and brownfield sites); (g) ecology (ecological value conservation and enhancement of the site); (h) materials (environmental implication of building materials, including life-4cycle impacts); and (i) water (consumption and water efficiency) (see www.breeam.org/).

The ratings on these criteria were then combined into an overall score (Pass, Good, Very Good, Excellent). The EcoHomes standard allowed for some compensation of under-performance on one criterion by over-performance on another. The EcoHomes method was introduced as a voluntary scheme in 2000, since when 10,000 houses have been rated by the method. From 2003 The Housing Corporation, which funds the building of social housing, set the EcoHomes pass level as the mandatory minimum for housing associations, and recommended they achieve the Good level.

In 2005 the Office of the Deputy Prime Minister introduced a draft Code for Sustainable Homes (CLG, 2005). It resulted from the working of the Sustainable Buildings Task Group whose aim had been a code for all buildings. It failed to achieve this and the term 'Sustainable Homes' in the Code's title was thus unintentional. Like the EcoHomes method, the Code was intended to encourage practice above the minimum standards contained in the Building Regulations. The assumption was that information and exhortation would be effective. For housing built by the private sector, the Code, like EcoHomes, would be voluntary. However, for social housing built with funding from The Housing Corporation (or from 2008 the Homes and Communities Agency), the EcoHomes Very Good level became obligatory from April 2006. The effect was that speculative houses built by the private sector did not need to be built to the same standard as social housing, and did not need to be assessed.

In December 2006, two months after publication of the Stern Report (2006), a set of new sustainable housing proposals under the banner 'zero carbon housing' was announced for consultation ending in March 2007. Among these was a new proposed system for rating new homes that would be incorporated into the final version of the Code for Sustainable Homes, and would replace the EcoHomes method (CLG, 2006a). There would be six levels, with Code level 3 (the EcoHomes Very Good level) the target for 2010, Code level 4 for 2013 and Code level 6 for 2016.

This proposal was new in two ways. The final Code introduced mandatory rating for all new homes from April 2008. However, mandatory rating refers to the *reporting* of environmental standards, not the *achievement* of these standards beyond the social housing sector. The Code is quite clear on this:

> The Code is essentially a *voluntary* set of environmental standards
> – we are not proposing that any development or building should

be required to meet these higher standards (except where public funding is involved…). (CLG, 2006a, p 13)

Second, each Code level requires a specified improvement in energy efficiency towards 'zero carbon', and a specified reduction in water consumption (which will fall from 120 to 80 litres/person/day between Code levels 1 and 6). This reduces the scope for compensation for under-performance between areas. In addition, each Code level corresponds to a certain number of 'points' that can be obtained in a wide variety of ways[6] – here the idea of compensation or tradeability still applies.

The last measure is the introduction of energy efficiency reports on all houses sold, a requirement of the European Commission (EC) Energy Performance of Buildings Directive by 2009. After a delayed start, these were introduced in August 2007 as part of 'Home Information Packs'. In May 2010 these packs were suspended, but energy efficiency reports will continue to be necessary. They are produced by 'home inspectors' on the basis of a visual inspection. Whereas, previously, house buyers had no way of knowing the energy efficiency of a house, these reports are intended to help raise awareness of energy efficiency issues. They do not themselves require achievement of a particular level of energy efficiency.

In sum, these rating systems and codes have introduced the idea of mandatory rating for new and existing houses for sale, but only the EcoHomes Very Good/Code level 3 requirement applied to social housing (which makes up around 20 per cent of new housing) requires the achievement of a specific level of sustainability.

Building Regulations: an example of regulation

The concept of Building Regulations is to set a 'level playing field' of minimum standards that all new buildings must meet. Building Regulations concern the structure of the building, its ventilation, lighting, heating, insulation, electricity, etc so sustainability has been a factor, but recently it has become a more explicit driver of changes. In 2002, higher standards were introduced for insulation, thermal bridging and air-tightness, and energy efficient lighting was required. In 2005, condenser boilers became mandatory. In 2006, in response to the EC Energy Performance of Buildings Directive, a new method for assessing CO_2 emissions was introduced, together with a 20 per cent improvement in the conservation of fuel and power in new buildings or extensions. Improvements in ventilation were also introduced. In 2007, improvements in fire safety came into force.

As we have seen, the Code for Sustainable Homes set out a six-level rating system but did not require all new (or existing) houses to achieve specific levels. However, the July 2007 Housing Green Paper contained a promise to amend the Building Regulations to include the Code's energy efficiency requirements for 2010, 2013 and 2016, which are needed to progress towards 'zero carbon by 2016'. This implies a 25 per cent improvement in the energy/carbon performance of new housing by 2010, a 44 per cent improvement by 2013 and the achievement of 'zero carbon' by 2016 (CLG, 2006b, pp 14–16). This change from the voluntarism of the Code to the compulsion of Building Regulations is a turning point in policy. The pressure for this change was apparent in responses to the government's consultation on its new policy (CLG, 2006c, para 3.35). After the usual consultation process the Code's energy efficiency requirements were incorporated in the 2010 Building Regulations that took effect in October 2010. This should help bring about higher sustainability levels outside social housing. However, the wider range of sustainability features outlined in the final Code for Sustainable Homes will remain optional, except in social housing.

It should be noted that recently the effectiveness of the Building Regulations has been questioned by BRE, which found that 32 per cent and 60 per cent of two samples of new houses failed to meet Building Regulations requirements on air permeability (HoCEAC, 2005, para 114). This is considered to reflect a lack of resourcing and technical expertise for building inspection. According to BRE, 'building control officers are not really trained nor do they have the resources to check on environmental aspects' (HoCEAC, 2005, para 113). Thus it appears that the Building Regulations are far from fully effective in areas where specialist environmental expertise is needed, and that enforcement is rare and costly. This is in line with studies of enforcement which argue that inspectors prefer to rely on education and negotiation, and see legal action as costly, as something which exposes them to public gaze, as well as being an admission of failure (Hawkins, 1984; Lowe et al, 1997; Fineman, 2000). The 2010 Building Regulations draw attention to this 'performance gap'.

Local government planning powers: an example of regulation

Power over planning lies with the Department for Communities and Local Government (CLG) that operates through Regional Development Agencies and local government. For example, it is responsible for the targets for development on brownfield sites (which include gardens) (50 per cent in 1995, 60 per cent in 1997) and for setting regional house building targets. CLG expresses its guidance through Regional Spatial Strategies and Planning Policy Statements (PPSs). Their topics range from general sustainability considerations that councils should follow, as in *PPS1: Delivering sustainable development*, to very specific conditions. For example, *PPS22: Renewable energy* states that:

> Local planning authorities may include policies in local development documents that require a percentage of the energy to be used in new residential, commercial or industrial developments to come from on-site renewable energy developments. (CLG, 2004, p 10)

Local councils are expected to operate within these national and regional planning guidelines in drawing up their own Local Development Framework and Local Development Documents. These are subject to public enquiry, and direction by the CLG. There is also an appeal system against refusal of development.

The most enterprising local authorities have proved creative in using explicit powers or areas of discretion in legislation. (UK local government does not have a Scandinavian-type general power to act for the benefit of the local population.) Some have pioneered sustainable housing by introducing as planning conditions sustainability requirements which are in excess of Building Regulations. For example, Merton Borough Council is well known for the 'Merton rule' that requires developers to ensure at least 10 per cent of all energy production for new development comes from renewable energy equipment on site. Woking Borough Council has developed a series of innovations involving combined heat and power plants for its own office buildings and council housing. It is also introducing planning conditions that constrain developers to use on-site renewable energy, and uses innovative legal arrangements ('single purpose vehicles') to avoid placing long-term obligations on developers who provide such installations, and to limit the risk to the Borough. Enfield Borough has pioneered the checklist approach to sustainability. By 2010 90 per cent of all local councils had signed the Nottingham Declaration in support of action to mitigate and adapt to climate change. As Mark Whitehead and Harriet Bulkeley, Mike Hodson and Simon Marvin also describe in their chapters (Chapters Two and Six, respectively), some urban localities are therefore important sites of innovation and variation.

In December 2007, the government published the definitive *Planning Policy Statement: Planning and climate change – Supplement to Planning Policy Statement 1* (CLG, 2007d), after the zero carbon target and proposed changes in Building Regulations had been announced. Local authorities are now encouraged more explicitly 'to set out a target percentage of the energy to be used in new development to come from decentralised and renewable or low-carbon energy sources where it is viable', to set higher targets where appropriate (CLG, 2007d, p 16), and to set 'levels of building sustainability in advance of those set out nationally' (CLG, 2007d, p 17). However, there remain constraints: 'Any policy relating to local requirements for decentralised energy supply to new development or for sustainable buildings should be set out in a [Development Plan Document]' (2007d, p 18), which has to be approved by an inspector.

Clearly, local government planning powers are used in innovative ways by some councils, but the national government balances between encouraging this and keeping it under control.

Other measures

The 2006–08 period also saw a variety of governance measures especially involving industry as partners:

- A National Centre for Excellence in Housing was formed in December 2006 by BRE and the National House Building Council (NHBC).
- A Green Building Council was formed in February 2007 to bring together 36 larger building firms and link them to the government sustainable building objective. Its aims include promoting sustainable building, influencing government sustainable building policy and assessment tools, setting standards for new products, developing technical knowledge and providing training.
- A '2016 Task Force' was announced in July 2007 with the Home Builders Federation.
- In July 2007 the government announced its 'Eco-towns Initiative' (CLG, 2007e) (also known as the Carbon Challenge) under which 10 small new towns of 5,000–20,000 homes are to be built with the housing reaching Code levels 5-6. In 2010 this was scaled down to 600 homes to be built in four towns by 2016 at Code level 4 at a cost to government of £60 million.
- In August 2007 the CLG announced its '2016 commitment', 'to build 240,000 new zero carbon homes a year by 2016'. The first four signatories were the Home Builders Federation, the Local Government Association (LGA), the UK Green Building Council and WWF.
- In 2008 the Zero Carbon Hub was created as a body representing the industry and with support from the BRE and government, to facilitate the move to zero carbon at the same time as the announcement of the government consultation on the definition of zero carbon (CLG, 2009).

In sum, over the period from 2002 a range of sustainable housing measures has been introduced as well as structures to facilitate their implementation. The targets have been the house building industry, the energy industry, equipment suppliers, local authorities and households. The measures used have been economic (for example, subsidies to households for the introduction of energy-saving measures and alternative energy production), regulation (for example, compulsion on the energy industry, rating of the energy efficiency of dwellings, higher sustainability standards incorporated in the Building Regulations) and persuasion (for example, through the '100 per cent zero carbon for new homes by 2016' slogan, the Code for Sustainable Housing and the encouragement of pioneering local authorities).

Explaining sustainable housing policy

A series of questions can be asked about a policy; for example, why any policy at all is introduced in a given field, what forms it takes (exhortatory, regulatory, economic), what the scale of spending is, which government departments are responsible and what lobbies exist in its field. A variety of explanatory approaches can be taken which address one or more of these questions and a mix of approaches is necessary to make sense of the various questions about policy. The approaches refer to dominant ideas (interventionism versus laissez-faire), structural features (for example, state 'openness' to external influence, state capacity to make and deliver policy, whether central policy coordination is strong or weak), socioeconomic conditions (social divisions, resource availability), party politics (party political calculation about taking up an issue, the proximity of elections) and group behaviour (pressure from lobbies) (John, 1998). In addition, cross-national studies reveal how, in more 'open' states (such as the UK), 'insider' groups which are treated as expert and broadly in sympathy with the government are given access, whereas 'outsider' groups have to rely on their ability to mobilise opinion outside the state to influence policy (Rawcliffe, 1998). They also reveal differences in national policy styles (Vogel, 1986), although policy styles also vary between issue domains.

Before explaining why UK sustainable housing policy has the features described above, it needs to be pointed out what the policy does not include:

- The main forms of policy are exhortation and regulation. The approach to regulation has been very tentative: social housing is used as a pioneer sector and the zero carbon requirements added to the Building Regulations in 2010 are limited to energy and water use, rather than the full range of features of sustainable housing.
- The spending commitment has been modest and the main element in it is the Warm Front social policy. There has been much comment on the lack of financial incentives to the building industry and the low incentives to households, except for those in fuel poverty.[7] The cost of the tax reliefs for zero carbon houses and on income from selling surplus micro-generated electricity is likely to be insignificant, and the new policy of feed-in tariffs will be paid for by electricity consumers.
- The zero carbon target focuses on new housing. Although Warm Front, incentives to micro-generation and the 'Decent Homes by 2010' housing

policy all apply to existing houses, there is no systematic effort to raise the energy efficiency of the existing stock.
- There is a shortage of personnel trained in sustainable housing technology or building methods. This is apparent among employees in local government (building inspection, planning) and the building industry.
- Sustainable housing policy has been presented as 'technical', with little attention to the need to change people's lifestyles.

This section puts forward some elements of an explanation for particular policy developments, drawing on evidence on the positions of different actors as shown by their evidence to House of Commons Committees, from surveys and from their own publications.[8]

International commitments

The existence of a sustainable housing policy derives primarily from the international commitments since Rio of successive UK governments to cut GHG emissions. Since 'houses' produce 24 per cent of all GHG emissions the link can be portrayed as a close one. However, it is notable that this has led to a policy concerned with changing the physical features of housing. The role of changes in lifestyles has been de-emphasised, although human activity plays a key part in the total of emissions from 'houses'. The political riskiness of sustainable housing policy was reduced in 2006 when David Cameron, the new Conservative leader, adopted the green agenda as a way of repositioning the party in the centre of political spectrum, thus creating a consensus among all three major parties in favour of environmental policies.

National-level interest groups and pressure groups have also had an impact on both the form and the content of the policy, as follows.

The house building industry

The house building industry has several positions (see Chapter Five, this volume, for a discussion of the wider property development industry). First, it is against anything that adds to costs, or which, in its view, hampers the sale of houses. The industry's primary concern is with the additional costs of sustainability features, which it sees as imposing costs but without corresponding benefits since consumers do not value them (HoCEAC, 2006, Ev 35-37).[9] The industry's view is that new house prices cannot deviate from existing house prices and that in the short term builders (and, in the longer term, landowners) will bear the cost of energy-saving improvements (CLG, 2006b, p 17). One estimate of these extra costs is 5 per cent for the 2013 standard, and 13-16 per cent for the 2016 standard, that is, £15,000 or £44,000 for a £300,000 house; savings are estimated at £360 per year in

2016 with onsite alternative energy (CLG, 2007c, pp 23-5; see also Sweett, 2007). The proposed stamp duty exemptions will cover the net costs of achieving the 2010 standard but not of the higher levels.

Second, the house building industry prefers change to be introduced via the Building Regulations since they are constant across the whole country, rather than by local governments using planning policy which results in locally varying standards. Statements by the industry's representative body, the Home Builders Federation, make this clear. The industry, as reflected by the Federation, is also in favour of the idea that the Code for Sustainable Housing should be voluntary, even though it acknowledged that a voluntary Code would not be followed by all builders (HoCEAC, 2006, Ev 44-46).[10] A government document articulates the argument very well:

> If we allowed every local planning authority to set different standards for building methods and materials, so that developers faced hundreds of varying standards across the country, we believe industry would find it extremely difficult to build the capacity it needs and to adapt its supply chains and practices so as to meet the challenging new national framework…. And this could also jeopardise the economies of scale that can be realised by setting national environmental standards. So we might end up with a higher cost to meet our environmental goals, and greater difficulty in achieving them…. Such a variable approach could also mean that prices of new development would rise, and fewer homes would be built – particularly if there is a risk of authorities setting unrealistically high standards. (CLG, 2006b, p 18)

Taken at face value, the house building industry's preference for the Building Regulations over variable planning conditions is a textbook-like preference for a 'level playing field'. However, this may not be the whole story. Changes to the Building Regulations involve a consultative process led by the CLG Building Regulations Advisory Committee which has a large membership including the main industry and professional groups. The different sections of the Building Regulations are revised on a cyclical basis every three to five years, and revision is a slow process, taking some four years, as it involves informal consultation, formal consultation, regulatory impact assessment and consultation on proposals. The industry's preference for the Building Regulations as a policy tool, therefore, is also preference for a familiar process, involving slow change, over which it has some influence. Its influence is very much less direct in the case of planning policy.

Some indirect evidence of house building industry behind-the-scenes influence comes from the consultation on *Building a greener future*, the government's zero carbon policy document. The analysis of the responses to the survey shows that of 218 participants in the consultation, only 11 were developers (CLG, 2007b, p 6). This is compatible with (but does not prove) the view that house builders had an insider status in the preparation of the policy, so did not need to take part in the open-to-all consultation.

Lastly, as mentioned above, the weak enforcement of the Building Regulations reduces pressures on house building firms, and presumably the industry is not unhappy with that.[11]

In one sense one can argue that the house building industry has been a strong influence on policy: its strong preference for change to be introduced via the Building Regulations has been very influential; it has prevented the Code for Sustainable Housing from mandating higher standards; and constraints have been placed on local government planning powers. However, it has not been strong enough to secure incentives to introduce sustainable housing features, a measure advocated by a variety of interests from local government to the industry itself, as reported in various surveys. Pickvance with Chautard (2006) found that financial incentives to households, building firms and housing associations were supported by majorities of councils, as well as by builders and housing associations. (See also the surveys by CLG, 2007b; LGA, 2006b.) Finally, from a government viewpoint, the house building industry's very conservatism is a source of weakness since the industry is an obstacle to reform, and the government has to look elsewhere for support. This is why central government needs to encourage pioneering local authorities.

Building supplies and energy industries

These industries, while closely dependent on the house building industry, take a different stance. The house is a market for supplier industries, which are more innovative on the whole. For example, suppliers of condenser boilers, insulating material, triple-glazed windows, etc all have an interest in their products being specified in houses. They are therefore a force for innovation. Incentives to install micro-generation equipment benefit producers in this sector, and measures to improve roof insulation benefit materials producers and fitters. Equally important is the broader question of the public image of energy companies who are under government injunction to promote energy efficiency thereby reducing consumption of their product. They want to be seen as 'green' to counter their image as rapacious in their pricing, and insensitive to the needs of the poor. (The Warm Front policy has the effect of taking some public pressure off them.)

At the international level, the World Business Council for Sustainable Development, which treats sustainable development as a business opportunity, has 200 member companies. Building suppliers and energy companies are prominent; house builders are not (see www.wbcsd.org). In the UK, building suppliers and energy companies are an active influence on government both as individual firms and through a pressure group, the Association for the Conservation of Energy (ACE). Created in 1981, ACE has 19 member companies drawn from the insulation, building materials and power supply fields. Many of these are large corporations, for example, EDF Energy, E.On UK and Pilkington. Its stated aim is to reduce overall energy demand and increase the use of energy-saving measures (ACE, 2006). Essentially it is a lobby group advancing the interests of industrial groups operating in some of the building supplies and energy markets created by sustainable housing. It lobbies both at Westminster and Brussels. It claims its efforts have helped bring in a 5 per cent VAT for energy-saving building materials (2000), the Warm Homes and Energy Conservation Act 2000 (promoting council energy efficiency strategies and the Warm Front anti-fuel poverty campaign), the Sustainable Energy Act 2003 (targets, monitoring of CO_2 emissions and energy conservation, £60 million funding for developing renewable energy) and the Climate Change and Sustainable Energy Act 2006 (promotion of micro-generation by national targets, amended Building Regulations, and simplified planning). ACE also promoted energy audits for home buyers as early as 2000. In most cases ACE promotes specific measures as private bills that are incorporated into omnibus government acts.

Unlike the house building industry, which has mostly been trying to avoid or delay change, the building supplies and energy industries have wanted specific changes that would expand markets for them. They have been relatively successful.

Housing associations

Housing associations are in an unusual situation. As commissioners of social housing built with government funding, they cannot claim to be fully independent of government. For this reason they have been given a leading role by the Code for Sustainable Housing. However, any extra costs of sustainability features have to be met by government grant or increased rents (and Housing Benefit). They are thus not totally shielded from the market forces that affect private builders. As a group they are represented by the National Housing Federation which lobbies on their behalf. However, the Federation is primarily occupied in defending housing associations against government centralisation. Sustainable housing is not a major concern.

In practice, some housing associations are strong supporters of sustainable housing and would like the government to raise standards faster, while others are less enthusiastic. This depends very much on their size, resources and technical expertise, and whether they are building new houses or simply managing a fixed stock. In recent years there has been a process of concentration, and a channelling of funding to the largest associations, but there remain many small associations.

Local authorities

Over the last 30 years local government has been subject to the increasing centralisation of its financial and decision-making powers, and has lost functions to non-elected bodies. It treats planning policy as an irreducible function, since, as an elected territorial authority, local government has no legitimate rival. As explained above, there is a small group of local governments which have been proactive in using the planning system to encourage alternative energy and green building methods, for example, by making planning approval conditional on extra conditions. Together with professional bodies, local government was the main source of responses to the consultation on the *Building a greener future* document (CLG, 2007b).

In 2006, aware that the government was planning new measures on sustainable housing, the Local Government Association (LGA), the lobby group for local government, in conjunction with the Society of Planning Officers, produced draft proposals to improve the sustainability of housing by imposing more demanding planning conditions. The report noted that 'the planning system is empowered to go beyond building regulations in standards and topics' (LGA, 2006a, para 2.7). It refers to *PPS1: Delivering sustainable development*, and notes that its statement that 'sustainable development is the core principle underlying planning ... provides the key policy hook on which to hang policies for sustainable building' (LGA, 2006a, para 2.1). The report ends by proposing policies in 10 areas, each of which would 'require' (rather than 'encourage') developers to meet certain standards. However, the report notes the lack of expertise among planning officers (one third felt unable to advise on sustainable construction), the lack of resources for monitoring, the lack of capacity of the building industry in some areas and the risk that developers would be frightened off by demanding standards (LGA, 2006a, paras 1.1, 3.5, 4).

In the event, the government went a little way towards LGA's 2006 policy proposals in its new policy (CLG, 2007c). The limited influence local government has derives from its reputation for innovation.

Pressure groups

The sole major environmental group that has operated in the field of sustainable housing is World Wildlife Fund-UK (WWF-UK). It is one of the largest such organisations in the UK, with 330,000 supporters and an income of £39 million in 2006. It has had a long history of involvement with industry and government and can be considered an 'insider' group (Rootes,

2006). It launched its Campaign for One Million Sustainable Homes (in the UK by 2012) in Johannesburg in 2002. Its approach was to work with government, the building industry and other 'stakeholders' to raise the profile of sustainable housing. (It was not therefore a campaign that depended on mobilising public opinion.) To this end it undertook, in collaboration with the bank HBOS, two audits of the progress toward sustainability of 12 large house building firms in 2004 and 2005, took part in the government Sustainable Buildings Task Group (the only non-governmental organisation to do so), developed a 'Regional Sustainability Checklist' with BRE, gave advice to the Building Regulations Advisory Committee, lobbied for the Sustainable and Secure Buildings Act 2004 and advocated stamp duty relief for sustainable homes, 5 per cent VAT for green building goods, full VAT for new homes and 5 per cent VAT for sustainable homes. WWF was also the first party to be interviewed by the House of Commons Environmental Audit Committee in their hearings on Sustainable Housing in 2006. This confirms their position as a major participant in discussions but from a position willing to do business with government and which does not demand radical changes in lifestyles.

Understandably, WWF describes the government announcements of December 2006, which were made at WWF headquarters, as a victory for WWF:

> WWF's campaign for more sustainable homes has won government support today with the announcement that all new homes will be "zero carbon" in less than ten years…. The announcement in Gordon Brown's pre-budget report follows more than four years of campaigning on the issue by WWF through its One Million Sustainable Homes (OMSH) campaign. (www.wwf.org.uk/ news/n_0000003280.asp, accessed 2 May 2008)

In its support, WWF quotes The Housing Corporation as saying 'The WWF One Million Sustainable Homes campaign has pushed sustainable homes into the mainstream' (www.wwf.org.uk). And at the 13 December 2006 policy launch, Ruth Kelly, Minister of Communities and Local Government, said, perhaps predictably, that "no one over the decades has done more to raise awareness of how precious and fragile our environment is than WWF". In February 2007, Paul King, Director of the OMSH campaign, left WWF to become chief executive of the UK Green Building Council. This Council is likely to play a critical role in negotiating building industry support for government measures designed to achieve the zero-carbon target.

In contrast, there have been no mass public movements around sustainable housing. It is an issue with low political salience. Instead, individual household practices have changed, as seen in the enthusiastic take-up of solar heating and wind turbines by small numbers of well-off people.

Conclusions

This chapter has argued that the UK government has pursued sustainable housing policy by exhortation, regulation and fairly modest economic measures. The Code for Sustainable Homes introduced mandatory sustainability standards for social housing but not private housing. The major July 2007 commitment to gradually raise the energy and water efficiency of houses in line with the 'zero carbon by 2016' goal has been incorporated in the 2010 Building Regulations and will extend these standards to all new housing. At the same time a series of economic incentives (and most recently funding by electricity consumers) has been used to increase the use of alternative energy sources, improve home insulation, etc. Paradoxically, the largest element of the policy in terms of spending, and, no doubt, impact on energy consumption, has been Warm Front, the social policy.

It has been shown that sustainable housing policy has mainly been driven by (a) government commitments to international targets; (b) proactive local governments; and (c) efficient lobbying by the building supply and energy industries, backed up for a period by the WWF campaign. On the other hand, the house building industry has taken a defensive position, objecting to extra costs and reluctantly accepting higher building standards. Paradoxically, this has undermined its influence and made central government more open to lobbying by the other industries and to local government. Spending on the policy has been kept down to a modest level and calls for large incentives to business or households have been resisted. The modest spending can be attributed to the lack of influence of environmental groups or consumers (either as residents, as energy consumers or as potential energy micro-producers) and to the policy's resultant low political profile. The fact that the largest element of spending is on Warm Front, a social policy with considerable public prominence, supports this view. All the interested parties identify a key obstacle to sustainable housing as the lack of a campaign led by central government, local government or the building industry (Pickvance with Chautard, 2006; LGA, 2006b; CLG, 2007b).[12]

The broader economic climate since 2007 has been unfavourable for sustainable housing policy. The financial crisis of 2008 and the subsequent recession in the UK had an immediate effect on the housing market. House building levels fell from 37,000 in the second quarter of 2007 to 21,000 in the second quarter of 2010, the supply of mortgages shrank as foreign banks stopped offering them and remaining banks became more risk-averse, house prices stagnated and the survival of many house building firms was threatened. The house building industry, which has always argued that buyers are unwilling to pay the extra initial costs of sustainability features, pursued its opposition through the Zero Carbon Hub, where it is seeking to weaken the definition of zero carbon housing by pressing for payments to be allowed for off-site carbon reduction to compensate for insufficient carbon reduction on site. This would, in effect, undermine the intentions of the 2010 Building Regulations.

The election of the Conservative–Liberal Democrat government in May 2010 abolished regional housing targets and promised to strengthen local control over house building. This is likely to encourage opposition to new housing and will add to the difficulties of the house building industry, therefore reducing the prospects for sustainable housing. Whether existing pioneering local councils will flourish under the new government's claimed policy of giving power back to local people remains to be seen.

Finally, it is notable that sustainable housing policy is a field in which 'sustainable' has been subject to very precise definition. At the same time it is a policy which has been framed as about changing buildings rather than about changing lifestyles, and it has ignored the social justice element associated with the Brundtland definition. This is probably the price of its emergence as a policy in the absence of wide social movement support.

Key conclusions

- There are four main types of UK sustainable housing policy: domestic energy-saving measures, sustainability rating schemes, Building Regulations and planning policy.
- The main forms of policy have been exhortation and regulation, and spending has been modest.
- The policy has focused on technical aspects of housing rather than changing lifestyles or social justice.
- Policy has mainly been driven by (a) government commitments to international targets; (b) proactive local governments; and (c) efficient lobbying by the building supply and energy industries, backed up for a period by the WWF campaign. The house building industry has taken a defensive position, objecting to extra costs and reluctantly accepting higher building standards.

Notes

[1] Strictly speaking, this chapter refers to policies applying in England. Scotland has a separate planning system and there are more limited differences between policy in England and Wales, but many grant schemes operate throughout the UK under different names or with different funding channels.

[2] The Brundtland Report defined 'sustainable development' as 'development that meets the needs of the present without compromising the ability of future generations to meet their own needs' (WCED, 1987, p 43) This concept has given rise to much debate (Connelly, 2007). Needs can mean everything, from what people have now to what future generations might want. Development can be economic/quantitative or socioeconomic/qualitative. Desirable features such as social justice and social stability can be treated as intrinsic to sustainability.

[3] The zero carbon standard is extremely high: 'For a new home to be genuinely zero carbon it will need to deliver zero carbon (net over the year) for all energy use in the home – cooking, washing and electronic entertainment devices, as well as space heating, cooling, ventilation, lighting and hot water. This will require renewable or very low carbon energy in addition to high levels of insulation, etc' (CLG, 2006b, para 2.33). This is above the continental 'PassivHaus' standard, to which only 6,000 houses had been built by 2006 (www.passivhaus.org.uk/). This proposal therefore involves a quantum jump. In May 2011 the zero carbon standard was weakened by omitting cooking, washing and domestic electronic equipment energy use.

[4] Stamp Duty Land Tax is levied on the sale of all houses above £125,000. The rates are currently 1 per cent from £125,001, 3 per cent from £250,001 and 4 per cent above £500,000. The maximum value of this exemption per house is thus £15,000. It was later announced that houses above £500,000 would also receive the £15,000 exemption.

[5] For comparative information on the installation of PV systems see IEA, 2010.

[6] For example, energy-saving lights, cycle storage facilities, waste recycling capacity, eco-labelled white goods, renewable/low carbon technologies, a home office, areas of low flood risk, low rainwater run-off, home composting or sound insulation.

[7] CLG found that 29 out of 84 respondents to its consultation supported financial incentives of some kind (2007b, p 27).

[8] I have also benefited from conversations with officials.

[9] A small number of building firms have adopted a more 'green' image. Two of them, Crest Nicholson and Wimpey, say explicitly that they thought it would help with marketing and also enable them to pay less for land bought

from landowners who also had green views. However, both admitted that their decision had not been commercially advantageous (HoCEAC, 2006, Ev 32, 33).

[10] Williams and Dair's (2007) study of obstacles to sustainable housing reported a widespread ignorance of sustainability features and the lack of regulations requiring them.

[11] However, if planning policy was used to set building standards instead of Building Regulations, it is unlikely that enforcement would be much stricter since the monitoring of compliance does not have a high priority in typical council planning departments (Jowell and Millichap, 1987).

[12] See Chapters Four, Six and Eleven, this volume, for further examples of the importance of government in sustainability agendas.

Further reading

HoCEAC (House of Commons Environmental Audit Committee) (2006) *Sustainable housing: A follow-up report. Fifth report, Session 2005–6*, London: The Stationery Office.

Acknowledgement

This chapter is a considerably revised and updated version of the previous article by Chris Pickvance, 2009, 'The construction of UK sustainable housing policy', *Local Environment*, vol 14, pp 329-45, printed with the permission of the publisher, Taylor & Francis Ltd (www.informaworld.com).

It has benefited from presentations at conferences at the Universities of Toulouse and Saint-Etienne and at the International Sociological Association RC21 Conference on Urban Justice and Sustainability, Vancouver.

References

ACE (Association for the Conservation of Energy) (2006) Memorandum submitted to the House of Commons Committee on Environmental Audit, quoted in HoCEAC (2006) Ev 94-5.

CLG (Department for Communities and Local Government) (2004) *Planning Policy Statement 22: Renewable energy*, London: DCLG.

CLG (2005) *Proposals for introducing a code for sustainable homes: A consultation paper*, London: CLG.

CLG (2006a) *Code for sustainable homes: A step change in sustainable home building practice*, London: CLG.

CLG (2006b) *Building a greener future: Towards zero carbon development*, London: CLG.

CLG (2006c) *Consultation supplement to Planning Policy Statement 1: Planning for climate change*, London: CLG.

CLG (2007a) *Homes for the future: More affordable, more sustainable*, Housing Green Paper, London: CLG.

CLG (2007b) *Building a greener future: Towards zero carbon development – Analysis report*, London: CLG.

CLG (2007c) *Building a greener future: A policy statement*, London: CLG.

CLG (2007d) *Planning Policy Statement: Planning and climate change – Supplement to Planning Policy Statement 1*, London: CLG.

CLG (2007e) *Eco-towns prospectus*, London: CLG.

CLG (2009) *Sustainable new homes: The road to zero carbon*, London: CLG.

Connelly, S. (2007) 'Mapping sustainable development as a contested concept', *Local Environment*, vol 12, no 3, pp 259-78.

DECC (Department of Energy and Climate Change) (2009) *The UK Low Carbon Transition Plan*, London: DECC.

DECC (2010) *Impact assessment of feed-in tariffs for small-scale, low carbon, electricity generation*, London: DECC.

Defra (Department of Environment, Food and Rural Affairs)/DTI (Department of Trade and Industry) (2006) *The UK fuel poverty strategy: Fourth annual progress report 2006*, London: Defra/DTI.

DTI (Department of Trade and Industry) (2003) *Our energy future: Creating a low carbon economy*, Energy White Paper, London: DTI.

DTI (2007) *Meeting the energy challenge*, Energy White Paper, London: DTI.

Fineman, S. (2000) 'Enforcing the environment: regulatory realities', *Business Strategy and the Environment*, vol 9, no 1, pp 62-72.

Hajer, M.A. (1995) *The politics of environmental discourse*, Oxford: Clarendon Press.

Hannigan, J. (2006) *Environmental sociology*, London: Routledge.

Hawkins, K. (1984) *Environment and enforcement*, Oxford: Clarendon Press.

HoCEAC (House of Commons Environmental Audit Committee) (2005) *Housing: Building a sustainable future*, First report, Session, 2004-5, London: The Stationery Office.

HoCEAC (2006) *Sustainable housing: A follow-up report*, Fifth report, Session 2005-6, London: The Stationery Office.

House of Commons Environment, Food and Rural Affairs Committee (2009) *Energy efficiency and fuel poverty*, Third report, Session 2008-9, London: The Stationery Office.

IEA (International Energy Agency) (2010) *Trends in photovoltaic applications: Survey report of selected IEA countries between 1992 and 2009* (http://iea-pvps.org).

John, P. (1998) *Analysing public policy*, London: Continuum.

Jowell, J. and Millichap, D. (1987) '"Enforcement": the weakest link in the planning chain', in M.L. Harrison, and R. Mordey (eds) *Planning control: Philosophies and practice*, London: Croom Helm, pp 175-94.

LGA (Local Government Association) (2006a) *Planning policies for sustainable building*, London: LGA.

LGA (2006b) *Planning policies for sustainable building. Guidance for local development frameworks. Support Document 3: Consultation*, London: LGA.

Lowe, P., Clark, J., Seymour, S. and Ward, N. (1997) *Moralizing the environment*, London: University College Press.

ODPM (Office of the Deputy Prime Minister) (2003) *Sustainable Communities Plan: Building for the future*, London: ODPM.

Parker, P., Rowlands, I.H. and Scott, D. (2005) 'Who changes consumption following residential energy evaluations?', *Local Environment*, vol 10, no 2, pp 173-87.

Pickvance, C.G. with Chautard, G. (2006) *A comparative evaluation of incentives, obstacles and perceptions of sustainable housing in Kent and Nord/Pas de Calais*, Canterbury: University of Kent (www.kent.ac.uk/sspssr/ursu.htm).

Priemus, H. (2005) 'How to make housing sustainable? The Dutch experience', *Environment and Planning B*, vol 32, no 1, pp 5-19.

Rawcliffe, P. (1998) *Environmental groups in transition*, Manchester: Manchester University Press.

Rootes, C. (2006) 'Facing south? British environmental movement organisations and the challenge of globalisation', *Environmental Politics*, vol 15, no 5, pp 768-86.

Stern, N. (2006) *Stern Review on the Economics of Climate Change*, London: HM Treasury.

Sunikka, M. (2003) 'Fiscal instruments in sustainable housing policies in the EU and the accession countries', *European Environment*, vol 13, no 4, pp 227-39.

Sweett, C. (2007) *A cost review of the code for sustainable homes*, London: Housing Corporation.

Vogel, D. (1986) *National styles of regulation: Environmental policy in Great Britain and the United States*, Ithaca, NY: Cornell University Press.

WCED (World Commission on Environment and Development) (1987) *Our common future* (Brundtland Report), Oxford: OUP.

Williams, K. and Dair, C. (2007) 'What is stopping sustainable building in England? Barriers experienced by stakeholders in delivering sustainable developments', *Sustainable Development*, vol 15, no 3, pp 135-47.

Section 3

Placing sustainability: contexts and conflicts

Section 1

Placing sustainability concerns within conflicts

Urban ecological accounting: a new calculus for planning urban parks in the era of sustainability

Sarah Dooling

Introduction

This chapter explores the intersections of urban parks and green belts as a form of infrastructure that enhances a city's overall sustainability (in relation to human and ecosystem health), and homeless people, as one of the most economically and politically vulnerable people using parks. When sustainability is defined as providing for the needs of the present populations without compromising the ability of future generations to meet their own needs (WCED, 1987), then homelessness (as those people who lack adequate, or are without, shelter) emerges as a particularly challenging aspect of urban sustainability. In fact, homelessness defies characteristics of sustainability. While parks and green belts can be framed as contributing to social sustainability (by providing access to spaces of recreation and social interaction), ecological sustainability (by setting aside green spaces and parks for carbon sequestration, habitat connectivity and species migration), and economic sustainability (by increasing property values of adjacent properties and neighbourhoods), homelessness detracts from notions of sustainability. Instead, homeless people – being the most visible sign of homelessness – are more easily framed as vulnerable populations, with increased exposure to disease and street violence, resulting in an overall lower life expectancy.

Sustainability, in contrast to vulnerability, is often linked to the concept of resilience (see Chapters Two and Ten, this volume), which refers to the ability of a given system – including urban systems – to respond to change and return to a level of functional stability (Gunderson and Holling, 2002).[1] Through the lens of resilience, with its emphasis on multiple steady states, sustainability can be understood as an ecosystem process, rather than an end result, capable of supporting social and economic aspects (Berkes et al, 2003). These social and economic aspects are coupled with biophysical processes and ecological health (Harvey, 1996; Berkes et al, 2003). As both a condition and a state of being that is produced, maintained and regulated over time, vulnerability erodes the capacity of an individual or city to effectively respond to change (that is, resilience) in ways that meet needs of current and future populations (that is, sustainability). Vulnerability is the antithesis of sustainability.

Why is the intersection between parks and homelessness important to the designing of sustainable cities? Because the primary challenge facing cities is the tenuous negotiations between vulnerabilities and sustainability. The impacts of 'sustainable development' plans and proposals on vulnerable communities are rarely assessed. Scholars argue that the tensions between equity and other sustainability goals are poorly understood (Oden, 2010), and not addressed in plans and proposals intended to enhance a city's sustainability. It is these encounters – of a homeless camp in a green belt or of people sleeping along the wooded banks of an urban creek – that remind society about current limits of the rhetoric of sustainability. Homelessness, as a particular form and condition of vulnerability, is not routinely addressed in the sustainability literature focusing on developed countries. Typically, urban poverty (which focuses on issues of displacement which lead to homelessness) and sustainability are analysed in relation to developing countries (Davis, 1996; Pugh, 1996). Yet, in the US urban homelessness persists as a 'wicked social problem'[2] (Rittel and Webber, 1973; see Chapter Seven, this volume). For some scholars, homelessness is related to the lack of affordable housing (Shinn and Gillespie, 1994; Watson and Austerberry, 1996), co-occurring mental and physical illnesses (Koegel et al, 1996; Hopper et al, 1997), changes in economic opportunities (that is, shifting from industrial to service economy) and living wage issues (Susser, 1996).

Homelessness remains as one of the most politically charged and intractable issues facing cities. As a group of people enacting their private lives daily in public spaces – including parks and green belts – homeless individuals destabilise the perceptions among housed residents of *private* and *public*, of *park* and *home*, of that which is familiar and that which is not (drawing from Freud's notion of the *uncanny*). Thus the intersections of public parks and homelessness serve as a particularly challenging dialectic through which: concepts of urban sustainability can be challenged and re-imagined, in order to articulate the ways in issues of poverty (as a form of social equity) and 'green' are not integrated consistently; and how conceptions and management of parks as a form of infrastructure contribute to sustainability while also contributing to the production of a vulnerable group of users, thus undermining the core goal of sustainability. The goal of this chapter is to articulate the intersections of public parks and homelessness in the local context of Austin, Texas (considered by many to be a green or environmental city) as a means of calling for a more robust conceptualisation of urban sustainability.

Austin: the environmental city and urban sustainability

Austin, Texas, is imagined to be, and framed as, 'the environmental city', both within Texas and the US. Austin, the state capital of Texas, has transformed from a sleepy college in the mid-20th century to a sprawling city in the 21st century. Part of this transformation includes the cultivation of a specific quality of life that marks Austin as unique among cities in Texas, and among cities in the US. The city is bisected by the Colorado River running east to west and bounded by two creeks on the west and east. The confluence of hills and creeks were the geographic features that shaped the early development of the city (Swearingen, 2010). The idea of Austin as the environmental city has been developed, contested and deepened over many decades, and parks play a particular role in this history.

One of the defining points in Austin's environmental history does not have to do with parks *per se*, but with the natural environment writ large. The 'Save Our Springs' (SOS) ordinance is one of the major hallmarks of Austin's identity as an environmental city. Resulting from environmental battles that pitted land speculation and rapidly increasing land values in the 1980s (referred to as the 'Austin Boom') against citizen concern about the impact of development on Austin's watersheds and neighbourhood urban creeks (Swearingen, 2010), the SOS ordinance was passed in 1992. This required future development to be set back from sensitive riparian areas in an effort to limit the amount of impervious cover, and protect water quality within the ecologically sensitive Barton Springs watershed (Trust for Public Land, 2000).[3, 4] The passage of this ordinance, known nation-wide as one of the most stringent water quality protection ordinances at that time, was the largest public show of support for an environmental issue in the city's electoral history (Swearingen, 2010). The SOS ordinance was a critical evolution in perception that Austin was an environmental city, where the natural environment – including urban creeks fed by cold springs, the Colorado River, the fertile soils of blackland prairie to the east and the rolling hills of the Edwards Plateau with its host of rare endemic species to the west – defined a very particular quality of life. Led by community advocates, the SOS campaign was framed as protecting a very special place from unprecedented development pressures, thus symbolising Austin's sense of place around one particular feature (Barton Springs) (Swearingen, 2010). Although the rule-making authority of the SOS was largely stripped away by grandfathering legislation passed by the Texas State legislature in the mid-1990s – that allowed much of the larger subdivisions to be removed from Austin's jurisdiction and thus outside the realm of the SOS ordinance (Swearingen, 2010) – the symbol of the natural environment emerged as an essential piece, if not the foundational piece, of the city's identity.

The effort to protect Barton Springs led to the first 'green city council' in the 1990s, where council candidates successfully ran on quality of life campaigns. The ideology of growth, so prominent in the 1980s, began to lose potency as environmental advocates assumed local positions of political power. In the 1990s, the environmental movement became the main organising structure, and the environment became the main organising symbol (Swearingen, 2010). However, issues other than watershed protection emerged, including energy policy. In 1994, Austin's Green Building programme became a charter member of the US Green Building Council, and energy efficiency became, and remains, a touchstone of environmental activism. Concepts also related to smart growth principles, that attempted to unite environmental and economic concerns, were promoted by the Green Council. Following the results of a commissioned study that outlined Austin's national economic competitiveness in terms of investments in economic, environmental and social equity opportunities, the Green Council began promoting the three-legged stool of sustainability. This situated the role of environmentalists as key players in planning Austin's future with developers. The previous dichotomy of environmentalists opposing developers gave way to a more coordinated effort between environmental and economic concerns.

During this time, the Green Council put forward a bond proposal that requested funding for each leg of the sustainability (referred to as smart growth) stool. Citizens voted to: purchase 15,000 acres of land in the Barton Springs watershed to protect against development; construct a downtown convention centre and a walkway along an urban creek to the centre; and to fund libraries, parks and social services in underserved neighbourhoods (Swearingen, 2010; see Chapter Ten, this volume, for the importance of such infrastructure investment in low-income areas). While the SOS alliance campaigned for downtown development, the business community supported the land acquisition. Environmentalists were concerned about downtown creeks and restoring their ecological functionality; developers, too, were also becoming more interested in downtown (as compared to generating profits through the construction of suburban housing). Tax subsidies and tax breaks were granted to hi-tech corporations who opted to locate downtown instead of over the ecologically sensitive aquifer. Thus emerged Austin's ideas and policies related to urban sustainability.

City in a park

Unlike other cities – including Seattle, Portland and Buffalo – which had park plans designed by the landscape architect Frederick Law Olmsted, Austin did not begin formally planning its park system until the late 1920s. The city purchased its first park in 1840, which was the first of three public squares that are still located in the downtown core (Austin Parks and Recreation Department, undated). Barton Springs, the future location of the popular Barton Springs pool, was purchased in 1918. A series of donations occurred between 1845 and 1929, including an initial 350 acres for what is now the largest metropolitan park in the city. The 1929 Master Plan described Austin, which lacked an industrial economic base, as a primarily cultural and educational city (Swearingen, 2010). A primary role of parks, according to this plan, was to preserve the natural beauty of the geography and the creeks – specifically Waller and Shoal Creeks that bounded the city along the east and west respectively – were features around which to plan for the city's parks. The Recreation Department in the city was established in 1928 with funding provided only for the superintendent and the Department relying extensively on volunteers (Austin Parks and Recreation Department, undated). A shift from a primarily aesthetic emphasis to ideas that parks added economic value to residential neighbourhoods began to be documented in the early 1960s. In a 1958 Planning Commissions report (which then served as the basis for the city's 1961 plan), parks were seen as amenities that stabilised neighbourhoods and protected property investments that would insure that 'Austin will continue to grow to improve its physical environment on the basis of long range public interest' (City of Austin, 1958, p 1).

Yet, the economic and ecological preservation value of city parks was not always upheld, and many parks became vulnerable to the emerging growth ideology that prioritised the construction of highways and urban development. During this time period, dedicated parkland was often given or leased to developers (Swearingen, 2010). Bureaucratic indifference and inadequate funding were two major obstacles to not only acquiring new but also retaining existing parkland. Parks were rarely a high priority for the city council. Administratively, the Recreation Department was subsumed as part of the Public Works Department, which leveraged parks as financial assets by transferring money from parks to public works projects. Residents, especially those with financial and political influence, emerged as a form of civic infrastructure that profoundly influenced the acquisition of parks and green belts (this also casts a new perspective on the limited role for local residents in sustainability planning in the UK identified by several other contributors to this volume). The city's first green belt along Shoal Creek, referred to as a hike and bike trail, was the result of a local woman who used her own financial resources to hire the Parks Department as a contractor to landscape the property. The Parks director during this time (1946-73) was a strong advocate for green belts and parks in downtown. While many city officials and administrators were promoting rapid urban development and economic growth, Beverly Sheffield worked with environmental activists to preserve and extend public land. One of the main efforts of the Sierra Club in the 1960s was fighting against the construction of highway bridges over

Austin's parkland adjacent to creeks; they were only moderately successful. The historic pressures stemming from rapid economic development in a state and city lacking regulatory frameworks to direct and constrain development in relation to the conservation of open space, as well as the persistent pressures related to inadequate funding of the Parks Department, worked in concert to render parks as highly prized amenities that were vulnerable to the city's commitment to expansion.

The Parks Department has been able to acquire large tracts of land, including the Barton Creek green belt, totalling approximately 1,700 acres (Trust for Public Land, 2010); however, the number of downtown parks has remained low and they have suffered from inadequate funding for maintenance. Edwin Waller, the early pioneer who established the location of the city between Shoal and Waller Creeks, set aside four squares (Barnes, undated). Originally designated as parkland, Woolridge Park functioned as the early city's dump until 1909. Historically, Woolridge has been the location of political rallies; it was here that Lyndon Johnson announced his campaign for the US presidency. Between 1950 and 1960, another of these parks was converted into a parking lot, and through negotiations between the Parks Department and Sierra Club conducted in 1974, it was restored as a park (Austin Parks and Recreation Department, undated). Instead of working to acquire additional downtown parks, the Parks Department focused on establishing green belts to link downtown parks, including the Shoal Creek hike and bike trail and the green belt along Waller Creek.

Now, Austin is a city with almost 800,000 residents and the Parks Department manages approximately 16,700 acres of land, including 206 parks, 12 preserves and 26 green belts (Crompton, 2008). This equates to approximately 16.7 per cent of the city's land area per 1,000 residents (Trust for Public Land, 2010). The Parks Department is considered by other cities to be a leader in park systems, and recently earned national certification from the Commission for Accreditation of Parks and Recreation.[5] However, total park expenditure translates to only US$69 per resident (Trust for Public Land, 2010),[6] and the desired goal of having each resident live within one mile of a park or green belt has not been met. Access to public parks in the historically underserved neighbourhoods continues to be limited (Crompton, 2008).

In many ways the history of Austin's parks and green belts is not drastically different from other cities. What is unique about Austin, given its past and current emphasis on sustainability planning, is the lack of strong regulatory frameworks that direct development and redevelopment. States with growth management policies require the development of a comprehensive plan in order to secure funds for municipal services and infrastructure, and to concentrate development within urban growth boundaries. In contrast, Texas lacks enabling legislation to support growth management planning, or even comprehensive planning; it is a weak planning state. In the absence of state policy levers, local plans and ordinances are the only tools localities have available to shape land use. The first comprehensive plan in Austin was developed in 1979; another plan based on extensive public participation was developed in the late 1980s but was never approved by city council. Austin is the fifth fastest growing city in the US (Downtown Austin Alliance, 2010): in the greater Austin metropolitan region population increased approximately 48 per cent during 1990–2000,[7] with projections for an additional 1.3 million people by 2030 (Austin Chamber of Commerce, undated). Questions about how the city will accommodate a rapidly increasing population and future growth have spurred a planning frenzy; currently, there are eight regional plans in the process of being developed, and Austin is once again in the process of developing a comprehensive plan (Gregor, 2010). The city is focusing on the densification of urban neighbourhoods and in particular increasing housing units in the downtown core. This reflects a dominant idea in the development of, and planning for, sustainable cities, that argues that concentrating growth in urban cores will inhibit the outward expansion of residential neighbourhoods and the concomitant expense of providing services and constructing infrastructure. In 2008, just over 5,000 residents lived in downtown; by 2015, the city hopes to have 25,000 residents (Downtown Austin Alliance, undated). Currently, there are 24 condominium developments under construction or planned, which, when completed, will add an additional 4,319 housing units (Downtown Austin Alliance, 2008).

Urban parks and green belts are assuming renewed attention in response to the downtown densification efforts. Over the past 10 years, Woolridge Square, once a gathering place for political rallies and politician speeches, has become a place where homeless people congregate during the day and are given a free early evening meal by a local not-for-profit organisation. Likewise, the Waller Creek green belt and trail, once described as contributing economic and ecological value to downtown, is now described as a ditch used mostly by homeless people for sleeping (Waller Creek Redevelopment Plan, 2008). Along Shoal Creek there are condominium developments that look down onto homeless people's camps tucked away from view alongside the hike and bike trail. As the city attempts to attract residents to the downtown core, homelessness is also receiving renewed interest. While in many ways the intersections of parks and homelessness has a long history in the development and revitalisation of cities, what makes this intersection even more problematic now is how notions of sustainability, and sustainable development, are currently being used to isolate homelessness from larger visions of what constitutes a sustainable city. This, in effect, situates issues of homelessness outside the scope and beyond the purview of what are considered legitimate issues to address in planning for sustainable cities.

Yet, within the context of a deepening national recession, the connections between how parks are valued, designed and managed to create 'sustainable cities', and urban homelessness, becomes particularly acute.

Hard times: homelessness, urban parks and redevelopment in the recession

National estimated increases in homeless populations have been attributed to the economic recession; specific causes include reduced income due to job loss, the lack of affordable housing and housing foreclosures (Bensenia, undated). Approximately 10 per cent of homeless Americans helped by social service agencies in 2009 lost their homes to foreclosure (National Coalition for the Homeless, 2010). Another study estimates that, based on the duration of the current recession, an additional 1.5 million Americans will experience homelessness over the next two years (National Alliance to End Homelessness, 2009). On average, American cities have reported a 12 per cent increase in homeless populations since 2007 (US Conference of Mayors, 2008). These increases come in the wake of local planning efforts (known as the Ten-year Plans to End Homelessness) around the country that were having significant impacts: between 2005 and 2007, the National Alliance to End Homelessness (2009) estimated a 10 per cent reduction nationwide.

Austin has been relatively protected from the economic recession stemming from the mortgage crisis in the US. While many cities are struggling with high rates of foreclosed homes and unemployment, Austin's economy has emerged as the third[8] most robust in the US, with a stable housing market that avoided the bubble and crash cycle and an economy rooted in higher education, government and high technology (Brookings Institute, 2010). In the first fiscal quarter of 2010, Austin's gross metropolitan product was 5.3 per cent, with an unemployment rate of 7.1 per cent (as compared to the national unemployment rate of 9.7 per cent) (Brookings Institute, 2010). The median house price for Austin in 2009 was US$187,400 while the national median house price was US$173,200 (National Association of Realtors, 2009). Characterised as the 'next frontier' (along with eight other metropolitan regions), Austin is portrayed as being economically sustainable in times of global and national economic downturn (Brookings Institute, 2010).

However, similar to the rest of the country, Austin's homeless population has been increasing. Prior to the recession, Austin's estimated homeless population was already increasing, jumping from 3,789 in 2004 to 5,281 in 2007[9] (US Department of Housing and Urban Development, 2004, 2007). A local not-for-profit organisation documented that between 2005 and 2006, 6,242 unique individuals received services from Austin-area homeless service providers (Homeless Management Information Service, undated). The annual One Night Count, which is a concurrent point-in-time street and shelter count, estimated that in 2004 approximately half of Austin's homeless individuals were found downtown (1,900 out of 4,000) (Homeless Count, 2004). Austin's Homeless Task Force estimated that in 2006, approximately 15-20 per cent of the population was chronically homeless, meaning they had been continuously without shelter for at least a year or temporarily homeless at least four times over a three-year period.[10] This local increase is attributed to Austin having the highest housing costs of any city in Texas (Texas A&M Real Estate Center Report, 2005) and low job wages (of the top 10 occupational categories in the Austin area, nearly 30 per cent of the jobs have a median wage under US$10 an hour; WorkSource, undated).

In addition, the State of Texas currently faces a predicted US$21 billion shortfall (Fikac, 2010), and Austin faced a US$28 million shortfall for the 2010–11 municipal budget (Cappola, 2010). Inadequate funding continues to be an impediment for the Parks Department. In response to current and predicted budgetary constraints, a master plan for downtown open spaces and parks has been recently developed (ROMA Austin, 2010). A key element to the plan is the creation of strategic public and private investment strategies to enhance the quality of downtown parks. In an effort to densify downtown, and to make the lifestyle choice to live in the urban core attractive, city officials and developers are prioritising parks as a critical element in creating a sustainable Austin. The redevelopment of Waller Creek is also a central focus of the city's agenda to clean up downtown and restore an ecologically degraded creek. In many ways, addressing the eroded quality of downtown parks and the ecological degradation of urban creeks represent conventional strategies in creating walkable, liveable, vibrant and (socially and ecologically) healthy urban cores – which are all key concepts in the creation of sustainable cities. However, a closer analysis of the parks master plan and the Waller Creek redevelopment proposal reveals the inconsistencies between holistic notions of sustainability and the exclusion of the most vulnerable human populations to these proposed changes.

Downtown parks and open space master plan

Austin's downtown parks are smaller and more highly programmed than those in the suburbs. The use and design of the downtown parks are described as not promoting the kinds of activities consistent with dense, mixed-use areas as they are poorly programmed for families and lacking a coherent design identity (ROMA Austin, 2010). As a result, the parks are described as having 'no regular users that can be ... stewards' and have been 'taken over by the homeless population' (ROMA Austin, 2010, p 34).

The master plan evolved in response to the undervaluing and underfunding of Austin's downtown parks over the past decades. Recognising these parks as unique in their management strategies compared to other parks in less urban neighbourhoods requires renewed 'advocacy and leadership' (ROMA Austin, 2010, p 5). The larger vision of downtown, which the parks master plan seeks to advance, identifies the 'need to bolster Downtown's competitive advantage in the region, to support compact and liveable high-density development ... where everyone is welcome' (ROMA Austin, 2010, p 5). The vision of the parks master plan states:

> Austin's downtown parks and open spaces will augment our identity and bolster our economy by creating signature, high-quality places that serve the community's diverse population, connect it to nature and provide it with unique opportunities for active and passive recreation and entertainment. This will be achieved through strategic public, private and non-profit investments in parks and open space improvements and new parks, synchronized with a high standard of programming and upkeep. (ROMA Austin, 2010, p 5)

Five challenges are identified: chronic underfunding of capital, operations and maintenance budgets; limited staffing to address downtown parks; limited stewardship; poorly designed parks; and the lack of coordinated planning with surrounding properties (ROMA Austin, 2010). As a strategy to deal with reduced and inadequate funding for city parks, public–private partnerships are defined as one of the guiding principles associated with achieving 'great public spaces' (ROMA Austin, 2010, p 15). While the Parks Department recognises that 'public revenues remain the essential component of a strong parks system', they also claim that 'additional sources of funds should always be pursued in order to achieve maximum leverage' (ROMA Austin, 2010, p 26). Downtown parks, in particular, require an even higher level of investment and management oversight than other parks in the system and rarely depend on public funds alone. Referring to examples in other cities (including the High Line Project and Central Park in New York City), where public funds were complemented with for-profit businesses, not-for-profit groups and private fundraising, the master plan identifies the creation of corporate and private sponsorships as a key implementation strategy for the creation of great public spaces. The merging of funds blurs the distinction between publicly and privately managed spaces, and emphasises the increasingly closer alignment of government and business interests.

The first policy priority seeks to reduce the impact of the homeless population on downtown parks, although the impact is not explicitly defined. Woolridge Square, one of the original downtown squares, is prioritised within the plan; this park is a gathering place for homeless individuals and is also a site for a local not-for-profit social outreach ministry that distributes 75 sack lunches daily around Austin. The lines of homeless people waiting for food have grown longer over the past two years. Given that the plan defines a key role of downtown parks as promoting economic development and increasing property values, the exclusionary treatment of homeless people is not surprising, and reflects strategies in other cities (Gibson, 2003; Dooling, 2009). The plan defines the success of Austin's downtown as dependent on a 'public realm and a downtown park system that can be enjoyed by the whole community' (ROMA Austin, 2010, p 14); however, it is clear that the intention of the plan, and of the Parks Department, is to remove all visible signs of homeless people and homelessness from the public realm.

Waller Creek redevelopment proposal

While the parks master plan focuses on parks as conveying economic benefits and while also promoting the densification of downtown, the Waller Creek redevelopment proposal focuses on conveying ecological and economic benefits. Waller is one of the most densely developed creeks in the city, with just over 50 per cent impervious cover (Scoggins, 2002). Most of the development was completed before the 1950s and in 1974 Waller was designated as the 'most seriously polluted of Austin's urban creek' (City of Austin, 1975). Wastewater lines are located down the middle of the channel in many places and illegal dry weather discharges have been observed throughout the storm sewer system. The water flow starts and stops along the approximately seven-mile length of the creek; some sections are persistently dry while other sections have intermittent flow. Loss of base flow detrimentally impacts aquatic life while it is also perceived as aesthetically displeasing (City of Austin Watershed Protection and Development Review, undated). According to the City of Austin ordinances, Waller Creek is considered an urban watershed and thus falls into one of the desired development zones in which restrictions on water quality or impervious cover are not applied. The creek contributes more than 10 per cent of the Town Lake (created by the damming of the Colorado River) load of the common run-off pollutants while only representing 4 per cent of the Town Lake drainage area (City of Austin, 2001). Analysis of 10 years of water quality data shows that there has been little to no significant changes in water chemistry and that Waller is consistently in the bottom 30 per cent of water quality among Austin creeks (Scoggins, 2002).

The most important aspect of Waller Creek, from the city's perspective, is that it is within a 100-year floodplain; numerous severe floods in 1915, 1985 and 2007 have resulted in deaths (Willis, 2010). The local media recently portrayed the creek as: '… a mess. There's trash from homeless folks who camp-out nearby. Trees are uprooted and erosion has washed away virtually everything' (Willis, 2010, p 1). Previous floods have removed most of the soil and bank erosion stabilisation efforts. In addition, the risk of flooding has deterred development within the floodplain; the major goal of the redevelopment proposal is to remove one million square feet of land (equivalent to 28 acres), thus 'making more room' for development and economic activity (Willis, 2010, p 2). The Waller Creek Master Plan (developed in tandem with the redevelopment proposal, and approved by City Council in 2010) reads:

> Waller Creek still remains essentially a negative element in the city, plagued by flooding, homeless encampments, pollution and neglect. It is an ecologically and sociably unsustainable environment still burdened by past attitudes which relegated the lowest value uses to the creek, or replaced it with more 'exciting' but aggressively artificial reinterpretations of place. (Waller Creek Master Plan, 2010, p 2)

In 2008, the city initiated a community process for articulating a vision for redevelopment. The vision focused on replacing the creek from essentially a storm channel to 'a more ecologically diverse, authentic and resilient environment, capable of serving multiple roles simultaneously … the value of the creek will be extended to the surrounding community' (Waller Creek Master Plan, 2010, p 2). Approved in 2010, the redevelopment project addresses flood control, base flow and economic development within the former floodplain. A storm water by-pass tunnel, dropped below the creek bed, has been approved. The mile-long tunnel will begin with an inlet structure at a park a mile from the river and enter the Colorado River through an outlet structure. A water pump, located in the park, will maintain constant water flow during the dry season. The initial cost estimate for the tunnel project is approximately US$127 million (2006 dollars) (Waller Creek Tunnel Project, undated).[11] It is important to note that the tunnel project only focuses on the most urban part of the creek; upstream impacts and issues are not part of the redevelopment focus. In addition to the tunnel project, the Waller Creek Master Plan emphasises improving the quality of open space along the creek corridor by creating pedestrian and bicycle links to the Colorado River and to the University of Texas (located just north of the park). It is anticipated that along the green belt that businesses, including restaurants and music venues, will attract people and enhance economic vitality.

Similar to Woolridge Park, the Waller Creek green belt is used predominantly by homeless people wanting to sleep, eat and avoid interacting with the Austin Police Department. Following other cities (for example, Las Vegas and Seattle), Austin voted in 2005 for a no–sit, no–lie ordinance that is intended, according to city officials, to keep doorways free, and not intended to explicitly discriminate against homeless individuals.

The ordinance makes it illegal to sit, sleep, lie down or block entrances to businesses (McHenry, 2010). Local business owners and community association members consider sitting down an issue because 'it also promotes panhandling', which discourages potential customers (McHenry, 2010, p 1). Also similar to the Woolridge Park Master Plan, eradicating homeless people is an explicit part of the Waller Creek Master Plan. The Downtown Parks Master Plan, which also addresses the Waller Creek green belt, states that the Austin Police Department 'should provide more consistent enforcement of existing anti-camping and vagrancy laws that prohibit overnight camps within the corridor' (ROMA Austin, 2010, p 58). With an estimated shortage of approximately 1,900 supportive housing units city-wide (Ball, 2010) and a downtown shelter with only 100 beds, many homeless individuals resort to living outside (G. Gibson, Director, Austin Travel County Integral Care, personal communication, 2 September 2010). Increasingly, encampments are appearing on private property with absentee landlords; occasionally verbal contracts are made between the campers and the property owner (G. Gibson, Director, Austin Travel County Integral Care, personal communication, 2 September 2010). These camps are composed mostly of chronically homeless men, and recently these camps have become more permanent and more structurally elaborate (G. Gibson, Director, Austin Travel County Integral Care, personal communication, 2 September 2010). With the increase in construction downtown, homeless people are beginning to move out to outlying areas. The Waller Creek green belt is one of the last remaining transitional places where homeless people can sleep, sit down and eat without risking being ticketed for violating the no-sit no-lie ordinance.

Leaving Waller Creek and the green belt in its current state is not desirable, for both ecological and social reasons. Although limits to the master plan and the inadequacies to the tunnel project are debated, the ecological conditions the redevelopment effort intends to address (that is, reduce flooding, regulate storm water and improve water quality) are critical components to the creation of a more sustainable city. What is deeply problematic, however, is the intentional focus on the removal of a vulnerable population of people who have the fewest options and resources to respond to future changes. The plan, which is being hailed as contributing to Austin's image of, and experience as, a green and economically vibrant city, reflects a consistent pattern among many plans and policies aimed at urban sustainability – that is, the failure to rigorously address issues of social equity, a point made, in different contexts, by, for example, Mark Whitehead and Chris Pickvance in their chapters in this volume (Chapters Two and Eight respectively). Due to the very fact homeless people are users of urban green spaces, including parks, issues of social equity demand to be addressed. By failing to address homelessness as a systemic problem that is embedded in the planning for parks and green spaces, and homeless people as current users of park spaces, sustainability plans serve to ultimately undermine the very goals of integrating ecology, economics and equity.

Changing the calculus of planning: sustainability, vulnerability and urban ecological accounting

The intersections of homelessness and public parks pose a particularly difficult challenge for policy makers, planners and the housed public. Parks are associated with active and passive recreation; they are understood to increase property values and the desirability of neighbourhoods; they are created and mapped to reduce habitat fragmentation and enhance carbon sequestration (Sutton, 1971; Cranz, 1982; Young, 1995; Low et al, 2005). Situated in Austin's history, parks and green spaces are equated with ecological protection and ecosystem health; they are also equated with a unique quality of life where people feel connected to nature. In many ways, the perceptions and values of parks stimulate the uniting and collaborating of housed residents and park staff, as well as for-profit companies and not-for-profit agencies that have invested in the stewardship of particular parks. In contrast, homelessness, and homeless people, possesses a deeply polarising effect, which is related to ideological notions of home, and in the case of parks, ideological notions of public space (Dooling, 2009). With the lack of permanent supportive and affordable housing, and unsafe and occasionally unhealthy conditions in shelters, oftentimes homeless individuals opt to remain outside because all other options are inadequate (Dooling, 2009). As individuals who enact their private lives in public because they have no place to go, homeless people confuse the boundaries between private and public, making housed residents uncomfortable. In the Austin context, the alignment of economic and ecological interests related to the planning of downtown parks and green belts work to define and treat homelessness as an issue primarily about safety (that is, homeless people decrease experiences of safety for other park users) and that the concentration of homeless people in parks excludes other (housed) park users. Ultimately, the alignment of economic and ecological interests works to increase the vulnerability of homeless people by planning to remove their access to food (that is, the mobile meal programme at Woolridge Park) and to shelter (that is, in the Waller Creek green belt) that is currently found in specific city parks. With the increased construction of condominiums in formerly wooded areas of downtown, there are fewer public (and private) places for homeless people to enact their daily lives.

However, theories and ideas related to sustainability are founded on the idea of integrating ecological, economic and social equity issues. In the Austin context, the parks master plan and the Waller Creek redevelopment proposal both fail to integrate one of the most serious social equity issues associated with the recession – urban homelessness. What each plan does, in effect, is ultimately reinforce a narrowly defined notion of homelessness as a social equity issue (as individuals to expel and regulate) that is separate from the ecological and economic aspect of public parks and green belts. Parks Department staff and community residents clearly consider dealing with homelessness – other than excluding or regulating it out of public spaces – as beyond the purview of master planning and redevelopment efforts; they perceive homeless people as users to remove from park spaces. Yet, for sustainability planning to reflect theories about sustainability, these difficult dialectics between social equity and the environment – including homelessness and public parks – must be addressed.

Some scholars argue that the integrated vision of sustainability is, at best, only approximated through constant negotiation of conflicts between goals related to economics, ecology and social equity (Campbell 1996). Specifically, in the development and implementation of urban plans intended to enhance sustainability, issues of social equity are often neglected (Campbell, 1996). The challenge, then, is not only to integrate social equity into sustainability-related plans explicitly and meaningfully, but to also recognise the deeply complex relationships between equity, economics and ecology (that is, between public parks and homelessness). Oden (2010) proposes framing the lack of attention to equity in discussions of urban sustainability using Walzer's concept of 'complex inequality', where power in one realm of urban politics crosses over into another realm, resulting in the systematic exclusion of marginalised groups (Walzer, 1983). In this way, local political agendas are set that reflect the simultaneous interest of members of urban governing regimes wanting to intensify development while also defining the terms of development to minimise or neglect goals related to equity. Similar to the concept of complex inequality, researchers have demonstrated that vulnerability to one type of harm often increases the likelihood of being vulnerable to other sources of harm. Findlay (2005) refers to 'vulnerable spatialities', where people and places are made vulnerable and maintained in a state of vulnerability through a series of implemented political economic agendas. In the Austin context, the alignment of economic and ecological interests related to the planning of downtown parks and green belts work together to exacerbate the exclusion and expulsion of homeless people, thus contributing to their overall vulnerability within a context that frames homelessness as mostly related to safety and constraining the use of parks for housed residents.

Vulnerability and sustainability are two faces of the same coin related to the future of cities. Designing and planning for resilient cities rests on minimising vulnerability (for example, networks of green belts to reduce habitat fragmentation, displacement funds to mitigate impacts on residents who lose housing resulting from the construction of condominiums) by recognising the deep complexities of spatial dynamics resulting from relationships among economics, ecology and social equity. Current scholarship related to vulnerability calls for assessing exposure to harm and hazards in relation to both social and ecological dimensions, thus reflecting the similar concept of holism in designing and planning for sustainable cities (Pelling, 2003). Specifically, conceptualising vulnerability as an ongoing *process* highlights the historical origins of current problems (Hogan and Marandola, 2005). The production of vulnerability is an antonym of sustainability; the production of vulnerability challenges the assumption that plans and redevelopment proposals generate benefits for all community residents, both existing and future.

It is not enough to simply call for the inclusion of social equity issues into plans and redevelopment proposals, especially related to the intersections of public parks and homelessness. What is needed is the recognition that not only is homelessness a housing issue, but that public spaces, including parks and green belts, are also related to, and deeply embedded in, urban homelessness as an urban ecological phenomenon. It is in the institutional framing and political engagement of these intersections where the development of plans related to sustainability fall woefully short in addressing 'complex inequalities' compared to the theories of sustainability. In order to critically address and integrate social equity relationships, including urban homelessness, into strategies for future design and use of public spaces a new calculus of planning must be developed. Drawing from the concept of vulnerability as a condition that is produced over time can alert planners to analytic strategies that can be leveraged in the analysis of potential impacts related to proposed plans and policies. In Austin, as in other cities, sustainability plans are framed in terms of change that targets future users of a revitalised green belt or downtown parks. While this future orientation in and of itself is not problematic, what is problematic is the lack of analysis these proposed policies and plans have for existing *vulnerable* populations.

In Austin, a city that lacks an institutionalised larger vision of future growth and development, the challenge remains how to develop and implement plans that are able to critically engage issues of social equity in the context of powerful economic and political forces that conspire to limit concerns of social equity. Vulnerability assessments are one analytic strategy that might lead to creative strategies to integrate issues of social equities, ecology and economics. Assessing redevelopment proposals and master plans both in terms of desired outcomes and predictions for enhancing ecological function and economic vitality with an analysis of potential impacts on current vulnerable populations is a form of urban ecological accounting (Dooling, 2009; see Chapter Four, this volume, for a discussion of calculating and constructing the carbon city). While urban ecological accounting does not necessarily transform the ideological notions of *public* and *private* urban spaces, or of *home* and *homelessness*, which drive narrowly defined concepts of sustainability in the development of plans and proposals, it does offer an analytic strategy that can be leveraged in political and institutional processes of planning for sustainable cities. Assuming the Brundtland Commission's (WCED, 1987) vision of sustainability as meeting the needs of the current generation without compromising the needs of future generations, urban ecological accounting holds the potential for a robust analysis of needs related to poverty. Assuming Campbell's (1996) argument that sustainability is fundamentally about the assessment of trade-offs, then urban ecological accounting can make those trade-offs explicit and transparent in the planning process.

Conclusions

Austin's history reveals a city whose residents value ecological processes in their rapidly developing urban landscape; this history also reveals how leadership among residents emerged in response to ensuring the experience of a unique quality of life that values the role of parks and green spaces in connecting people to the environment and to the economic vitality of the city. Yet, ecological change is never socially neutral, and social change is never ecologically neutral (Harvey, 1996). This chapter is a call for planners to resist the 'mutually exclusionary discourses' (Harvey, 1996, p 357) of ecology and social equity by integrating vulnerability assessments into an urban ecological accounting strategy. If sustainability is to be a meaningful guiding heuristic that influences the future growth of cities, then recognising the deeply dialectical relationships among, for example, public parks and homelessness, is the first step towards creating cities that take seriously designing and maintaining spaces of health, vitality and prosperity.

Key conclusions

- The intersections of urban parks and homelessness are some of the most intractable challenges facing cities today.
- Sustainability, as a conceptual framework, espouses the maximum integration of economic, equity and environmental components. Yet, in practice, realising the full integration of the three components of sustainability is thwarted by powerful influences of politics, economics and value systems.
- While it is clear that homelessness and parks are intimately connected, they are maintained as non-overlapping and unrelated phenomena in planning for sustainable cities. The disconnection results in a persistently fragmented, non-ecological approach to a fundamentally ecological system.

Notes

[1] The engineering concept of resilience refers to a system's ability to resist disturbance and speed of return to the steady state equilibrium point. A second definition, referred to as ecosystem resilience, emphasises that there are conditions in a given system that exist far from a state of equilibrium and that instabilities can flip a system into another regime of behaviour. Resilience in this case is measured as the magnitude of disturbance that can be absorbed before the system changes its structure (Gunderson and Holling, 2002). For the purposes of this chapter, I refer to ecosystem resilience.

[2] Rittel and Webber (1973) define a 'wicked social problem' for the field of urban planning as having no definitive formulation, no stopping rule, with solutions that are better or worse (rather than right or wrong), lacking an immediate test of a solution, and considered to be a symptom of an oftentimes larger problem.

[3] The ordinance has been challenged in court. In 1995, some of the larger subdivisions were removed from Austin's jurisdiction by a bill passed by the Texas State legislature. Another bill allowed for owners of more than 1,000 acres to create a 'water quality protection zone' that would be exempt from the SOS ordinance. The Texas Supreme Court, however, ruled that water quality protection zones were unconstitutional (Trust for Public Land, 2000).

[4] Barton Springs, located within the Edwards Aquifer, has been identified as the most endangered aquifer in Texas, being highly vulnerable to pollution because of its relatively small size, geology (highly porous) and land development pressures (Trust for Public Land, 2000).

[5] To be accredited, a city must meet 36 fundamental standards and over 85 per cent of additional standards. Fundamental standards are categorised as: agency authority, role and responsibility; planning; organisation and administration; human resources; finance; programme and services management; facility and land use management; security and public safety; risk management; and evaluation and research. Austin met the fundamental standards and obtained 97 per cent of the additional standards.

[6] Total park expenditures per resident range from US$259 (Washington, DC) to US$26 (Tulsa, Oklahoma) (Trust for Public Land, 2010).

[7] In 1990, there were 585,051 residents; in 2000, this number jumped to 1,249,763 (Austin Chamber of Commerce, undated).

[8] Albany, New York and Augusta, Georgia are ranked as the first two strongest-performing metropolitan areas by the Brookings Institute's Metropolitan Policy Program in 2010. Economic performance was measured as gross metropolitan product, which is defined as the market value of all goods and services produced within a given metropolitan area. The Brookings Institute report identified 21 metropolitan areas that exhibited stable housing and labour markets and posted gains in economic activity.

[9] Numbers are based on US Census Bureau data for 2004 and 2007.

[10] This is definition of chronically homeless as established by the US Department of Housing and Urban Development.

[11] A tax increment financing (TIF) district has been established and will be effective for 20 years. Property values are expected to rise with the reduction of flood risk. The taxes collected on the increased value of properties will pay for the tunnel project (and not for the improvement of the green belt).

Further reading

Campbell, S. (1996) 'Green cities, growing cities, just cities? Urban planning and the contradictions of sustainable development', *Journal of the American Planning Association*, vol 62, no 3, pp 296-312.

Cranz, G. (1989) *The politics of park design*, Cambridge, MA: The MIT Press.

Crompton, J. (2008) 'Empirical evidence of the contributions of park and conservation lands to environmental sustainability: the key to repositioning the parks field', *World Leisure*, vol 50, no 3, pp 154-72.

Harvey, D. (1996) *Justice, nature and the geography of difference*, Oxford: Blackwell Publishing.

Low, S., Taplin, D. and Scheld, S. (2005) *Rethinking urban parks: Public space and cultural diversity*, Austin, TX: University of Texas Press.

References

Austin Chamber of Commerce (undated) *Population and population growth* (www.austinchamber.com/do-business/greater-austin/greater-austin-profile/population.php).

Austin Parks and Recreation Department (undated) *A living legacy: Honoring our past, celebrating our present and creating our future 1928–2003*, Austin, TX: Austin Parks and Recreation Department.

Ball, A. (2010) 'Low-cost housing for homeless remains in short supply', *American Statesman*, 3 July (www.statesman.com/news/local/low-cost-housing-for-homeless-remains-in-short-784629.html).

Barnes, S. (undated) 'Historic downtown parks. Austin, Texas' (www.austinparks.org/Downtown/ParksWiFi.html?history.html~mainFrame).

Bensenia, L. (undated) *Issue brief 14: Homeless today*, Alexandria, VA: CAF America.

Berkes, F., Colding, J. and Folke, C. (2003) *Navigating social-ecological systems: Building resilience for complexity and change*, Cambridge: Cambridge University Press.

Brookings Institute (2010) *Metromonitor: Tracking economic recession and recovery in America's 100 largest metropolitan areas* (www.brookings.edu/~/media/Files/Programs/Metro/metro_monitor/2010_09_metro_monitor/0915_metro_monitor.pdf).

Campbell, S. (1996) 'Green cities, growing cities, just cities? Urban planning and the contradictions of sustainable development', *Journal of the American Planning Association*, vol 62, no 3, pp 296-312.

Cappola, S. (2010) 'Austin faces $28 million budget shortfall', *American Statesman*, 21 April (www.statesman.com/news/local/austin-faces-28-million-budget-shortfall-597404.html).

City of Austin (1958) *Planning Commission report*, Austin, TX: City of Austin.

City of Austin (1975) *Preliminary ecological assessment of Waller Creek, under the Comprehensive Drainage Plan and Study*, Prepared by URS/Forrest and Cotton, Inc and Espey, Huston and Associates, Inc, CIP project no 7029 0, Austin, TX: City of Austin.

City of Austin (2001) *Watershed protection master plan: Phase 1 Watersheds report*, COA-WPD 2001-02, Austin, TX: City of Austin.

Cranz, G. (1989) *The politics of park design*, Cambridge, MA: The MIT Press.

Crompton, J. (2008) *Park location and amenities in Austin, Texas*, Austin, TX: School of Public Affairs, University of Texas.

Davis, M. (1996) 'The political ecology of famine: the origins of the Third World', in R. Peet and M. Watts (eds) *Liberation ecologies: Environment, development, social movements*, New York: Routledge, pp 48-63.

Dooling, S. (2009) 'Ecological gentrification: a research agenda exploring justice in the city', *International Journal of Urban and Regional Research*, vol 33, no 3, pp 621-39.

Downtown Austin Alliance (2008) *Downtown condominium study*, Austin, TX: Downtown Austin Alliance.

Downtown Austin Alliance (2010) *Austin: 5th largest growing city*, Austin, TX: Downtown Austin Alliance.

Downtown Austin Alliance (undated) *Predicting Austin's future growth*, Austin, TX: Downtown Austin Alliance.

Fikac, P. (2010) 'Projected state budget shortfall reaches $21 billion', *Houston and Texas News: Austin Bureau*, 14 September (www.chron.com/disp/story.mpl/metropolitan/7199592.html).

Findlay, A.M. (2005) 'Editorial: Vulnerable spatialities', *Population, Space and Place*, vol 11, no 6, pp 429-39.

Gibson, T. (2003) *Securing the spectacular city: The politics of revitalization and homelessness in downtown Seattle*, Lanham, MD: Lexington Books.

Gregor, K. (2010) 'Plans in play: the big eight', *The Austin Chronicle*, 16 July (www.austinchronicle.com/gyrobase/Issue/story?oid=oid%3A1056094).

Gunderson, L. and Holling, C.S. (2002) *Panarchy: Understanding transformations in human and natural systems*, Washington, DC: Island Press.

Harvey, D. (1996) *Justice, nature and the geography of difference*, Oxford: Blackwell Publishing.

Hogan, D.J. and Marandola, E. (2005) 'Toward an interdisciplinary conceptualization of vulnerability', *Population, Space and Place*, vol 11, no 6, pp 455-71.

Homeless Count (2004) *Austin's Homeless Task Force*, Austin, TX: Homeless Count.

Homeless Management Information System (undated) *Plan to end chronic homelessness in Austin/Travis County*, Austin, TX: Chronic Homelessness Working Group and Community Action Network's Homeless Task Force.

Hopper, K., Jost, J., Hay, T., Welber, S. and Haugland, G. (1997) 'Homelessness, severe mental illness, and the institutional circuit', *Psychiatric Services*, vol 48, no 5, pp 659-64.

Koegel, P., Burnam, M. and Baumohl, J. (1996) 'The causes of homelessness', in J. Baumohl (ed) *Homelessness in America*, Phoenix, AZ: Oryx Press, pp 24-33.

Low, S., Taplin, D. and Scheld, S. (2005) *Rethinking urban parks: Public space and cultural diversity*, Austin, TX: University of Texas Press.

McHenry, C. (2010) '"No sit, no lie" ordinance frustrating. City Council committee recommends changes', *Austin News*, 17 August (www.kxan.com/dpp/news/local/no-sit-no-lie-ordinance-frustrating).

National Alliance to End Homelessness (2009) 'Homelessness looms as potential outcome of recession', Federal Policy Brief, 14 January.

National Association of Realtors (2009) *Austin-Round Rock area: Local market report* (www.realtor.org/wps/wcm/connect/f326c38041b373ba8917fda3819af93a/lmr_tx_austin_Q22010.pdf?MOD=AJPERES&CACHEID=f326c38041b373ba8917fda3819af93a).

National Coalition for the Homeless (2010) *Foreclosure to homelessness 2009: The forgotten victims of the subprime crisis*, Washington, DC: National Coalition for the Homeless.

Oden, M. (2010) 'Equity: the forgotten "E" in sustainability', in S.A. Moore (ed) *Pragmatic sustainability: Theoretical and practical tools*, New York: Routledge.

Pelling, M. (2003) 'Paradigms of risk', in M. Pelling (ed) *Natural disasters and development in a globalizing world*, New York: Routledge, pp 3-16.

Pugh, C. (ed) (1996) *Sustainability, the environment, and urbanization*, Sterling, VA: Earthscan Publications Limited.

Rittel, H. and Webber, M. (1973) 'Dilemmas in a general theory of planning', *Policy Sciences*, vol 4, no 2, p 155-69.

ROMA Austin (2010) *Draft: Downtown parks and open space master plan*, Austin, TX: ROMA Austin.

Scoggins, M. (2002) *Waller Creek status report 2002*, Austin, TX: City of Austin Watershed Protection.

Shinn, M. and Gillespie, C. (1994) 'The roles of housing and poverty in the origins of homelessness', *American Behavioral Scientist*, vol 37, no 4, pp 505-21.

Susser, I. (1996) 'The construction of poverty and homelessness in US cities', *Annual Review of Anthropology*, vol 25, pp 411-35.

Sutton, S. (ed) (1971) *Civilizing American cities: A selection of Frederick Law Olmsted's writings on city landscapes*, Cambridge, MA: The MIT Press.

Swearingen, W. (2010) *Environmental city: People, place, politics and the meaning of modern Austin*, Austin, TX: University of Texas Press.

Texas A&M Real Estate Center Report (2005) *Market report 2005* (http:// recenter.tamu.edu/mreports/2005/AustinRRock.pdf).

Trust for Public Land (2000) *2000 watershed report* (www.tpl.org/tier3_cdl. cfm?content_item_id=917&folder_id=745).

Trust for Public Land (2010) *2010 City Park facts* (www.tpl.org/publications/ books-reports/ccpe-publications/city-park-facts-report-2010.html).

US (United States) Conference of Mayors (2008) *Hunger and homelessness survey: A status report on hunger and homelessness in America's cities*, Washington, DC: US Conference of Mayors.

US Department of Housing and Urban Development (2004) *Continuum of care assistance programs*, Washington, DC: US Department on Housing and Urban Development.

US Department of Housing and Urban Development (2007) *Continuum of care assistance programs*, Washington, DC: US Department of Housing and Urban Development.

Waller Creek Master Plan (undated) (www.ci.austin.tx.us/wallercreek/ wcmp_home.htm).

Waller Creek Redevelopment Plan (2008) (www.ci.austin.tx.us/ wallercreek/).

Waller Creek Tunnel Project (undated) (www.ci.austin.tx.us/wallercreek/ wctp_home.htm).

Walzer, M. (1983) *Spheres of justice: A defense of pluralism and equality*, New York: Basic Books.

Watson, S. and Austerberry, H. (1996) *Housing and homelessness: A feminist perspective*, London: Routledge and Kegan Paul.

WCED (World Commission on Environment and Development) (1987) *Our common future*, Report of the World Commission on Environment and Development, New York: WCED.

Willis, C. (2010) 'Waller creek could get a facelift: before upgrade, Waller needs major cleanup', *Austin News*, 5 June (www.kxan.com/dpp/news/local/kxan-austin-waller-creek-could-get-a-facelift).

WorkSource (undated) quoted in C. Smith (2006) 'Homelessness: the big picture', *The Austin Chronicle*, 15 December, Austin, TX.

Young, T. (1995) 'Modern urban parks', *Geographical Review*, vol 85, no 4, pp 535-51.

ten

Neighbourhood sustainability: residents' perceptions and perspectives

John Flint

Introduction

Two defining characteristics of UK policy rationales linked to sustainability have been an emphasis on neighbourhoods and communities as the arenas in, and through which, sustainability will be achieved and a focus on the social sustainability of deprived urban areas (ODPM, 2003; Raco, 2007; Manzi et al, 2010). In these rationales, physical renewal and housing regeneration programmes have been allied to attempts to strengthen the cohesion and fabric of the social dynamics within neighbourhoods and, to a lesser extent, the connectivity between neighbourhoods. However, as Manzi et al (2010) suggest, the conceptualisation of social sustainability remains weak, and there is very limited evidence to underpin key policy techniques such as building mixed communities or enhancing social capital. This chapter seeks to complement the analysis and critique of policy presented in the other chapters of this volume by exploring how residents themselves understand and conceptualise neighbourhood change and the components of, and prospects for, ensuring that localities are sustainable in economic, social and environmental terms (see also Bashir and Flint, 2010).

The chapter presents qualitative evidence from six low-income neighbourhoods in Britain to explore residents' perceptions of, and perspectives on, neighbourhood change and sustainability. It begins with an overview of previous research findings and key policy concepts and a brief description of the research methodology. It then describes the drivers, symbols and indicators of sustainability identified by residents and the impacts of change on them. Finally, the chapter presents residents' conceptualisations of how neighbourhood sustainability may be achieved or enhanced and the policy implications of these findings.

Neighbourhood change and sustainability

It has long been established that conceptualisations of neighbourhood sustainability need to be viewed within a framework of neighbourhoods having 'careers' during which they are subject to periods of stability or transformation and trajectories of growth or decline (Park et al, 1925; Zorbaugh, 1929; Jacobs, 1961). The current sociological and political focus on neighbourhood sustainability is, in part, driven by a belief that the scale and pace of change within 'liquid modernity' (Bauman, 2000) or the 'vertigo' of 'late modernity' (Young, 2007) have led to a widespread 'ontological insecurity' (Giddens, 1984) among individuals as their previous certainties and sense of place and belonging, and the localities where they live, are subject to rapid transformation and reconfiguration as a result of contemporary social and economic forces (Hall, 2007).

Although such narratives tend to somewhat overlook previous historical periods of similar anxiety and fluid neighbourhood conditions (see Hunt, 2004; Overy, 2009), a number of processes have impacted on lower income neighbourhoods in the UK and elsewhere. These include the residualisation of neighbourhoods, with growing concentrations of disadvantaged populations and social problems (Murie, 1997); the gentrification of particular working-class districts (Martin, 2005; Hall, 2007); rapid population turnover (Livingston et al, 2008); and major changes to areas' housing tenure mix (Atkinson and Kintrea, 2001; see Chapters Five and Eight, this volume, for a further discussion of housing) and ethnic profile (Watt, 2006; Hall, 2007).

Previous research has found that lower income groups are more likely to state that their neighbourhood has deteriorated (Burrows and Rhodes, 2008; Feitjen and van Ham, 2008), and studies have identified complex narratives of neighbourhood decline, weakening social conditions, community fragility and the loss of landmark buildings, shops, facilities and work places (Andersen and Munck, 1999; Wood and Vamplew, 1999; Charlesworth, 2000; Watt, 2006; Hall, 2007; Blokland, 2008; Robertson et al, 2008). These narratives often contrast a previous 'golden age' of neighbourhoods (Ravetz, 2001; Watt, 2006) with what Martin (2005, p 16) terms 'a constellation of material issues that residents perceive as impeding their day to day existence'. Importantly, even positive perceptions of neighbourhoods (grounded in emotional attachment, satisfaction with conditions, social and familial networks and ontological security) are often qualified by awareness that the current situation may not be sustainable due to contemporary processes of change (Shon, 2007).

The area effects literature has sought to demonstrate the impacts of changes to the physical, environmental, economic, social and cultural characteristics and dynamics of neighbourhoods on their sustainability (see Ellen and

Turner, 1997; Atkinson and Kintrea, 2001; Kearns and Parkinson, 2001). A series of theories have been developed to explain the relationship between neighbourhood change and sustainability, including cultural transformation (Wilson, 1987; Murray, 1990); social capital and belonging (Putnam, 2001; Livingston et al, 2008); the arrival of new social groups (Elias and Scotston, 1994; Wood and Vamplew, 1999); the broken windows thesis linking physical disorder and population turnover to neighbourhood decline (Wilson and Kelling, 1982; Skogan, 1990); and the relationship between satisfaction and propensity to leave neighbourhoods (Shon, 2007).

Similar conceptualisations have informed urban policy programmes in the UK which have sought to establish 'sustainable communities' (ODPM, 2003; CLG, 2007; see also Raco, 2007) through a process of (internalised) neighbourhood regeneration and achieving 'mixed' and 'cohesive' communities that would, presumably, become stable over time, for example as epitomised in the 'lifetime neighbourhoods' agenda (ODPM, 2003; see CLG et al, 2008; Lupton and Fuller, 2009). Without overstating the point, one can identify an interesting trajectory in urban and neighbourhood policy in the UK, dating from an ambition of achieving an urban renaissance and neighbourhood renewal (Urban Task Force, 1999; Social Exclusion Unit, 2001) through community sustainability (ODPM, 2003) to a more recent emphasis on the resilience of communities (Cabinet Office, 2009; Mohaupt, 2008; Innes and Jones, 2006; Day, 2009; see also Chapters Two and Nine, this volume). This lowering of policy goals (at least rhetorically) appears to reflect a retrenchment in the face of economic and social conditions within low-income areas, what the Conservative Party (2010) terms 'Broken Britain' and the uncertainties of environmental emergencies, terrorism and social conflict (Cabinet Office, 2009).

The current Prime Minister (Cameron, 2010) argues that 'huge cultural changes [are] required within communities', and this is largely based on a belief that deprived communities lack an ability to cope with modern life (for a critique, see Johnston and Mooney, 2007; Mooney, 2009). This retains a focus on social sustainability, but is also influenced by the concept of the Big Society and a new localism (Cameron, 2010) as a mechanism for securing neighbourhood sustainability. Although the link is somewhat implicitly and incoherently made between the critique of state intervention, urban planning and the Big Society (Cameron, 2010; Conservative Party, 2010), it is evident that the voluntary endeavour that also underpinned conceptualisations of sustainability and urban renewal in previous Conservative and New Labour rationales of governance are now allied to an emphasis on the private sector and local 'ownership' replacing, rather than complementing, state provision. The new localism espoused by the Coalition government is somewhat contradictory in its spatial imaginings, on the one hand promoting residential mobility as a key mechanism for linking individuals to sustainable employment and on the other continuing to locate citizenship within local communities.

These sociological theories and policy programmes influenced by them conceptualise enhanced sustainability as being dependent on changing the social interaction and population compositions of neighbourhoods. However, as Shon (2007) argues, residents' accounts of their neighbourhoods' trajectories and perceptions of their futures are often missing from studies of place and urban sustainability (although see, for example, Charlesworth, 2000; Watt, 2006; Hall, 2007). Large-scale quantitative longitudinal studies have sought to capture residents' perceptions of (short-term) neighbourhood change and its impacts (see, for example, Beatty et al, 2009; Batty et al, 2010a). This chapter now attempts to complement this evidence base through a qualitative exploration of residents' perspectives, including a longer historical period of reference and their views on how neighbourhood sustainability may be achieved in the future.

Background to the study

The findings presented in the following sections are drawn from a Joseph Rowntree Foundation-commissioned longitudinal study of neighbourhood change in six lower income neighbourhoods in Britain. The six neighbourhoods were:

Amlwch: an isolated rural town in Anglesey, with an industrial heritage including copper mining and chemical works, which have now closed. The town has a large indigenous Welsh-speaking population, but there has been considerable in-migration from the North West of England.

Hillside/Primalt: an estate in Knowsley, Merseyside, built to accommodate populations from the Liverpool slum clearance programmes. The area has experienced economic decline since the 1980s. The population is predominately White British. The estate is a New Deal for Communities programme and there has been substantial demolition activity in an attempt to diversify housing stock and tenure, but redevelopment has largely halted as a result of the recession and the current crisis in the construction industry.

Oxgangs: an estate in the southern suburbs of Edinburgh, adjacent to some very affluent areas of the city. It formerly comprised predominately local authority housing but there is now considerable tenure diversification with council, housing associations and owner-occupied (including Right to Buy) properties. The high-rise flats in the centre of the estate were demolished and there are new build developments on the northern edge of the estate. The population is predominately White Scottish, although there is considerable residential mobility on the estate.

West Marsh: a neighbourhood adjacent to Grimsby town centre. Historically its economy was based on fishing and food production, but these have been in rapid decline. The population is predominately White British. There is a high proportion of private-rented and low-rise housing.

Wensley Fold: a neighbourhood located near Blackburn town centre, with a large (but not majority) South Asian population. The on-street terraced housing which dominates the neighbourhood has been subject to substantial refurbishment and redevelopment as part of the housing market renewal programme and properties now have back yards or gardens.

West Kensington: an ethnically diverse neighbourhood in West London, adjacent to the Earl's Court complex and surrounded by areas of considerable affluence. The neighbourhood comprises two estates, West Kensington and Gibbs Green, consisting of predominately high-rise flats. The neighbourhood is a New Deal for Communities area and the properties have been modernised. It has been proposed that, within the post-Olympic Games redevelopment of Earl's Court, both estates will be demolished.

The research study comprised two waves of semi-structured interviews with 30 residents in each neighbourhood in 2007 and 2009 and a third wave of interviews in 2010 with six residents in each neighbourhood. Attempts were made to retain wave one participants in the subsequent fieldwork stages to provide a longitudinal element at the individual as well as neighbourhood level. A full account of the research methodology, information about the case study neighbourhoods and a series of research papers, photographic images, audio clips and films are available at the study website (http://research.shu.ac.uk/cresr/living-through-change/index.html). The real names of residents have been changed in order to protect their confidentiality.

Drivers, symbols and indicators of sustainability

It is important, when reading the narratives of residents, to acknowledge that individuals' perceptions of the scale and nature of change, the impacts of these changes and the future sustainability of the localities varied within, as well as between, each case study neighbourhood. Residents also used various temporal and geographical scales of reference in framing their accounts (see Bashir and Flint, 2010, for a fuller discussion). However, a number of common themes emerged, including the key drivers and symbols that residents identified in assessing neighbourhood sustainability.

The economy

Residents used a long historical time frame in assessing the changes within their neighbourhood and its likely future sustainability (confirming the findings of Watt, 2006; Robertson et al, 2008). This was based on an awareness of wider structural economic changes, linked to the loss of key local employers and industrial sectors and reduced opportunities for employment:

'We didn't need the tourist industry and it was very self-sufficient, there was farming, the sea but those have depleted and we've got to bridge that gap because Amlwch's dying on its feet.' (Wendy, aged 45-64, Amlwch)

'For the young people here, without [work] … they'll have to go into England maybe to find work or whatever.' (Harold, aged 65+, Amlwch)

'The food industry here it's gone down. It used to be a thriving town, now it isn't any more.' (Harold, 35-44, West Marsh)

This industrial restructuring was in turn linked to a narrative of decline in the social status and social conditions of the neighbourhoods:

'The people that live next door to me, they've been here, they've grown up here, the three lads there with their mum and the lads are all in their 40s and 50s and they said it's gone downhill. They're all wanting to move and it's so sad when they've been here all their lives and they're thinking they want to move and its just shows the ways the area's going.' (Doris, aged 30-34, West Marsh)

Residents also identified a more immediate economic impact from the current recession:

'This recession is hitting. There's more people out of work; it's harder to get a job.' (Maureen, aged 65+, Wensley Fold)

'The work situation has become a lot worse. There isn't any work, they've closed down the factories, they've replaced them with other buildings.' (Khaliq Ahmad, aged 30-34, Wensley Fold)

'West Kensington is going down to the floor [due to the recession].' (Christina, aged 30-34, West Kensington)

Many residents described the nature and pattern of local retail provision as a symbol of the economic strength and sustainability of their neighbourhood. In some of the neighbourhoods the loss of a diversity of retail provision was linked to a wider sense of decline which impacted directly on quality of life:

> 'When I first moved here, there was quite a lot of shops, there was a baker's, there was a newsagent, there was a butcher's shop … all of that's gone now.' (Betty, aged 35-44, Oxgangs)

> 'There was a shop on every corner whereas now you've got to go on the bus to town.' (Kathleen, aged 65+, West Marsh)

Residents in Amlwch in particular, identified the rapid turnover in retail units as an indicator of the economic fragility of the town:

> '[Shops] constantly changing, opening and closing, opening and closing, I suppose it's the same in most small towns.' (Lorna, aged 30-34, Amlwch)

Figure 10.1: Changing retail provision

"Dorringtons, which is a local shop, it's been here for about 30 years. Its got everything from paint to seeds, to compost, to food and hopefully someone will be taking over it in the next couple of months to save it from closing."

Amlwch residents identified the closure of specialist food and goods shops in the last three years and their replacement with charity shops, cafes and restaurants and supermarkets: "there seems to be a lot of them and not enough other shops". These residents also articulated a concern about the appropriateness and sustainability of these shops against the backdrop of economic decline:

> 'There's a great influx of outlets for eating but not everybody can afford … it's a high unemployment areas so I don't know how they're all going to survive.' (Rose, aged 16-24, Amlwch)

These narratives identify the nature of retail provision as a key indicator of the sustainability of a locality, in which charity shops and food outlets symbolise an unsustainable local economy that is not built on secure or well-paid employment or the viability of small goods retailers. Conversely, changing retail provision could be read as being indicative of a renewed economic vibrancy, which in turn increased the social sustainability and quality of life of a neighbourhood, as in Wensley Fold:

'Shop keepers seem happier and more established, there's not shops opening and closing as much as there were … shops like Netto have come along so people seem to shop and live much easier than they did before, there's a lot more choice.' (Martha, aged 35-44, Wensley Fold)

'I suppose it's for the better because we've got some different shops now.' (Artur Novotny, aged 45-64, Wensley Fold)

Population

Perceived shifts in the populations of the neighbourhoods featured prominently in residents' accounts of social change and sustainability. This included a perception that 'incomers' and 'strangers' were changing the local social dynamics (see Elias and Scotston, 1994, for a historical precedent and sociological analysis of this). Particularly in Amlwch, this was linked to a generational effect and a sense of weakening social ties:

'They've all grown up and most of those have left the village, you don't see the parents as much at the school gates and, you know, everyone just drifts apart.' (George, aged 45-64, Amlwch)

The growing ethnic, religious and cultural diversity of some of the neighbourhoods (most prominently Wensley Fold), including migration from Eastern Europe, was a key indicator of profound change for many residents, although they varied in their responses to these trends. In Wensley Fold, some residents suggested that the arrival of Eastern Europeans had helped the existing Asian community feel more established and had added to the vibrancy of the neighbourhood:

'What's really changed is the sounds on the street, the sound was always Bengali or Jukati, now it's goodness knows how many different languages.' (Martha, aged 35-44, Wensley Fold)

However, other residents viewed increasing diversity as an economic and cultural threat to social and economic sustainability:

'Far too many Asians putting other people at risk because they're taking a lot of jobs.' (Maureen, aged 65+, Wensley Fold)

Beyond the issue of diversity, there was a common identification in most of the neighbourhoods of an increasingly transient population. For example, one resident in West Marsh described how:

> 'The population seems to change regularly, you don't see them, perhaps a year, perhaps six months and there's one house, I don't think it even goes six months, you don't know whose living there, you see somebody turn up with a van, furniture in, furniture out.' (Isobel, aged 65+, West Marsh)

Similarly, some residents in Oxgangs identified a rapid turnover on individual stairs in flats and "a lot of semi-constant residents":

> 'There's a lot of folk coming in that weren't in the area that are moving in and some of them can get overpowering.' (Betty, aged 35-44, Oxgangs)

This perception of new populations and the transience of many residents was perceived to undermine the certainties of the past and created a sense of volatility and often anxiety about the future of neighbourhoods and individuals' social status and connections within them (see Hall, 2007). In particular, social housing allocation policies, which, as with local economic restructuring, residents were powerless to influence, were regarded as threatening the social dynamics and status of neighbourhoods and were strongly linked to perceived increases in levels of anti-social behaviour and crime:

> 'It seems as though they are letting to any old people that are trouble makers where they've moved them from.' (Francine, aged 16-24, West Marsh)

> 'The top end of this estate is a disgrace now which it wasn't before, you know what I mean? Families have been moved from ... they must have been problem families ... the anti-social behaviour's actually worse.' (Irene, aged 65+, Hillside/Primalt)

Anti-social behaviour was a common indicator for residents in all neighbourhoods of the fragility of social control, and a loss of cohesion and a perceived increase in drugs misuse in public space symbolised this:

> 'They are more open taking it [drugs], so I think we tend to see it more....I think it's more so the increase in visibility, I think I mean it's always been here but I think because they're more open about it now.' (Olive, aged 35-44, Oxgangs)

'Drugs are more visible, it's a change from alcohol.' (Brenda, aged 35-44, Amlwch)

Although perceptions of trends in anti-social behaviour were complex and contradictory (see Bashir and Flint, 2010, for a fuller account), it was evident that public disorder was central to residents' assessment of the sustainability and trajectory of their neighbourhoods. Residents in Hillside/Primalt and West Marsh often linked increasing crime and disorder to the wider decline of their neighbourhood:

'For us it's actually deteriorated in as far as conditions and your quality of life.' (Irene, aged 65+, Hillside/Primalt)

'There is a change. I think some of it's for the worse.' (Julie, aged 45-64, West Marsh)

'I personally think it's got worse ... it just seems at the moment every week there's a car burnt out and there's yobs around.' (Doris, aged 30-34, West Marsh)

Housing, the physical environment and neighbourhood services

The strength of neighbourhood infrastructure was a key determinant of residents' perceptions of sustainability:

'It's gone down an awful lot. We've had a railway station here, we had the bus station here, we've neither now.' (Lloyd, aged 65+, Amlwch)

In other neighbourhoods, the closure of key facilities, like youth clubs, or play parks for children or the decline of key community events, such as carnivals or street parties, and less people in public houses, were perceived as symbolising deterioration in the social vibrancy of communities (see Robertson et al, 2008). Conversely, the provision of new facilities, such as play areas, could indicate a more positive future, although this could be complex. For example, although a new children's play area was welcomed in West Marsh, the use of security lights reinforced fears of crime and, in some neighbourhoods, the vandalism to, or deterioration of, recently provided play areas or youth shelters indicated to residents the fragility of the possibility of renewal.

The decimation of neighbourhood infrastructure and its affect on perceptions of sustainability was most stark in Hillside/Primalt, and was summarised in the account of one resident:

'The neighbourhood has not improved ... all the shops have closed, including the post office. [There are] lots of undeveloped areas, lots of top soil everywhere and lots of problems with kids on the building sites. There are for sale signs everywhere but given the current state of the area and lack of facilities, they are not selling.' (Marie, aged 35-44, Hillside/Primalt)

Regeneration programmes were central to residents' perceptions of change and sustainability in three neighbourhoods – Hillside/Primalt, Oxgangs and Wensley Fold – and recently announced regeneration plans were also prominent in the narratives of residents in West Kensington. Changes to the physical condition and tenure of the housing stock were important symbols of the trajectory of neighbourhoods. Large-scale demolition and redevelopment could cause major disruption and anxiety, which was most evident in Hillside/Primalt:

'Beachwood, that's still going on, the building there but on the opposite site the demolition took place and they're supposed to, Lowry were supposed to be building there, but they've stopped on the site now ... and there's some people still waiting to move into the Lowry homes, those people are still waiting to be re-housed.' (Irene, aged 65+, Hillside/Primalt)

'It's [the redevelopment] just all stopped and there hasn't been any work going on in Hillside for the longest time, not that I remember anyway, it's like a big waste ground.' (Kyle, aged 16-24, Hillside/Primalt)

Similarly, residents in West Marsh described the numbers of boarded-up empty properties as indicating a wider sense of decline. The stalled regeneration initiative in Hillside/Primalt was a stark example of the risks of an over-reliance on private sector, housing-led neighbourhood renewal. The credit crunch and crisis in the construction industry resulted in new build projects being halted indefinitely and had left residents with very little basic services and amenities.

Figure 10.2: The uncertainties of regeneration

This is my old home. I lived with my husband, and family, in this house for 47 years. we had very happy times, there, sadly we had to leave in nov. 2006 Due to demolition. we left a lot of memories there.

In contrast, in Wensley Fold, residents were generally positive about the regeneration and redevelopment of residential areas:

'Beforehand everybody had done what they thought was a good renovation on the property but everything was different so some people had stone cladding, some people had rendered fronts, some people hadn't done anything at all, some people had new windows, some people had white windows, some people had wood windows, everything looked like a patchwork, whereas now it looks like an integrated area in the sense that they don't look the same, there are differences between the houses but there's a much more uniform look and a uniform feel about it.' (Martha, aged 35-44, Wensley Fold)

'Before the street used to be totally fenced off which I don't agree with and people do mix so I think that's a better way of structuring a street where we don't segregate the people in housing association with privately owned. I think it makes more tension in the neighbourhood so I think that is a better way.' (Sajid Khan, aged 30-34, Wensley Fold)

The findings from Wensley Fold are very important in that they indicate how well planned and sensitive physical redevelopment and redesign can create a sense of positive future and sustainability within a neighbourhood:

'I think there's been a general feel of there being a lift in the area, people have a brighter attitude to the area, I certainly do ... it's an upward step, a forward step, it's definitely in the right direction.' (Martha, aged 35-44, Wensley Fold)

'I'd say it's hell of a lot better, much better.' (Khaliq Ahmad, aged 30-34, Wensley Fold)

Of equal importance, our findings challenge the links often made between ethnic and religious diversity and weakening social cohesion and reduced social interaction:

'It's changed, it changes more because the children tend to play together; they get out together.' (Saima Mirza, aged 16-24, Wensley Fold)

'Generally speaking I think it's becoming, there's a lot more cohesion amongst people, before when the Asians moved in it was hard to integrate but now people are just starting to accept that ... you see English people moving to Asian areas, Asians moving into English areas and it shows that times are moving forward.' (Faizal Hussain, aged 16-24, Wensley Fold)

'I think it is more a community than it was when I moved back, it was still pretty new, the new housing, a lot of the houses were still being sold, people hadn't moved into them … there's that kind of second and third families moving into these new houses, so in that sense its more established as a community … a lot of people feel like they've established roots I think here, there's not as many people in and out, people are not doing moonlight flits.' (Martha, aged 35-44, Wensley Fold)

What appears to be occurring in Wensley Fold is a stabilising of the population, allied to a maturing in the relationships between social groups, which has been supported by the new physical design of residential spaces. These are important lessons in exploring how diversity may be achieved alongside a sense of strengthened neighbourhood stability. Interestingly, the arrival of new migrants, particularly from Eastern Europe, appeared to have enhanced the 'social legitimacy' and sense of historical belonging of South Asian groups. Although only one case study example, this suggests that the policy rhetoric viewing multiculturalism as a threat to the sustainability of social relations does not take account of the temporal dimension through which such relations change and become embedded in local communities.

Securing sustainability?

Residents identified a number of factors that would be central to ensuring the future sustainability of their neighbourhoods. Just as the local economy was recognised as the primary driver of neighbourhood change, so economic development was viewed as underpinning a positive trajectory for the localities:

'Maybe more employment, that's the biggest thing.' (Robert, aged 25-29, Amlwch)

Crucially, residents articulated a belief that, without economic development, other forms of policy intervention would not be sufficient to secure sustainability:

'Where's your economy?…You see the thing is they need to develop the people along with the plans, because there is funding the people as communities can access but if they're not developing the people along with the project, where's your sustainability?' (Irene, aged 65+, Hillside/Primalt)

'All this trying to change the shopping centre to bring new housing in and trying to have better, new, ... it's all basically cosmetic.' (Maureen, aged 65+, Wensley Fold)

Residents recognised that the traditional industries that had been lost were not going to easily be replaced, so there was a need for neighbourhoods to link to new economic opportunities:

'What industries are there here? Very few is your basic answer, tourism is going to be your main one so you need to get [it] ... but for tourists you need to go back into your history ... the history is fantastic ... it's about its industrial heritage.' (Ashley, aged 45-64, Amlwch)

But there was also an acknowledgement that localities were in fierce competition to offer something distinctive and that the geographical location and particular heritage offered a very unequal legacy for different neighbourhoods:

'We're right at the end of the road. If you want tourists to come here you've got to beat all the other places that are trying to get tourists.' (Robert, aged 25-29, Amlwch)

Residents identified a number of key elements that would be required to ensure the sustainability of their neighbourhoods, including enhanced provision of retail outlets, public spaces, transport links and facilities for children and policing (see also Chapters Five and Seven, this volume). The provision of key facilities and services remains crucially important and lower income neighbourhoods require a level of infrastructure to function:

'It's going to make a difference, it's going to look nice and everything, a new health care centre, we've just had £82,000 for the library, that will make a big difference, other little things, calming traffic zones, different things for different areas, different people.' (Lorna, aged 30-34, Amlwch)

Two other themes emerged very strongly in residents' narratives of their futures and the futures of their neighbourhoods. The first was the very strong interlinking of the two. The majority of residents viewed their futures, and indeed in many cases the futures of their children, as being played out in their current places of residence. This was often linked to strong familial and social ties in which residents were embedded within their neighbourhoods, with an attachment and sense of belonging and security, even if these were challenged by population change and more specifically physical degradation and social disorder. One of the most prominent aspects of residents' accounts of sustainability was the detrimental impact that public policy (through housing allocation systems or demolition programmes) or economic forces (through limiting employment opportunities, particularly for young people) had on these social networks and the emotional and practical support that they provided for lower income households.

The second theme, which was exacerbated by residents' commitment to their current locality, was a pervading sense of powerlessness to influence the decisions and drivers generating the forces of change impacting on the neighbourhoods (see Chapter Six, this volume). Residents understood that they were reliant on other actors and factors to bring about positive change and to secure the sustainability of the arenas in which they were committed to living their lives in the future. In Hillside/Primalt, despite the communication strategies of the New Deal for Communities programme, residents were uncertain about when they personally would be re-housed, the phasing of redevelopment and the timescales for completion:

'The house we were living in is under demolition so it's getting revived here, I've moved into the new houses that have been built … it was two years going on and not knowing if I was going to get a new house straight away.' (Rebecca, aged 25-29, Hillside/Primalt)

It is no exaggeration to suggest that these residents were in a limbo over which they had no sense of ownership or control. Similarly, residents' responses to the proposed future demolition in West Kensington were characterised by a lack of awareness about the details of the programme and the inevitability of planning process decisions (although there were some organised opposition groups):

'But there's nothing I can do. I don't like it but I don't have the power, the people might say but when the government has made up its mind that this is what they're going to do.' (Gary, aged 45-64, West Kensington)

If, as Raco (2007) correctly argues, active citizenship and strengthened communities are viewed within policy rationales as essential to delivering neighbourhood sustainability, then our findings in these case studies suggest that these have not been achieved. Importantly, the findings also indicate flaws in conceptual models that link a sense of belonging and social ties in a linear relationship to social capital, empowerment and strengthened communities. Rather, there is a disconnection between the attachment and future commitment residents express towards their neighbourhoods and their ability to translate this sense of belonging into ownership and influence.

Conclusions

Even in previous regeneration programmes premised on an assumption of economic growth and increasing public expenditure, too much attention was given to addressing the population mix and physical infrastructure (primarily housing) of lower income communities and not enough emphasis on defending or securing the other elements necessary for a neighbourhood to function (see Chapter Eleven, this volume). Although previous research has suggested the need to improve service provision and facilities (Parkes et al, 2002; Power and Mumford, 2003; Andersen, 2008), there is a case for a more ambitious agenda here, that extends, for example, to retail provision. The absence of local shops selling essential and affordable goods, post offices and pharmacies exacerbated the experience of poverty and exclusion for many residents and indicates the need to ensure that all neighbourhoods have a minimum standard of retail and health, as well as housing, infrastructure.

This also suggests, contrary to the theory expounded in the Conservative's 'two nations' thesis (Conservative Party, 2010), that public provision of core services remains crucial to the residents of deprived neighbourhoods and the substantial cuts in services will exacerbate this problem. The central flaw in the (albeit sketchy) conceptualisation of the Big Society (Cameron, 2010) is the notion of the *substitution* of public policy and investment by the voluntary, community and private sectors rather than an awareness of their *complementary* relationship with public services. The localism and voluntary endeavour envisaged as essential to achieving economic and social sustainability within the Big Society are dependent on neighbourhoods having an economic, physical and social infrastructure as a prerequisite. Our study has revealed the extent and importance of community organisations and volunteering to low-income neighbourhoods (see Crisp, 2010). But, as demonstrated in Hillside/Primalt, these will not deliver sustainability if they function as a desperate attempt to compensate for the absence of core basic services and facilities (see Chapter Nine, this volume, for a similar analysis). Hillside/Primalt also offers a salutary lesson about the extent to which the vagaries of private sector investment, so central to the present government's economic and social policy, are unlikely to deliver many of the elements required for urban sustainability.

The attachment and future commitment that residents have to their existing neighbourhoods also undermines the current policy interest in residential mobility as a mechanism to link populations to more economically sustainable settlements or regions (for example, reforms to social housing tenancy conditions and Housing Benefit allowances), and indicates the continuing need for regional development and spatial strategy in urban sustainability planning, as discussed further by Allan Cochrane and Peter Newman in this volume (Chapters Three and Eleven, respectively). There is a tension and incompatibility at the heart of sustainability policies that was present under New Labour and has been exacerbated by the new Coalition government. It is simply not possible to square the circle of, on the one hand, promoting labour market flexibility and unregulated private capital as the drivers of economic sustainability and, on the other hand, emphasising localism, sense of belonging, cohesive communities and social capital as the drivers of social sustainability. The Chicago School identified almost a century ago that zones of transition were not arenas of urban sustainability (Park et al, 1925; Zorbaugh, 1929).

Our study confirms, as residents themselves identify, the centrality of the wider economy to neighbourhood change and the limited sustainability of responses to economic change. Residents were well aware that neighbourhood change continues to be driven by forces and factors external to the neighbourhoods, including the lack of affordable housing, social housing allocation policies and migration. The implicit premise of the neighbourhood renewal and mixed communities agendas of the last decade, that internal housing and population restructuring and enhanced service provision will result in sustainable positive change in deprived neighbourhoods, is challenged by our findings. It is not clear therefore how, within the proposed Big Society agenda, individuals, families or communities may be empowered to take control of their lives. A focus on strengthening families, schools and the welfare system (Conservative Party, 2010) will not, in itself, address the centrality of worklessness (and low-paid and insecure employment) to the prospects of economic or social sustainability of low-income neighbourhoods (see Batty et al, 2010b).

There is also a need to address the lack of empowerment and ownership that residents feel about public policy formation and urban restructuring and the sense of uncertainty that this generates about the viability and sustainability of neighbourhoods and their own futures and quality of life. This is, perhaps, indicative of the fact that, despite decades of academic research and urban regeneration initiatives, there remains at the heart of visions of sustainable city futures an inherent disconnection between urban planning and policy formulation and the perspectives of those subject to the outcomes of these processes.

Key conclusions

• Residents identify a range of drivers, symbols and indicators of neighbourhood sustainability. There is a disconnection between the attachment and future commitment residents express towards their neighbourhoods and their ability to translate this sense of belonging into ownership and influence.

- All neighbourhoods require a minimum standard of retail, service and housing infrastructure. This requires a combination of public policy and investment and contributions from the voluntary, community and private sectors. The vagaries of private sector investment will not deliver sustainability in lower income urban neighbourhoods.
- There is an inherent tension between policy aims of promoting labour and housing market flexibility and simultaneously emphasising localism, sense of belonging and social cohesion as drivers of sustainability.

Further reading

Bashir, N. and Flint, J. (2010) *Residents' perceptions of neighbourhood change and its impacts*, Research Paper No 2, Sheffield: CRESR.

Manzi, T., Lucas, K., Lloyd Jones, T. and Allen, J. (eds) (2010) *Social sustainability in urban areas: Communities, connectivity and the urban fabric*, London: Earthscan.

Robertson, D., Smyth, J. and McIntosh, I. (2008) *'Whaur are you fae?' A study of people, place and identity in Stirling*, York: Joseph Rowntree Foundation.

References

Andersen, H.S. (2008) 'Why do residents want to leave deprived neighbourhoods? The importance of residents' subjective evaluations of their neighbourhood and its reputation', *Journal of Housing and the Built Environment*, vol 23, no 1, pp 79-101.

Andersen, H. and Munck, R. (1999) *Neighbourhood images in Liverpool: 'It's all down to the people'*, York: York Publishing Services for the Joseph Rowntree Foundation.

Atkinson, R. and Kintrea, K. (2001) 'Disentangling area effects: evidence from deprived and non-deprived neighbourhoods', *Urban Studies*, vol 38, no 12, pp 2277-98.

Bashir, N. and Flint, J. (2010) *Residents' perceptions of neighbourhood change and its impacts*, Research Paper No 2, Sheffield: CRESR.

Batty, E., Beatty, C., Foden, M., Lawless, P., Pearson, S. and Wilson, I. (2010a) *Making deprived areas better places to live: Evidence from the New Deal for Communities Programme*, London: Department for Communities and Local Government.

Batty, E., Beatty, C., Foden, M., Lawless, P., Pearson, S. and Wilson, I. (2010b) *The New Deal for Communities experience: A final assessment*, London: Department for Communities and Local Government.

Bauman, Z. (2000) *Liquid modernity*, Cambridge: Polity Press.

Beatty, C., Foden, M., Grimsley, M., Lawless, P. and Wilson, I. (2009) *Four years of change? Understanding the experiences of the 2002-2006 New Deal for Communities Panel: Evidence from the New Deal for Communities Programme*, London: Communities and Local Government.

Blokland, T. (2008) '"You've got to remember you live in public housing": place-making in an American Housing Project', *Housing, Theory and Society*, vol 25, no 1, pp 31-46.

Burrows, R. and Rhodes, D. (1998) *Unpopular places? Area disadvantage and the geography of misery in England*, Bristol/York: The Policy Press/Joseph Rowntree Foundation.

Cabinet Office (2009) *Draft strategic national framework on community resilience: Consultation document*, London: Cabinet Office.

Cameron, D. (2010) 'Big Society' speech, Liverpool, 19 July (www.number10.gov.uk/news/speeches-and-transcripts/2010/07/big-society-speech-53572).

Charlesworth, S. (2000) *A phenomenology of working class experience*, Cambridge: Cambridge University Press.

CLG (Department for Communities and Local Government) (2007) *Homes for the future: More affordable, more sustainable*, London: CLG.

CLG, DH (Department of Health) and DWP (Department for Work and Pensions) (2008) *Lifetime homes, lifetime neighbourhoods: A national strategy for housing in an ageing society*, London: CLG.

Conservative Party (2010) *Labour's two nations*, London: Conservative Party.

Crisp, R. (2010) *Work, place and identity: The salience of work for residents in six neighbourhoods*, Research Paper no 10, Sheffield: CRESR.

Day, K. (2009) *Communities in recession: The reality in four neighbourhoods*, York: Joseph Rowntree Foundation.

Elias, N. and Scotston, J.L. (1994) *The established and the outsiders*, London: Sage Publications.

Ellen, I. and Turner, M. (1997) 'Does neighbourhood matter? Assessing recent evidence', *Housing Policy Debate*, vol 8, pp 833-66.

Feijten, P. and van Ham, M. (2009) 'Neighbourhood change.... Reason to leave?', *Urban Studies*, vol 46, no 10, pp 2103-22.

Giddens, A. (1984) *The constitution of society*, Cambridge: Polity Press.

Hall, P. (2007) *London voices, London lives: Tales from a working capital*, Bristol: The Policy Press.

Hunt, T. (2004) *Building Jerusalem: The rise and fall of the Victorian city*, London: Weidenfield and Nicolson.

Innes, M. and Jones, V. (2006) *Neighbourhood security and urban change: Risk, resilience and recovery*, York: Joseph Rowntree Foundation.

Jacobs, J. (1961) *The death and life of great American cities*, Harmondsworth: Penguin.

Johnston, C. and Mooney, G. (2007) '"Problem" people, "problem" places? New Labour and council estates', in R. Atkinson and G. Helms (eds) *Securing an urban renaissance: Crime, community and British urban policy*, Bristol: The Policy Press, pp 125-40.

Kearns, A. and Parkinson, M. (2001) 'The significance of neighbourhood', *Urban Studies*, vol 38, no 12, pp 2103-10.

Livingston, M., Bailey, N. and Kearns, A. (2008) *People's attachment to place: The influence of neighbourhood deprivation*, York: Joseph Rowntree Foundation.

Lupton, R. and Fuller, C. (2009) 'Mixed communities: a new approach to spatially concentrated poverty in England', *International Journal of Urban and Regional Research*, vol 33, no 4, pp 1014-28.

Manzi, T., Lucas, K., Lloyd Jones, T. and Allen, J. (eds) (2010) *Social sustainability in urban areas: Communities, connectivity and the urban fabric*, London: Earthscan.

Martin, G.P. (2005) 'Narratives great and small: neighbourhood change, place and identity in Notting Hill', *International Journal of Urban and Regional Research*, vol 29, no 1, pp 67-88.

Mohaupt, S. (2008) 'Resilience and social exclusion', *Social Policy and Society*, vol 8, no 1, pp 63-71.

Mooney, G. (2009) 'The "Broken Society" election: class hatred and the politics of poverty and place in Glasgow East', *Social Policy and Society*, vol 8, no 4, pp 437-50.

Murie, A. (1997) 'Linking housing changes to crime', *Social Policy and Administration*, vol 31, no 1, pp. 22-36.

Murray, C. (1990) *The emerging British underclass*, London: WEA.

ODPM (Office of the Deputy Prime Minister) (2003) *Sustainable communities*, London: ODPM.

Overy, R. (2009) *The morbid age: Britain and the crisis of civilisation 1919-1939*, London: Allen Lane.

Park, R., Burgess, E.W. and McKenzie, R.D. (1925) *The city*, Chicago, IL: University of Chicago Press.

Parkes, A., Kearns, A. and Atkinson, R. (2002) 'What makes people dissatisfied with their neighbourhoods?', *Urban Studies*, vol 39, no 13, pp 2413-38.

Power, A. and Mumford, K. (2003) *Eastenders: Family and community in urban neighbourhoods*, Bristol: The Policy Press.

Putnam, R. (2000) *Bowling alone: The collapse and revival of American community*, New York: Simon & Schuster.

Ravetz, A. (2001) *Council housing and culture: The history of a social experiment*, London: Routledge.

Raco, M. (2007) *Building sustainable communities: Spatial development, citizenship, and labour market engineering in post-war Britain*, Bristol: The Policy Press.

Robertson, D., Smyth, J. and McIntosh, I. (2008) *'Whaur are you fae?' A study of people, place and identity in Stirling*, York: Joseph Rowntree Foundation.

Shon, J.-L.P.K. (2007) 'Residents' perceptions of their neighbourhood: disentangling dissatisfaction, a French survey', *Urban Studies*, vol 44, no 11, pp 2231-68.

Skogan, W.G. (1990) *Disorder and decline: Crime and the spiral of decay in American neighborhoods*, New York: Free Press.

Social Exclusion Unit (2001) *A new commitment to neighbourhood renewal*, London: Social Exclusion Unit.

Urban Task Force (1999) *Towards an urban renaissance*, London: Department for the Environment, Transport and the Regions.

Watt, P. (2006) 'Respectability, roughness and "race": neighbourhood place images and the making of working-class social distinctions in London', *International Journal of Urban and Regional Research*, vol 30, no 4, pp 776-97.

Wilson, W.J. (1987) *The truly disadvantaged*, Chicago, IL: University of Chicago Press.

Wilson, J.Q. and Kelling, G. (1982) 'Broken windows: the police and neighbourhood safety', *The Atlantic Monthly*, March, pp 29-37.

Wood, M. and Vamplew, C. (1999) *Neighbourhood images in Teeside: Regeneration or decline?*, York: York Publishing Services for the Joseph Rowntree Foundation.

Young, J. (2007) *The vertigo of late modernity*, London: Sage Publications.

Zorbaugh, W. (1929) *The Gold Coast and the slum: A sociological study of Chicago's Near North Side*, Chicago, IL: Chicago University Press.

eleven

Global city planning

Peter Newman

Introduction: Global city London

The idea of the global city is contested in academic discourse. Questions are raised about the value of, and indeed the intellectual justification for, distinguishing a special group of cities in a world of increasingly interconnected cities. Sassen (2006, p x) attempts to hold on to the special place of the global city seen as '... an analytic construct that allows one to detect the global as it is filtered through the specifics of a place, its institutional orders, and its sociospatial fragmentations'. But such an indiscriminate definition cannot step clear of the main problem with the global city and the historically older usage 'world city'. The problem is, of course, that the idea of global cities is not only an academic construct but has global reach as a popular label for successful and aspiring cities and importantly as a foundation for public policy in self-defined global cities around the globe. Unconcerned about disputatious academic papers and books the Mayor of London has no problem with the idea of a London 'that excels among global cities' (Mayor of London, 2009a, p 7).

The belief that London is in competition with other major business centres and latterly has become, and needs to maintain its position as, 'business capital of the world', is a powerful driver of public policy. Rivalry with other cities has a long history but the current concern with London as a world or global leader can be traced back to the mid-1980s when the revival of New York City and the claims of Paris and Frankfurt in an integrating Europe seemed to threaten London's economic prospects. The City Corporation funded research into London's competitiveness and the cross-borough London Planning Advisory Committee (LPAC) (that advised government on strategic policy in the years following abolition of the Greater London Council in 1986) published a report on London World City and was concerned that the London boroughs were not doing enough to support this world city role (Newman and Thornley, 1997). The Government Office for London (GOL) published its own study in 1996, benchmarking London against New York, Paris and Tokyo (Llewelyn Davies, 1996). Government was concerned about 'the UK's number one asset', and in 1996 issued its own strategy statement and encouraged more coordinated marketing and lobbying by leading businesses in the city. Over the past 20 years the claims of London as a world or global city have stayed at the forefront of national and regional policy.

Whatever the validity of claims about the London position relative to other major cities, 'global city London' has had a major impact on public policy. This chapter examines current policy priorities, in particular for planning and economic development. As a global economic crisis grew in 2008 it was widely thought that the problems of banks and the financial services industry more widely would be most severely felt in the global banking centres. Economic crisis spilled out onto the streets of London as staff of Lehman Brothers carried their cardboard boxes of personal belongings out of the bankrupt bank. But in the case of London the economy has performed no worse that the rest of the UK, and indeed it has been manufacturing centres that are most affected by falling demand. However, the economic position of London remains uncertain, as do the effects of any potential changes in the re-regulation of financial services on the wider planning of a global city around what has been perceived for the past two decades as its core industry. Early commentary on global financial crisis also talked up a return of the state, as national governments embarked on expensive stimulus packages and in many cases found themselves to be owners of previously private banks and other enterprises. What soon became clear in the last months of 2008 was that the fortunes of cities would depend not just on markets but on how governments were responding to market failure. Thus, in making sense of the present for global city London, we need to take a careful look at public policy, and this chapter concentrates on the role of strategic planning.

Prioritising the global city

Many commentators argue that the most important factors in London's success as a financial centre from the 1980s onwards were light touch regulation and relatively low taxes (see, for example, Barber, 2007), but alongside this favourable business climate ran the replanning and redevelopment of the city to support financial services and other perceived global assets. During the 1980s substantial resources were directed to the conversion of London Docklands into a secondary financial centre and to house a new middle class. London's 'riverside renaissance' saw new housing investment taking over the warehousing and industry that had served an older economy (Davidson and Lees, 2005). The attempt to protect areas of low-cost housing around the centre of London that featured in the draft Greater London Development Plan in 1984 was abandoned as the Greater London Council (GLC) was abolished and government took control of London-wide strategy and oversaw the plans made by the boroughs. In the 1984 draft Greater London Development Plan a tightly drawn Central Activities Zone (CAZ) sought to contain offices and other world city functions. This CAZ has since expanded, and in the 2004 London Plan extensive areas south of the river, in Battersea, Lambeth and Southwark, and Spitalfields and Shoreditch, and around the mega-projects at King's Cross and Paddington, were zoned as 'opportunity areas' to accommodate the demands of the central area. London was fitted around a global city spine running from Heathrow through the West End and City and on to Canary Wharf. In his first London Plan Mayor Livingstone accepted the arguments that London should grow, densities increase and that necessary infrastructure should be constructed. The Plan functioned as a lobbying tool as the case was made to central government for the infrastructure to reshape a growing city.

Vital to the 2004 London Plan was transport investment (see Chapter Seven, this volume, for further discussion). Onto this imaginary global city structure that linked the main airport to the business centres priorities for public transport investment could be mapped. Some of this thinking was not new. Transport planning for over 20 years has been concerned with the routing, and particularly the financing, of Crossrail that would give a direct connection between the airport and the City and destinations further east. The other transport investment priority from the 1980s was to retrofit public transport to London Docklands, including extensions to the Jubilee Line and Docklands Light Railway, and to re-route the Channel Tunnel Rail Link from Waterloo to St Pancras with a potential additional London station at Stratford.

During the 1990s the case for global city London was made by the government Minister for London, by the City Corporation, by the newly formed London First business lobby and supported by LPAC in its advice on strategic guidance. For some these multiple voices represented an institutional weakness in the governance of London and a weakness that undermined London's competitive position. The revival of New York City could be ascribed to a strong mayor and the Greater London Act in 1999 proposed a new, more coordinated, transparent and inclusive model of city-wide government. But the streamlined 'strong mayor' model of government also allowed the global city case to continue to dominate urban policy.

While the Mayor was strong in relation to the scrutiny role assigned to the elected Greater London Assembly, unlike mayors in other major cities the new Mayor of London had very little financial autonomy, few staff and had to negotiate policy with central government departments and the 32 boroughs, City Corporation and numerous quasi-government agencies that deliver many local services. Elected in 2000 the new Mayor was not supported by central government, and Livingstone's first term was marked by conflict, in particular over control of the upgrade of the tube network.

There was, however, less conflict between the Mayor and London's business lobbies. Business organisations set up a London Development Partnership to provide an economic development strategy for the Mayor and the Mayor's first official economic strategy drew heavily on this (West et al, 2003). The London Tourist Board and London First were convinced that London would be the 'undisputed World City by 2004'. The economic strategy set an agenda for the London Plan, which supported a growth strategy with necessary infrastructure investment. The economic emphasis reflected both the influence of business and the government's restrictions on the Mayor's budgets (Gordon, 2004). At the heart of the Plan was enhancement of the central area for international business.

The global city had high visibility in the 2004 Plan's approach to tall buildings. The Mayor favoured more tall buildings in the central area, conflicting with the previous policies supported, among others, by English Heritage. According to the Plan tall buildings 'can offer a supply of premises suited to the needs of global firms – especially those in the finance and business services sector' (Mayor of London, 2008a, p 249). Tall buildings would signal London's ambition, but also such high-density building could generate substantial benefits through exactions from developers and help to meet the Mayor's aims for constructing affordable housing and other benefits. Further and substantial 'planning gains' could also be achieved from hosting an Olympic Games. The Mayor had some experience of lobbying central government over prestige projects in the campaign to secure the new Wembley stadium, which was located in a much wider regeneration project that could deliver local benefits. In 2003 Livingstone lobbied hard for the 2012 Olympic Games. Securing sites for the Games would bring forward land reclamation and basic infrastructure investment and prioritise public transport projects. Locating the Games in East London also fitted well with the London Plan's overall ambition to steer development eastwards. In the east Canary Wharf was beginning to be successful as a tourist destination as well as a business centre, and development of Olympic facilities nearby might bring additional wider economic benefits.

Of lesser weight in the 2004 Plan were the aspirations for a more inclusive style of governance and broader policy ambitions heralded in the Greater London Act. While in the early months and years of the new government of London numerous commissions had been set up to look at, among others, issues of social housing and sustainable development, the regime had a clear bias towards economic development and a global city agenda. But the idea of the global city did not extend into a global city region (see Chapter Four, this volume, on this issue in relation to other English cities). A perceived weakness of the London Plan arose from the failure of strategic planning in London to engage with planning and economic development strategies for the wider South East region. The Mayor was only required to inform neighbouring authorities about his plans and a first round of regional economic strategies for the South East and East regions were not well integrated with the Mayor's plans. Additionally at this time central government was developing its own planning and development strategy for the Thames Gateway, an area including parts of East London but extending into both neighbouring regions. The government of the Thames Gateway has been widely criticised for its overlapping jurisdictions, unsettled leadership and multiple regional and sub-regional strategies (NAO, 2007; Allmendinger and Haughton, 2008). For a global city strategy the Thames Gateway offered the prospect of government infrastructure and investment in spaces that may be needed for expansion in the distant future. In the short term the priority given by government to the Thames Gateway backed up the London Plan's eastward shift and priority for Canary Wharf and latterly Stratford and the Olympic Park.

London's planning promoted a competitive global city. Some new ideas and strategies on a broader front had emerged – in relation to waste management, air quality and above all for the management of traffic in the central area. The Congestion Charge zone restricted movement within a narrowly defined City and West End area, increased video surveillance of this area and raised a levy that could be reinvested in public transport. The cost on travel in the centre could benefit bus users throughout London and in that sense the Congestion Charge zone ran against the general flow of city-centric, global city priorities in public policy.

The right strategy?

The London Plan was reviewed in 2007 and again in 2009 by the new Mayor, Boris Johnson. This section examines these reviews and the consequences of global city planning in an economic downturn.

The London Mayor is required to keep the London Plan under review and the review process started almost as soon as the 2004 Plan was adopted. The review incorporated some updating of economic and demographic data, reinforced the main policies of the existing plan and then focused on new elements. Planning for the 2012 Olympic Games had to be included, but perhaps more important was the Mayor's new interest in climate change and London's response. The revisions gave emphasis to reducing emissions and decentralising energy generation. London would aim to be an exemplary world city in relation to climate change (see Chapters Two, Six and Nine, this volume, for further examples of cities seeking a role and image as exemplars of innovative urban sustainability).

However, the revised Plan continued the emphasis on the central area and London's globally competitive financial services industries. If there was to be a significant change of direction in planning a global city before the crash of autumn 2008 then it may have arrived with the election of a new mayor that May. The new Mayor initially proposed a review of policy on tall buildings and the role of the CAZ (Mayor of London, 2008b), a review of a proposed extension to the Congestion Charge zone and a revision of the affordable housing targets in the Plan.

Planning for a better London proposed an ambitious target of 50,000 affordable units over three years, and argued for removing the 'prescriptive and counter-productive' requirement for 50 per cent of housing in new developments to be affordable. Additionally the mayor wanted a new emphasis on suburban London. The revision would have more to say about sub-regions beyond the global city centre and the idea of a review of London's geography had new weight with the setting up of the mayor's Outer London Commission (OLC, 2009) to look in particular at economic development in suburban centres.

There was an idea that the new Mayor would be less prescriptive. Mayor Livingstone had argued for enhanced powers and the Greater London Act 2007 transferred responsibility for a London housing strategy from the GOL to the Mayor and replaced essentially negative powers of veto over some large development projects with positive planning powers. The Mayor could now influence housing developments of 150 units rather than the 500-unit limit up to 2007. Although the position of the Mayor could be said to be stronger in 2008 than 2000, the new Conservative Mayor announced his intention not to interfere in decisions being taken by the boroughs. The election of Boris Johnson therefore suggested a possible change of emphasis away from strategic direction and conflict with the borough councils (Young, 2006) and towards more joint responsibility. In the new City Charter drawn up with the boroughs the Mayor promised to 'take over planning applications only as a last resort' (Mayor of London/London Councils, 2009, p 4).

New relationships between the Mayor and the boroughs also had a spatial dimension (see Chapter Three, this volume, for an account of spatiality in planning policy in the UK). A new interest in Outer London suggested a weakening of the city-centric global city stance of the previous Mayor. New sub-regional divisions in the Mayor's draft plan suggest a pragmatic approach. The East London sub-region now crosses the Thames with the advantage of grouping together the boroughs most closely involved with the 2012 Games. In West London not all boroughs have signed up to a sub-regional approach, and the boundaries of North London have changed to accommodate a newly defined central London but with little evidence of alliances working across the Greater London boundary and into other regions. However, the Mayor and boroughs promised cooperation around a range of issues including transport and economic planning, and continuing to campaign for resources for the capital, because 'A successful London economy is vital for the successful economic performance of the UK as a whole' (Mayor of London/London Councils, 2009, p 9). Thus, however the spatiality of London was being re-imagined, little has changed. As far as the UK was concerned, the interests of capital should come first. In this context of the Mayor's early statement about planning London the city hit the economic downturn.

Responding to recession

In late 2008 there was uncertainty about the future strength of the financial services sector that had been the core of global city making. The Mayor issued an Economic Recovery Action Plan in December 2008 just as other city mayors and national governments took action to prevent collapse and prop up their leading cities. The government of Singapore produced a £9.5 billion stimulus plan in the face of 10,000 lost jobs in 2008 (BBC News, 2009). The French government allocated €1 billion to the Ile-de-France region to be split in thirds between infrastructure projects, skills and employment measures and social housing. The Regional Council and City Council targeted support on small businesses in the Paris region. The federal government in the US was most concerned with propping up Wall Street, with a consequence that the economic impacts of the downturn were more severely felt in other parts of the New York regional economy. A common theme among global cities vulnerable to a banking recession was the need to diversify economies. The London Mayor's economic strategy emphasised London's other assets – higher education, creative industries and tourism (Mayor of London, 2009a) – and the Deputy Mayor of New York stressed fashion, tourism, media and the potential job creation effects of a 'green economy' (Elmhirst, 2009). But Mayor Johnson was equally concerned with what he saw as the city's core business. There was uncertainty about the future of financial services in the face of European regulation (a plot by Paris and Frankfurt, according to the Mayor), and the spectre of a flight of specialist financial sectors from London. But by early 2010 there was some evidence that banking was surviving the crisis, demand for office space in prime locations was holding up and Canary Wharf was reporting rising rental income (*The Guardian*, 2010).

Whatever the uncertainty about financial services, perhaps the greater cause of anxiety was the future of public spending, especially on essential infrastructure and the continuing ability of planning to exact payments from development projects. At the very least Crossrail, so important to spatial strategy, was going to cost Londoners more in Council Tax in future years (*Building*, 2009). The flow of business tax to part-fund Crossrail looked less certain. More generally developers would want to renegotiate the Section 106 agreements that had been delivering a supply of affordable housing, and a smaller public sector would undertake fewer development projects (LSE, 2008).

Planning for housing had been an issue throughout the Livingstone mayoralty (see also Chapters Five and Eight, this volume). The boroughs and the Mayor since 2000 had been chasing social housing targets as gains from private sector development, achieved through Section 106 Agreements. Mayor Livingstone included a target for the delivery of affordable homes in the London Plan. The GLA calculated that targets were not going to be met (GLA, 2008), although the failure to achieve targets should be seen in a context of very limited government investment (Bowie, 2010). Planning strategy, as described above, argued that economic growth could deliver necessary physical and social infrastructure. Without growth the public sector had limited ability to respond. The Homes and Communities Agency's 'kickstart' programmes to rescue affordable housing schemes were quickly committed. The densification (hyperdensification, according to Bowie, 2010) of the Livingstone years left problems of unviable schemes and an oversupply of small flats. Planning permissions for unprofitable schemes would not be implemented but housing sites would not become available for social housing if house builders could afford to wait for land values to return to pre-recession levels. The Mayor revised the targets for affordable housing, expecting house builders to be more interested in supplying 'intermediate' affordable housing and wanting to avoid demands from the social sector. The apparent failure of the London housing strategy to provide for an adequate supply of social housing provoked the government to write to the Mayor urging more action (*London Housing News*, 2010). In academic debate in the 1990s London researchers argued that the polarisation in global cities fundamental to Sassen's concept (Sassen, 2006) was not an inevitable process and not as marked as in New York City. Rather than polarisation, the dominant trend in inner London had been gentrification and public policy, although council house sales had excluded some populations from the central city (Hamnett, 2008). Given the failure to deliver even minimal levels of social housing and if, even without economic growth, the population continues to grow (Bowie, 2010, p 248), there needs to be a new look at spatial and social polarisation.

Following up his early 'Better London' outline, in May 2009 the new Mayor launched three linked strategies, on economic development, transport, and new outline for a revised London Plan (Mayor of London, 2009a, 2009b, 2009c). A full draft of the London Plan was produced for consultation later in 2009 (Mayor of London 2009d). The programme provided for the new Plan to be ready by the end of 2011 and before mayoral elections in May 2012.

In the face of immediate uncertainties, the draft Plan looks forward to 2031. It optimistically envisages continued employment growth, including growth in financial services, and retains the global city emphasis. To achieve that the major infrastructure projects of Crossrail and the Olympics continue to be fully supported. The perceptible difference from the 2004 and 2008 Plans is one of style, a lighter touch from a mayor less willing to impose strategy on the boroughs.

But the draft Plan's relation to other strategies launched in 2009 is less straightforward. Objections to the London Plan include those who want to see more detail on employment planning and better coordination of actions in the strategic hubs and corridors identified beyond the centre (West London Partnership, 2010). While overall objectives aim to 'give all Londoners the opportunity to share in London's economic success; and invest to ensure growth is spread across London, and in particular outer London', there is still an emphasis on building the 'undisputed business capital of the world' that continues with the city centric focus of previous strategies (Mayor of London, 2009d).

As noted above, economic crisis undermines funding for transport infrastructure. The Mayor lost his battle with the private companies upgrading the tube, incurring additional costs for Transport for London (TfL) and scaling back the speed of renewal. Other transport schemes have also been dropped. The new mayor did not support Mayor Livingstone's plan for a Thames Gateway Bridge and decided not to pursue plans for a cross-river tram linking central London with Peckham in the south and for an extension of the Docklands Light Rail through Barking Riverside. Without this public transport link, large housing projects in Barking stalled. The funding is insecure but Crossrail remains essential to the Plan. Crossrail benefits the City and Canary Wharf without benefit for Outer London and it makes sense alongside employment growth predictions that suggest most development will occur in and around the CAZ and at Canary Wharf. Therefore economic and transport policy continues to favour a narrowly drawn global city. Any changed assumptions run up against questions of economic viability (Mayor of London, 2009b, p 55). Existing public investment in transport infrastructure proved vital to the viability of the King's Cross mega-project in 2008. The developers had to invest £400 million of their own funds to keep the project going but could point potential investors to the HS1 terminus, investment in Javelin trains between London and the Olympic sites and the substantial upgrading of the King's Cross and St Pancras Underground stations. A further boost for the central city comes with the government's plans for HS2 with a terminus at Euston (involving substantial demolition of social housing around Euston station).

Some transport projects are vital for the global city strategy; others less so. The draft Plan's approach to environment and climate change may be viewed in terms of a competitive global city. Mayor Johnson wants London to be a 'world leader' in environmental policy: 'London is well placed to help the world adapt. I am committed to making London a world leader in tackling climate change' (Preface to Mayor of London, 2008b, p x). The mayor's research had already shown how much more advanced metropolitan ideas were in London compared to attitudes in other UK cities (GLA Economics, 2008). Global cities may be more privileged in the global struggle for 'ecological security' (Hodson and Marvin, 2009). This ecological competition is accompanied by some cooperation. Some cities have become more active as players in international networks, both in the search for lessons from 'successful' cities and in offering lessons and assistance to others (Jouve, 2007; see Chapter Six, this volume, for an examination of competitive and cooperative paradigms). In the case of Paris, Jouve argues that this internationalism has emerged as the social base of city politics changed in the early 2000s. An international platform on environmental issues became important for Mayor Livingstone and in 2008 Mayor Johnson became honorary Deputy Chair of the C40 group (an international group of the largest cities committed to tackling climate change). Climate change policy has a competitive edge and global city mayors have to be seen as leaders. For example, in New York City the Mayor points out that New Yorkers produced about one third less CO_2 per capita than residents of other US cities and the city's PLANYC strategy aims to reduce emissions by 30 per cent by 2030. Another similarity New York shares with London lies in the fine-grain approach to neighbourhood quality. Environmentalism is interpreted as local quality of life and investment in green infrastructure. Quality of life can be used to measure the competitive advantage of global cities. With the same horizon of 2030, Paris also imagines itself as a 'Post-Kyoto metropolis'.

Conclusions

The medium and longer-term impacts of the 2008 economic crisis are unknown. London, like New York, Hong Kong, Singapore and other financial centres, prefers to be optimistic about economic recovery and continuing growth around the financial sector. These global cities also talk up the diversity of their economies and other competitive assets – in tourism, culture and education for example – and their environmental advantages over other cities. This chapter argued earlier that it is not so much economic crisis but government's responses to crisis that determine the fortunes of global cities. That China focuses its economic recovery expenditure on infrastructure rather than social support to encourage demand will have consequences for the future development of Chinese cities (Ho-Fung, 2009). But whereas a model of a developmental state may help us understand change in some cities, for others we need other models of urban politics. Different cities make their choices in different ways. In reviewing the recent history of planning London, it is clear that we need to understand relationships between national government, London-wide institutions and the London boroughs, and vital relationships between business and the strategic planning process. In Paris the strategic direction of the city reflects a changing city politics represented by an alliance of socialists and greens and the complex interactions of city, region and state scales. New York is best described as 'managed pluralism' (Vogel, 2010) between governments and powerful lobbies, but with considerable intervention from community interests (as explored in another context by Sarah Dooling in Chapter Nine, this volume).

Perhaps a contrast with London is the relative quiescence of opposition to the London Plans. Whereas business was well represented in Mayor Livingstone's plans, and business and property development interests express clear views on the new draft Plan (for example, RICS, 2010, argues against restriction of tall buildings), other voices are fragmented (see, for example the collection of objections by the academic/community lobby Just Space, 2010). It may be that the relative quiescence of alternative voices is to some extent a function of the procedures for making and revising London Plans. The initial stages open up to comment and some public events are held. But comment on the Plan is then interpreted, selected and represented in the technical forum of an Examination in Public. The independent chair of this event consults only some parties to construct an agenda and selects participants (Rydin, 2008). The contentiousness of global city politics disappears in the discussion of the Plan. The new institutions of London governance could be argued to have facilitated political changes that reflect a wider 'post-politics' of urban development (Swyngedouw, 2009). On the one hand, the techniques of participation close off contentious issues, and on the other, the populist politics developed by Mayor Livingstone and followed by his successor define a shared fate for the city in which growth is good for everyone.

New York's 'managed pluralism' is effective in delivering large infrastructure projects. Global city London has been effective in capturing national resources for the city, but the funding of essential infrastructure remains uncertain and the Mayor and boroughs need to continue making the argument that 'economic recovery and continuing global competitiveness (are) essential for the UK as well as London'. As the forms of London-wide government have changed, national government has retained its grip on spending on major infrastructure. The new national government in 2010 overturned a previous commitment to a third runway at Heathrow but continued to back Crossrail. In the government's plans are also new high-speed rail lines from London to the North of England. This may be a long-term project but a new terminus will need to be accommodated in London's plans. We might assume that the UK government will want to protect London's apparent advantages as a trading centre – low taxes and light touch regulation – and to continue to encourage international business to locate in London and not in rival cities. Strategic planning will need to continue to support national economic policy.

We might also assume continuing change in the institutions of government. The new government will abolish the GOL set up with other regionalised government departments in 1994. Responsibility for housing strategy had previously been transferred from the GOL to the Mayor and the Mayor wishes the housing budget of the Homes and Communities Agency to be transferred to his London Development Agency and control of the agency set up to manage the Olympic Park after the games. There is no commitment to regional government outside London, but there is potential for stronger city-wide government in London. However, a substantial part of the public sector lies outside the functions of the Mayor and the GLA and there is little prospect of national health services being devolved to the mayor. The management of hospitals and local healthcare, as with the management of schools, lies in complex and evolving forms of 'partnership' between providers, borough councils and community interests. The discussion about quality of life in London Plans therefore tends to focus on the physical quality of neighbourhoods. Many of the routine (and emergency) services important in daily life lie outside the scope of plans for the global city. It is perhaps the quality of those services that will diminish as government adjusts to recession. At the same time Londoners will be asked to make 'lifestyle changes' in response to climate change (Siemens, 2008). However, the Mayor will argue for Crossrail and other infrastructure for growth:'Without these, our capital cannot go on developing and attracting the business and wealth that can lead the country out of recession' (Mayor Johnson, quoted in *Planning*, 2010, p 3).

Key conclusions

- The future competitiveness of London as a global city is the main force behind successive plans for the capital.
- Over the past 30 years London-wide government has been abolished and then recreated as the Mayor and GLA. We should expect further changes in the relationships between national government, the boroughs and London-wide institutions.

Further reading

Bowie, D. (2010) *Politics, planning and homes in a world city*, London: Routledge.
Newman, P. and Thornley, A. (2011) *Planning world cities* (2nd edn), London: Palgrave Macmillan.

References

Allmendinger, P. and Haughton, G. (2009) 'Soft spaces, fuzzy boundaries and metagovernance: the new spatial planning in the Thames Gateway', *Environment and Planning A*, vol 41, no 3, pp 617-33.

Barber, S. (ed) (2007) *The geopolitics of the city*, London: Forum Press.

BBC News (2009) 'Singapore budget targets recovery', BBC News, 22 January (http://news.bbc.co.uk/go/pr/fr/-/1/hi/business/7844769.stm).

Bowie, D. (2010) *Politics, planning and homes in a world city*, London: Routledge.

Building (2009) 'Boris' brain: Sir Simon Milton interview', *Building*, 20 February.

Davidson, M. and Lees, L. (2005) 'New-build "gentrification" and London's riverside renaissance', *Environment and Planning A*, vol 37, no, 7, pp 1165-90.

Elmhirst, S. (2009) 'Metropolis now', *New Statesman*, 22 October (www.newstatesman.com/economy/2009/10/london-johnson-york-bloomberg).

GLA (Greater London Assembly) (2008) *Crunchtime for London's affordable housing*, London: GLA.

GLA Economics (2008) *London's environmental effectiveness – An update: Comparing London with other English regions*, London: GLA Economics.

Gordon. I. (2004) 'Capital needs, capital demands and global city rhetoric in Mayor Livingstone's London Plan', *GaWC Research Bulletin 145*, Loughborough: University of Loughborough.

Guardian, The (2010) 'Canary Wharf landlord back in profit as bankers stay put', *The Guardian*, 27 March, p 43.

Hamnett, C. (2008) 'The regeneration game', 11 June, *The Guardian* (www.guardian.co.uk/commentisfree/2008/jun/11/housing).

Hodson, M. and Marvin, S. (2009) 'Urban ecological security: a new urban paradigm?', *International Journal of Urban and Regional Research*, vol 33, no 1, pp 193-215.

Ho-Fung, H. (2009) 'America's head servant? The PRC's dilemma in the global crisis', *New Left Review*, vol 60, November/December, pp 5-25.

Jouve, B. (2007) 'Urban societies and dominant political coalitions in the internationalization of cities', *Environment and Planning C: Government and Policy*, vol 25, no 3, pp 374-90.

Just Space (2010) *The London Plan is being rewritten* (http://justspace2010.wordpress.com).

Llewelyn Davies (1996) *Four world cities: A comparative study of London, Paris, New York and Tokyo*, London: Llewelyn Davies.

London Housing News (2010) 'Healey publishes response to Mayor's affordable housing strategy', 3 March.

LSE (London School of Economics) (2008) *Local authorities and the downturn: A review of issues, experience and options*, LSE revised report, 17 December, London: LSE.

Mayor of London (2008a) *The London Plan: Consolidated with alterations since 2004*, London: Greater London Authority.

Mayor of London (2008b) *Planning for a better London*, London: Mayor of London.

Mayor of London (2009a) *A new plan for London. Proposals for the Mayor's London Plan*, London: Greater London Authority.

Mayor of London (2009b) *Rising to the challenge: Proposals for the Mayor's economic development strategy for Greater London*, London: Greater London Authority.

Mayor of London (2009c) *Way to go! Planning for better transport*, London: Greater London Authority.

Mayor of London (2009d) *The London Plan: Consultation draft replacement plan*, London: Greater London Authority.

Mayor of London/London Councils (2009) *London City Charter: The first charter*, 29 April, London: Mayor of London/London Councils (www. londoncouncils.gov.uk/policylobbying/londonmatters/publications/ LondonCityCharter.htm).

NAO (National Audit Office) (2007) *The Thames Gateway: Laying the foundations*, London: NAO (www.nao.org.uk/publications/nao_ reports/06-07/0607526es.pdf).

Newman, P. and Thornley, A. (1997) 'Fragmentation and centralisation in the governance of London', *Urban Studies*, vol 34 no 7, pp 967-88.

OLC (Outer London Commission) (2009) *The Mayor's Outer London Commission: Interim conclusions*, London: OLC (www.London.gov.uk/olc/ questions/interim-conclusions.jsp).

Planning (2010) 'Transport strategy aims for expansion', 1[4] May, p 3.

RICS (Royal Institution of Chartered Surveyors) (2010) *Royal Institution of Chartered Surveyors (London) response to the Shaping London consultation on the draft replacement London Plan*, 15 January, London: RICS.

Rydin, Y. (2008) 'Discourses of sustainability: an approach to governance research', Paper presented at the Governance and Sustainability Seminar, University of Westminster, London, 12 March.

Sassen, S. (2006) 'Foreword: Searching for the global in the urban', in M. Amen, K. Archer and M Bosman (eds) *Relocating global cities: From the center to the margins*, Lanham, MD: Rowman & Littlefield.

Siemens (2008) *Sustainable urban infrastructure: London edition view to 2025*, Munich: Siemens.

Swyngedouw E. (2009) 'The antinomies of the postpolitical city: in search of a democratic politics of environmental production', *International Journal of Urban and Regional Research*, vol 33, no 3, pp 601-20.

Vogel, R.K., Savitch, H.V., Xu, J., Yeh, A.G.O., Wu, W., Sancton, A., Kantor, P. and Newman, P. (2009) 'Governing global city regions in China and the West', *Progress in Planning*, vol 73, no 1, pp 1-75.

West, K., Scanlon K., Thornley, A. and Rydin, Y. (2003) 'The Greater London Authority: problems of strategy integration', *Policy & Politics*, vol 31, no 4, pp 479-96.

West London Partnership (2010) *West London Partnership consultation response to draft London Plan 2009: 12 January 2010*, London: West London Partnership.

Young, K. (2006) 'Postscript: Back to the past?', *Local Government Studies*, vol 32, no 3, pp 373-80.

Section 4

Conclusions

twelve

Towards a new politics of urban sustainability

Mike Raco and John Flint

Introduction

The credit crunch of 2008 and the economic recession that followed have brought into stark relief some of the core conceptual and policy tensions that exist in relation to sustainability planning. The chapters in this book have interrogated these tensions in a variety of policy fields and reflected on the implications of change for our understandings of sustainable urbanism. In this concluding chapter we explore some of the key conceptual and empirical challenges that now face researchers of sustainability, and identify the themes and issues that are in urgent need of study if academics are to play a significant role in shaping the future development of cities.

We argue that, while what Bevir (2007, p 42) terms 'situated agency' plays a key role in shaping political processes, structural changes to economies still wield enormous power over development trajectories, political possibilities and everyday life in cities. We concur with authors such as Janet Newman (2007, p 64) in her call for researchers to identify the 'incompleteness of governmental projects or the contradictory features of new regimes of power', but we also argue that structural economic changes can radically transform the form and character of dominant modes of thinking. As Mark Whitehead, Allan Cochrane, Tim Dixon, Iain Docherty and Jon Shaw, and Chris Pickvance all suggest in their chapters in this book (Chapters Two, Three, Five, Seven and Eight, respectively), the credit crunch and recession have undermined assumptions of market-driven economic growth.

In countries such as the UK, we are currently witnessing some of the biggest social, economic and political changes seen since 1945 and this is having an impact on all areas of policy; Sarah Dooling in her chapter (Chapter Nine) identifies similar processes and impacts in the US and elsewhere. Our conclusions begin by examining emerging trends and dilemmas in sustainability planning policy. We then turn to the implications of crisis for conceptions of the environment and its 'value', before outlining areas for further research and questioning the value of sustainability thinking.

Emerging trends and directions in sustainability planning

In this book various contributors have argued that while the full consequences of the economic crisis are as yet unclear, the early signs are that there has been an *intensification* of the tensions and dilemmas surrounding urban sustainability thinking and practice. There are two contrasting policy responses that carry particular resonance for the direction of future agendas.

There has been a new emphasis on growth-first policies as a response to the perceived crisis of competitiveness and profitability now facing neoliberal capitalism as a whole. As Iain Docherty and Jon Shaw correctly identify in their chapter (Chapter Seven), neoliberal-inspired rationalities continue to shape contemporary debates and visions of a sustainable future urbanism (although see also the chapter by Harriet Bulkeley et al, Chapter Six, which argues that neoliberalism coexists with the rediscovery of a more explicitly interventionist role for government in contributing to place-based transformation and sustainability). Governments have increasingly prioritised the mobilisation of private investment and job creation as the primary mechanism through which post-credit crunch economic and social cohesion will be restored.

Such measures represent a re-embedding of neoliberal rationalities and a broader attack on the legitimacy and capacities of governments and welfare states. As some of the chapters have also demonstrated, economic instability encourages the formation, in some places, of more entrenched modes of growth-first politics, to the point where, as Mark Whitehead argues in Chapter Two, we may be witnessing the death of sustainable urbanism as a meaningful construct. In this understanding economic recovery is prioritised over potential environmental impacts; or at best, traditional conceptualisations of economic growth either define such growth as the mechanisms for (somehow) addressing social and environmental problems, as Allan Cochrane discusses (Chapter Three), or identify technological developments to tackle climate change as the mechanism for the next wave of economic growth. Harriet Bulkeley, Mike Hodson and Simon Marvin (Chapter Six) provide the insight that the place-based competition that epitomised urban environmental sustainability policies under New Labour were resonant of the Conservative and New Labour urban regeneration funding regimes characterised by competition and positioning among cities as sites of excellence, experimentation and learning (and, for example, the liberalisation and privatisation of energy markets and housing and transport provision), with similar outcomes of a varied landscape of capacity, effectiveness and social justice implications. For example, Will Eadson (Chapter Four) describes the spatial carbon inequities that are a likely consequence of such approaches. Within such a context broader debates over managing and limiting development in the name of something called sustainability sound increasingly hollow. As Will Eadson argues in Chapter Four, a focus on sustainable cities in isolation from their regions and urban and rural hinterlands will also undermine decentralised planning solutions and will not reduce demands for transit between cities.

In a context where expectations of growth are lowered, it is also possible that *alternative forms of development politics may be adopted*, in ways that seemed impossible even a short time ago (see Chapters Two and Six). As Bourdieu (2003) argued, the power of neoliberal politics lies in its ability to establish legitimate and widely accepted visions of the world. Since the 1980s successive administrations have held out the promise that aspirational, creative and entrepreneurial individuals can, and will, receive unlimited economic rewards and high cultural status in return for being successful. Sufficient numbers of people have benefited from this politics, or had enough faith in it for it to become a conventional wisdom (cf Galbraith, 1988). The inability of post-recession governments to deliver on these expectations may, therefore, undermine a broader faith in the power of markets.

One possible outcome is a systematic erosion of support for neoliberalism from the bottom up as its claims are undermined by economic failure and new legitimation crises (cf Habermas, 1984). The irony of a future with less economic growth and less consumption is that neoliberalism may have inadvertently created the conditions promoted by some of the more utopian modes of sustainability of the 1970s and 1980s (see, for example, Schumpeter, 1973; McRobbie, 1990). One consequence is that broader agendas focusing on issues such as quality of life, equality of outcome and social and environmental justice, all of which are advocated by each of the contributions in this book, may take on a more prominent role in debates over development, in a context where the excesses of neoliberal capitalism are no longer so prominent.

It is not yet clear, therefore, as Iain Docherty and Jon Shaw discuss in Chapter Seven, whether any global economic recovery will be robust and resilient enough to facilitate a 'back to business as usual' approach to growth and competitiveness and the unproblematised linkages of these to urban sustainability, environmental protection and social justice. What, their chapter asks, will be the impact if 'boom discourses' are genuinely replaced by post-growth concepts of austerity, consolidation, retrenchment and reduction in the use of resources and state and private investment? Will the very notion of sustainability be reconfigured? What are the impacts of initiatives, such as the Transitions Movement discussed by Mark Whitehead, that assert that urban communities will have to face up to the prospect of contracting spheres of economic production? As John Flint's research indicates (Chapter Ten), there does appear to be a retrenchment of urban ambition among some policy makers and some urban communities, in relation to goals of renaissance and renewal, through to those of sustainability and resilience.

Putting a value on the environment

Despite the emergence of these new opportunities for alternative urbanisms to become established, the early indications are, as Mark Whitehead and Chris Pickvance note in this book, that the environment is becoming less of a priority for governments as they wrestle with economic crises and rapid changes to the global economic order. In the UK, for example, policy discourses have adopted a utilitarian approach by presenting environmental assets as an economic 'opportunity' space, through which new forms of growth can be mobilised and delivered. It has sought to establish a middle way under its so-called 'green economy' plans, in ways that echo the ecological modernisation discourses of the 1980s and 1990s. It now proclaims that:

> Sustainable development recognises the interconnections between society, the environment, and economy and aims to find solutions that deliver benefits for all of these whilst minimising negative impacts. (Defra, 2010a, p 1)

Explicit connections are made between the environment and quantitative economic outputs:

> For too long, we have been content to just limit the damage, rather than grow and enhance the value of a healthy natural environment. Globally, it is estimated that the degradation of our planet's ecosystems is costing us £50 billion each year – a figure that could rise to the equivalent of 7% of global GDP by 2050. We are choosing to lose the valuable benefits of a healthy natural environment on a massive scale. A vibrant natural environment is not a luxury for the good times – it is a necessity for economic recovery and sustainable growth for the long term. (Spelman, 2010, p 2)

The government's stated aim is therefore to:

> Grow a leaner, greener economy. One which properly reflects the true value of nature's services in the way it works – in its prices and markets. Working with the grain of nature will prevent the unnecessary costs of environmental degradation, open up new business opportunities, and create new jobs. (Spelman, 2010, p 2)

Such priorities underpin the Coalition's first major policy paper on the environment, *An invitation to shape the nature of England*, that begins by stating that 'deficit reduction and ensuring economic recovery are the government's top priorities' (Defra, 2010b, p 3). Within this context nature takes on a commodified form, as something that can be quantified, managed and regulated in terms of costs and benefits. The strategy states that:

> We can no longer afford the costs to our economy and quality of life which arise from a degraded natural environment.... Our natural environment underpins our economic prosperity, our health and our wellbeing. (Defra, 2010b, p 3)

Moreover, it argues that:

> The value of natural resources extracted for use in the UK economy in 2007 was £41 billion. There are also costs to economy and society from environmental degradation, for example, the annual cost of soil erosion in the UK is around £40 million. And there are opportunities to create additional value – for example, action to prevent degradation can have a benefit to cost ratio of as much as 100:1. (Defra, 2010b, p 4)

Such discourses represent the expansion of Third Way or post-political approaches to sustainability and nature in which a proliferation of consensual, 'non-political' terms are deployed to further growth agendas (see Chapter One for a broader discussion). Sustainability, in this reading, represents an attempt by governments and elites to colonise new areas of policy under the umbrella of environmental protection, social justice and a 'balanced' approach to economic development that, in reality, enables businesses to expand remorselessly (see Chapters Two and Nine for further discussion). It represents what Swyngedouw (2007) terms an 'impossible' construct, used to justify the rolling out of pro-market reforms in a context where, as Harvey (2009) notes, capitalism cannot 'abide' a limit to its ambitions for growth. Sustainability thus becomes a useful political tool to enable counter-claims and barriers to be overcome in the pursuit of profit.

The contributors to this book robustly critique this post-political landscape. As Mark Whitehead argues (Chapter Two), there is a need for an explicit recognition that demands for social justice, economic development and environmental protection cannot be delivered to all places and all populations all of the time. So, despite the linking of economic growth to urban sustainability and, as Allan Cochrane describes in Chapter Three, attempts in the UK to suggest that, for example, the interests of the Northern Way cities could be seamlessly reconciled with the needs of the South East, social and spatial inequalities will continue to be manifested, and impact on particular places and populations, be they the homeless populations of cities in the US studied by Sarah Dooling (Chapter Nine), the residents of deprived neighbourhoods covered by John Flint (Chapter Ten), or the cities unable to compete effectively for state or private sector investment. As Iain Docherty and Jon Shaw argue in Chapter Seven, this returns us to the politics of prioritisation and the rationing of goods and services. Or, as Sarah Dooling points out, sustainability politics becomes inherently about trade-offs and regions, cities and the places within cities are all constructed on ideological notions of space and its uses. As Will Eadson describes in Chapter Four, cities are viewed as a product of spatial calculation, based on a modernist notion of exerting control over nature, with a lack of attention given to the material and behavioural networks underpinning the politics of urban sustainability.

While such critiques capture a core part of what sustainability planning has become, and seems to be becoming in the wake of recession, the openness of the concept still provides political scope for its reformation and redefinition in a variety of contexts, which all of the contributors to this book identify. These constructions do not *necessarily* have to be post-political in form. The deployment of sustainability as a construct can have unintended and wide-ranging consequences for the politics of development planning and open up innovative new policy spaces. Many of the critiques used by post-political theorists are written at a relatively high level of abstraction, with a focus on policy rationalities rather than practices. They fail to account for the fact that in some instances sustainability goals have enabled deep and powerful relationships to be forged by civil society and state actors, often in unpredicted ways (see Chapters Five, Eight, Nine and Eleven, for example).

While sustainability is then, in many ways, an 'impossible' construct, so are other political terms such as equality, justice and fairness. Just because terms have a utopian element does not mean that they are groundless or unable to take on progressive forms. In the absence of in-depth empirical work it often remains unclear exactly who the agents of the 'post-political' condition actually are in different contexts, and how and why political constructs, such as sustainability, are framed the way they are. Contributors to this volume offer practical ways forward here in terms of developing frameworks, such as urban ecological accounting and vulnerability assessments, that provide a 'grid of legitimation' within which national governments, city regimes and others claiming to be acting 'sustainably' may be held to account.

New research agendas: re-thinking sustainability?

Overall, then, the book has highlighted areas where there is now an urgent need for new research, and here we conclude by identifying some of the most significant.

First, the current crisis has opened up debates over *the relationships between the state and civil society*. As Bevir and Trentmann (2007, p 7) note, 'all kinds of theories of governance remind us that the state alone can not realise its ends. State power involves the participation, even the collusion, of actors from civil society ... governance is an ongoing activity that involves the creation and recreation of meanings'. In the wake of recession and the rolling out of neoliberal–inspired reforms, the nature of such participation and collusion represents an area where researchers have a key role to play in both deconstructing the definitions of the powerful and outlining alternative ways of thinking. There is a need to explore what is meant by the 'state' and 'civil society' in a more engaged way. As Chapter One pointed out, one of the most significant legacies of governance reforms has been the emergence of new entanglements between the state, civil society and the private sector. The complexities inherent to these new arrangements are almost absent in debates in countries such as the UK, where simplified binaries of the state versus community are deployed to justify welfare reforms. Research is required that unpicks these entanglements and demonstrates where *political power* lies and the networks through which this power is mobilised and enacted, as argued by the chapters in this collection by Cochrane, Bulkeley et al, Dooling and Newman.

On a related point and as the contributions have demonstrated, some of the most significant, yet under-researched, dimensions of governance surrounding sustainability planning have concerned the *growing importance of multi-level scales of governance* (see in particular Chapters Four, Five, Six and Eleven). European legislation and directives such as the Water Framework Directive that requires local authorities and utility managers to ensure that water quality meets certain European Union (EU) standards have had a significant impact on development planning in urban areas, particularly where waterfront development plays a key role in new build projects. Other EU legislation, such as the Conservation of Habitats and Species Regulations, introduced in the UK in 2010 (HMSO, 2010), requires local authorities and other agencies to develop biodiversity plans and these, in turn, become statutory documents that shape planning at the local level. In addition, there are other regulations covering waste management and recycling, employment law, development subsidies and infrastructure which have had an enormous affect on the form and character of development planning, both in terms of plan making and implementation. Despite this, many studies of urban development and sustainability planning continue to understate this multi-level context and its implications for democracy and sustainable city building. This is particularly important for debates over accountability and community responsiveness, as many of these new regulations and rules are put together by expert panels and bureaucratic organisations that are removed from local experiences. Again, there is a clear research agenda here that emerges from the studies earlier in the book.

The emergence of welfare reforms across the Global North raises significant questions for academic researchers. Despite moves in many countries to develop an 'evidence base' to policy production (see Allen and Imrie, 2010), a combination of recession and austerity governance is likely to put pressure on researchers to produce more 'relevant', and less critical, research. It is worth noting that despite decades of critical writing on sustainability, the politics of post-recession planning in countries such as the UK has thus far demonstrated that neoliberal readings of society and sustainability are still very much in the ascendancy. There is a real challenge here for researchers in the longer term.

It is also critical to identify alternative trajectories for future development. For example, a focus on the technologies and practices surrounding the 'green economy' might provide a platform for more progressive readings of development, as well as opening up new opportunities for the drawing together of the technical and social sciences. Across the EU, North America and Asia governments are gradually promoting new technologies in the fields of energy generation and carbon reduction that have the potential to propagate a new wave of economic growth, albeit in a context of finite resources. At the same time, the recession may also open up more radical thinking on existing structures and systems. Questions over unequal land ownership and community rights and responsibilities may, for example, play an increasingly important role in sustainability and development politics in the Global North, again mirroring the debates that have been raging in cities in the Global South for decades. As Whitehead notes in Chapter Two, some of the experiments over Transition towns and other local forms of action in European countries have, as yet, generated uncertain results, but in the longer run there is a clear research and policy agenda that builds on forms of progressive localism.

There is, however, no simple 'magic bullet' in policy terms that will tackle some of the problems and issues identified in this book. The economic problems and uncertainties now afflicting western countries demonstrate just how vulnerable modernity has become (see Will Eadson's chapter,

Chapter Four). Many of the warnings set out by sustainability writers in the 1970s and 1980s, in relation to resource depletion, inequality and ecological limits to growth, look to carry a new authority despite the best efforts of post-political governments to generate more optimistic and consensual accounts of change.

References

Allen, C. and Imrie, R. (eds) (2010) *The knowledge business*, Aldershot: Ashgate.

Bevir, M. (2007) 'The construction of governance', in M. Bevir and F. Trentmann (eds) *Governance, consumers and citizens: Agency and resistance in contemporary politics*, Basingstoke: Palgrave Macmillan, pp 37-53.

Bevir, M. and Trentmann, F. (2007) 'Introduction: Consumption and citizenship in the new governance', in M. Bevir and F. Trentmann (eds) *Governance, consumers and citizens: Agency and resistance in contemporary politics*, Basingstoke: Palgrave Macmillan, pp 1-36.

Bourdieu, P. (2003) *Firing back – Against the tyranny of the market 2*, New York: The New Press.

Defra (Department for Environment, Food and Rural Affairs) (2010a) 'Sustainable development', 15 November (http://ww2.defra.gov.uk/environment/economy/sustainable/).

Defra (2010b) *An invitation to shape the nature of England*, London: The Stationery Office.

Galbraith, J.K. (1988) *The affluent society*, New York: Mariner Books.

Habermas, J. (1984) *Legitimation crisis*, Cambridge: Polity Press.

Harvey, D. (2009) *Cosmopolitanism and the geographies of freedom*, New York: Columbia University Press.

HMSO (Her Majesty's Stationery Office) (2010) *The Conservation of Habitats and Species Regulations 2010*, London: HMSO.

McRobbie, G. (1990) *Small is possible*, London: Abacus Press.

Newman, J. (2007) 'Governance as cultural practice: texts, talk and the struggle for meaning in the new governance', in M. Bevir and F. Trentmann (eds) *Governance, consumers and citizens: Agency and resistance in contemporary politics*, Basingstoke: Palgrave Macmillan, pp 54-69.

Schumpeter, E. (1973) *Small is beautiful: A study of economics as if people mattered*, London: Blond and Briggs.

Spelman, C. (2010) 'Foreword', in Defra, *An invitation to shape the nature of England*, London, The Stationery Office, p 2.

Swyngedouw, E. (2007) 'Impossible "sustainability" and the post political condition', in R. Krueger and D. Gibbs (eds) *The sustainable development paradox*, New York: Guilford Press, pp 13-41.

Index

Page references for notes are followed by n

Y

Z